To Grace, my number one star

Los Angeles | London | New Delhi
Singapore | Washington DC

SAGE Publications Ltd
1 Oliver's Yard
55 City Road
London EC1Y 1SP

SAGE Publications Inc.
2455 Teller Road
Thousand Oaks, California 91320

SAGE Publications India Pvt Ltd
B 1/I 1 Mohan Cooperative Industrial Area
Mathura Road
New Delhi 110 044

SAGE Publications Asia-Pacific Pte Ltd
3 Church Street
#10-04 Samsung Hub
Singapore 049483

Editor: Mila Steele
Assistant editor: James Piper
Production editor: Imogen Roome
Copyeditor: Rosemary Morlin
Proofreader: Leigh C. Timmins
Indexer: Adam Pozner
Marketing manager: Michael Ainsley
Cover design: Jen Crisp
Typeset by: C&M Digitals (P) Ltd, Chennai, India
Printed and bound by CPI Group (UK) Ltd,
Croydon, CR0 4YY

MIX
Paper from
responsible sources
FSC
www.fsc.org   FSC® C013604

Library of Congress Control Number: 2014941145

British Library Cataloguing in Publication data

A catalogue record for this book is available from
the British Library.

ISBN 978-1-4462-4926-0
ISBN 978-1-4462-4927-7 (pbk)

At SAGE we take sustainability seriously. Most of our products are printed in the UK using FSC papers and boards.
When we print overseas we ensure sustainable papers are used as measured by the Egmont grading system.
We undertake an annual audit to monitor our sustainability.

CELEBRITY CULTURES

an introduction

LEE BARRON

SAGE

Los Angeles | London | New Delhi
Singapore | Washington DC

CONTENTS

CELEBRITY CULTURES: AN INTRODUCTION

INTRODUCTION

To explain why the lives of famous people such as Rihanna, Madonna, David Beckham, Kate Middleton, Kareena Kapoor, Jennifer Lawrence, One Direction, or Miley Cyrus have such a cultural impact, James Houran, Samir Navik, and Keeli Zerrusen concluded that the 'worldwide popularity of celebrities indicate that nearly everyone enjoys temporary escapism associated with the fantasy of celebrities' (2005: 238). As indicated by this quote, we use celebrity to enhance our lives, whether in the form of fandom – of admiring and gaining pleasure from the talents, styles, and unique qualities of famous individuals, or from just 'loving to hate' particular figures. Thus, celebrity matters, and the idea of a worldwide celebrity presence is a key aspect of the cultural and media landscape of contemporary society. From film and rock/pop stars, to political figures, Reality TV contestants, celebrity-bloggers-turned celebrity figures, fans reaching YouTube millions with their bedroom-shot emotional celebrity-defences, to chefs, criminal figures, ice road truckers, and beauty pageant participants, the representation, possession, and quest for fame is more pervasive than ever.

But it always has been, as Leo Braudy (1986) demonstrates within his seminal history of fame within Western society, *The Frenzy of Renown*, in which he charts the desire to be publicly recognized as stemming from the ancient civilizations of Greece and Rome, through the rise of Christianity and the veneration of saints and prophets, through to the fame of monarchs, artists, poets, political figures and, ultimately, the 'democratic' era of widespread fame produced by the rise of mass communication technologies and best epitomized by Hollywood. Therefore, the desire for fame and a compulsion to stand out from the social multitude is as old as human society itself.

The concept of fame, especially in relation to concepts such as stardom, is a particularly limited status as stars are comparatively rare due to their 'extraordinary' quality. As such, it is figures, from Marlon Brando, Marlene Dietrich, Marilyn Monroe, John Wayne, Elizabeth Taylor, Jane Fonda, to Jack Nicholson, Bruce Willis, Tom Cruise, Julia Roberts, Angelina Jolie, George Clooney, Nicole Kidman, Matt Damon, Brad Pitt, Will Smith, or Sandra Bullock, who constitute the 'A-List' conception of star (Dyer, 1982; McDonald, 2013), but who are comparatively rare. Indeed, the idea of the mediums that create 'stars' being historically limited and stardom being quintessentially associated with cinema and originating with the Hollywood star system is a longstanding one (Gledhill, 1991; McDonald, 2000; deCordova, 2001).

In Martin Shingler's view, given the proximity of film stars to a range of other famous individuals, from popular music, sport stars and television personalities, the mark of the film star has been the primacy of performance in addition to issues such as glamour or photogenic physical attractiveness – in essence, the perceived possession of distinctive and singular talent, rare ability, star image, and their work. However, there are instances in which this is not always so clear, for example prior to her Oscar-winning performance in *Shakespeare In Love* in 1996, Gwyneth Paltrow was notable as a celebrity figure rather than as an actress due to her relationships with Brad Pitt and Ben Affleck in addition to the multiple times 'her image consistently adorned the cover of celebrity and fashion magazines such as *Vogue*, *Elle*, *Cosmopolitan*, and *Marie Claire*' (2012: 58). The example of Paltrow points to a differentiation between the concepts of stardom and celebrity, and it is a distinction that is essential to make as they are not the same categories, and indeed, fame and the concept of celebrity, while frequently overlapping, are ultimately unique. In this regard, Robin D. Barnes provides a cogent differentiation between fame and celebrity:

> Fame has traditionally been associated with individual demonstrations of superior skill or striking deeds as displayed by a select few, then chronicled by contemporary authors and historians. Celebrity, on the other hand, is more transient, relying on marketing, timing, and instant appeal. (2010: 19)

Consequently, in conjunction with a literature devoted to stardom and fame, a distinctive body of academic research has become established to chart the nature and multidimensional historical, cultural, and social contours of celebrity (Monaco, 1978; Gamson, 1994; Gabler, 1995; Marshall, 1997; Rojek, 2001, 2012; Turner, 2004, 2014; Cashmore, 2006; Inglis, 2010; Ferris and Harris, 2011; Redmond, 2014). Ultimately, while the possessors of superior skills or striking deeds frequently do make it into the ever-expanding pantheon of celebrity culture, the semantic difference is essential to make as celebrity admits a far wider array of figures than the more laudable definition of fame allows. While the film star's rise to fame is built upon the honing of a craft coupled with potentially years of 'making it', celebrity consists of individuals who range from those who have produced pop hits (or had pop hits produced for them), established themselves as televisual personalities, write books, enter politics, model clothes, appear as themselves within Reality TV, broadcast their thoughts from their bedrooms to global audiences via YouTube, become embroiled in sex scandals, or commit heinous, but judiciously media-covered, crimes (while in some cases merely being related to a famous person is enough to warrant media attention). Many celebrities possess talent and unique skills or looks, but talent and achievement is not mandatory and, for the more cynically-inclined critics, image is now everything and merit frequently secondary within a landscape in which the 'exorbitance of celebrity's contemporary cultural visibility is unprecedented' (Turner, 2014: 4).

With regard to definitions, the concept of celebrity is a multi-faceted term whose Oxford English Dictionary definitions, notes P. David Marshall (1997), cite meanings such as 'celebration', being 'extolled', in addition to 'famousness' and 'notoriety'. In the opinion of the cultural sociologist Chris Rojek – author of the ground breaking and influential book, *Celebrity* – the Latin root of the word celebrity is *celebren*, which has connotations with both 'fame' and 'being thronged'. Furthermore, *celebren* is related to the verb *celere*, which is in turn derived from the English term celerity, which means 'swift'. However, it is not just Latin from which celebrity has emerged, as, argues Rojek, it is also related to the French word *célèbre* which translates as 'famous' or 'well known in public' (2001: 9). In this regard, these definitions underscore the direct meaning of celebrity – to be well known, famous, and attract public attention; but also, somewhat presciently, the French roots of the word also flag the fleeting, time-bound quality of celebrity status, a definition that captures Rojek's influential category of the 'celetoid' – the individual who achieves short-lived fame in the form of 'lottery winners, one-hit wonders, stalkers, whistle-blowers, sports' arena streakers, have-a-go-heroes, mistresses of public figures' (2001: 21). These are the Warholian figures whose 15 minutes of fame are almost over before they begin to reflect James Monaco's earlier third category of celebrity (following the hero and the star), the 'quasar', who (like their astronomical namesake) 'appear to be much larger and moving much faster than the laws of physics allow' (1978: 10).

However, through the proliferation of Reality TV, social media, and blogging in the 2000s, the celetoid/quasar has mutated and, with reference to examples such as Paris Hilton, the Real Housewives of Orange County, Atlanta, New Jersey, Beverly Hills, New York, and Miami, Heidi Montag, Lauren Conrad, Perez Hilton, Snooki, Honey Boo Boo, or Kim Kardashian have become a dominant expression of celebrity culture and reflect arguably the first celebrity theorist, Daniel Boorstin, who, in 1962, predicted that the future of public renown was a cadre of individuals who were 'famous for being famous'. Therefore, Robert van Krieken argues that celebrity can be defined as:

> a quality or status characterized by a capacity to attract attention, generating some 'surplus value' or benefit derived from the fact of being well known (highly visible) in itself in at least one public arena. It can be either positive or negative, including notoriety. (2012: 10)

Furthermore, from P. David Marshall's compelling political and economic view of celebrity within *Celebrity and Power*, he argues that it is a force that valorizes individualism. Thus, celebrity has emerged as a potent source of cultural and social power and one that is diffused throughout the major institutions and cultural centres within contemporary societies to the extent that 'the power of celebrity status appears in business, politics, and artistic communities and operates as a way of providing distinctions and definitions of success within those domains' (1997: x). Moreover, the institutions that celebrity is entrenched within have become further enhanced due to the proliferation of celebrity discourses and presentational strategies afforded by digital technologies, especially social media networks that have enhanced fan/audience interaction with celebrity figures (Marshall, 2010) to ensure that their images and cultural presence are more ubiquitous than ever. This perception is deftly encapsulated by Sean Redmond when he states that:

> Celebrity matters because it exists centrally to the way we communicate and are understood to communicate with one another in the modern world. Celebrity culture involves the transmission of power relations, is connected to identity formation and notions of shared belonging; and it circulates in commercial revenue streams and in an international context where celebrated people are seen not to be bound by national borders or geographical prisms. (2014: 3)

Celebrity culture, therefore, has become such a pervasive force that it not merely serves as a focus of media and journalistic attention, but also represents a potent intersection point for many of the fundamental social factors that dominate twenty-first-century societies within national and international contexts. These intersections and their interrelationship with celebrity form the basis of this book's exploration and analysis as it examines celebrity in relation to history, theory, business, branding and advertising, politics and celebrity advocacy, globalized celebrity and non-Western celebrity cultures, journalistic practice and media law, fandom, social networking technology, fashion and the body, and criminality. As such, *Celebrity Cultures: An Introduction* synthesizes core components of contemporary celebrity culture and key issues and themes central to the dynamic between cultures and their celebrity systems. Furthermore, the book critically introduces and examines readings of celebrity in relation to reference to a range of key social and cultural theorists that will include Karl Marx, Max Weber, Theodore Adorno, Émile Durkheim, Zygmunt Bauman, Leo Braudy, Richard Dyer, Pierre Bourdieu, Erving Goffman, Manuel Castells, Daniel Boorstin, Jean Baudrillard, and Paul Virilio in order to critically analyse and evaluate historical and contemporary expressions, manifestations, and effects of celebrity cultures within a global context.

With regard to Adorno's thought, although it has arguably fallen from the theoretical and cultural vogue, their analysis of the mass culture industries is highly pertinent (if not prescient) to modern celebrity cultures, as it ably illustrates the mechanisms in which celebrity is marketed and the 'zones' of culture that celebrity has 'infiltrated' (popular culture, news media, brand culture, fashion, and politics), usually with the purpose of influencing and enhancing consumption of products and markets as an aspirational but distracting 'fantasy' lifestyle. To explore these ideas the discussion places the sociological/cultural analysis of celebrity within the context of a series of precise and specific (but varied) historic and contemporary studies and examples such as Alexander the Great, Julius Caesar, Cicero, Georgiana Cavendish, Angelina Jolie, the Kardashian family, Kate Middleton, Miley Cyrus, Lady Gaga, Paris Hilton, Shahrukh Khan, Barrack Obama, One Direction, Britney Spears, David 'the Son of Sam' Berkowitz, PSY, and Nazril Irham. As such, the analysis synthesizes conceptual and theoretical sociological and cultural approaches and critically applies them to a range of precise examples that reflect the vibrant celebrity culture that is flourishing in the second decade of the twenty-first century.

With regard to the structure and content of the book, Chapter 1 charts the historical roots of fame and celebrity, but from the position that the history of celebrity is one that has numerous beginning points. In the view of Fred Inglis, celebrity as we understand it emerged from the rise of the great metropolitan spaces of London, Paris, and New York with their 'zones' of visibility and centres of rising consumerism and the subsequent development of a mass communications industry. However, this chapter returns to the analysis of Leo Braudy and his classic contention that the history of fame truly begins with the life and military career of Alexander the Great. The reason to return to this analysis is the issues identified in relation to Alexander (the role of Callisthenes, for instance, Alexander's appointed 'PR agent') resonates through to contemporary celebrity culture, especially with regard to the modern relationship between celebrity, journalism, and promotion. However, the chapter will extend the Alexander analysis with a discussion of the later, but no less iconic, Roman military leader, Julius Caesar, and specifically his text, *The Conquest of Gaul*, a history in which Caesar takes on the role of publicist for himself, sparing no opportunity to emphasize his military genius to audiences in Rome.

There were other figures who consciously pursued fame in the ancient world, however, aside from military leaders of the stature of Alexander or Caesar, and a prime example was the lawyer and orator, Cicero, who also engaged in a systematic programme of self-publicity. The issue of visibility and fame will be further extended in a fourth historical example, that of Louis XIV of France, the 'Sun King', and his influence upon royal portraiture. As such, the chapter will contextualize these historical case studies in light of contemporary public relations practice with regard to celebrities and the celebrity industry.

Chapter 2 explores a range of sociological and cultural theoretical approaches that explain the function and cultural expression of celebrity. The chapter initially draws upon the work of Max Weber to respectively outline a key sociological basis for the existence of fame and why particular individuals are able to command the attention of large social groups, or even entire societies. Here, although an oft-used concept, Weber's conception of charisma will be cited to explain the reasons why individuals are able to apparently set themselves apart from wider populations. However, the chapter will also focus upon the link between his concept of status and why celebrity is such a desired social position (fame's associated material wealth being the dominant factor) and will refer to the critical approach articulated by the Frankfurt School, and more specifically that of Adorno and Horkheimer. The celebrity system fits well with the Frankfurt School's cultural and economic critique of what they dub the mass culture industry (cinema, radio, popular music, and television), and it provides both an updated application of Adorno and a critical view of contemporary celebrity cultures that will be explored and developed in many subsequent chapters. However, the chapter continues with a theoretical analysis of celebrity with an emphasis upon classic and contemporary sociological approaches. Initially, the chapter will cite Rojek's use of Émile Durkheim's theory in relation to celebrity as a form of secular us practice; however, it will then explore the efficacy of Durkheim's approach al solidarity in terms of the 'function' of celebrity. This will address the extent to which celebrity is a central and 'universal' presence within numerous cultures, and celebrity can be argued to act as a subject and concept that arguably 'binds' individuals together in terms of perception and discourses upon celebrity lifestyles and behaviours. However, to provide a contemporary view and critical complement to the solidarity issues, the chapter will then link this analysis with Zygmunt Bauman's 'liquid society' thesis to look at the ways in which celebrity perfectly reflects an ever-shifting 'liquid' social culture. As such, this will provide the means with which to apply Daniel Boorstin's classic, pessimistic (but prescient) study of the degradation of fame. Boorstin's analysis charts the shift from the celebration of the worthy to that of film stars and a system dominated by shallow publicity stunts or 'pseudo-events', and which sees a rapid cultural turnover of celebrated individuals. Thus, while the cultural roster of famous faces may change, in some instances with great rapidity, the celebrity system endures and proliferates.

Having explored the roots of celebrity and theoretical explorations of its nature and proliferation, Chapter 3 represents the first example of the trajectory of the rest of the book: to examine particular expressions of celebrity. This chapter, therefore, explores the business of celebrity to investigate the extent to which the world of celebrity is deeply embedded within wider industry and economics. In John Gray's (2004) wry opinion, 'the cult of celebrity has become one of the chief drivers of the economy . . . the core of the economy has come to be entertainment . . . an economy driven by the need to manufacture demand' (2004: 203). In one sense, this is nothing new. The rise of celebrity in the early part of the twentieth century in relation to the growing cinema industry saw nascent film 'stars' used as both a means to secure finance for film projects, and as attractors to the general public, or more specifically, 'fans'. However, this chapter will focus upon the ways in which celebrity is used as an economic tool. First, this takes the form of endorsing consumer projects, a longstanding relationship between celebrity and the advertising industry. Nevertheless, a significant development to be analysed within the chapter is that of the rise of the individualized celebrity 'brand'. As such, this chapter will focus extensively on the nature and practice of branding, a central factor within the marketing and advertising industry. The chapter will apply the classic mass communication concept of 'synergy' to individual celebrity figures who have successfully (in the main) diversified their public portfolios across a range of media. To critically examine this development, the chapter will focus specifically on the celebrity examples such as Justin Timberlake, and the Kardashians (among many others), all of whom have extended their brands into fashion design and perfume ranges. In this sense, many contemporary celebrities' careers mirror flexible capitalist economic approaches and the ways in which celebrity is a key contemporary component of the cultural industries.

Chapter 4 assesses the degree to which the contemporary social spheres of politics and celebrity have coalesced, and the repercussions of such a cultural fusion. In the analysis of Francesco Alberoni (1972) in his now-classic article, 'The powerless "elite"', film stars could wield considerable cultural power and influence (inspiring imitative behaviours in fans, for example), but they could never gain or exercise institutional or political power. However, the election of the actor Ronald Reagan to the office of Governor of California in 1966 and his election as the President of the United States of America in 1980 (and re-elected in 1984) illustrated the ways in which the lines between celebrity fame and political office could be blurred. But, while Reagan's transition from actor to politician and holder of political power is comparatively rare (repeated at the level of state governorship by Arnold Schwarzenegger in 2004, but by few others), the presence of celebrity in the world of politics has expanded significantly in recent years. From Bob Geldof and *Live Aid* in 1985 to Bono, the lead singer with U2, and his ongoing campaign role for an end to Third World debt, to George Clooney's role in anti-genocide campaigning in Darfur, politics and celebrity have become interwoven. This chapter explores the processes and implications of this combination (awareness-raising of political issues by celebrity endorsers/advocates, the 'dumbing down' of politics or whether unelected figures should have access to any form of political power) and the critical issue of the extent of celebrity power. To evaluate these questions, the chapter will critically focus on a key case study, that of the Hollywood actress Angelina Jolie and her appointment as UN High Commissioner for Refugees (the UNHCR) in the early 2000s to the present to investigate and report on the plight of refugees. It will also assess the ways in which politicians themselves have become intimately linked with the practices and discourses of celebrity.

Chapter 5 initially returns to classic ideas relating to fandom and contemporary expressions and developments of fan activity with regard to celebrity. While the view, identified by Jenkins within his now-classic book *Textual Poachers*, that fandom has never quite shaken off connotations of religious or political 'zealotry' or 'orgiastic excess' (1992: 12) finds expression in extreme celebrity fandom, for example the practice of stalking, the 'active' fan approach is of great significance apropos relationships with celebrity. This chapter will re-examine such classic views with an onus upon the field of fandom that has become exclusively tied to celebrity: the para-social relation. The chapter explores this concept within the context of positive and individually enriching outcomes for fans, but also considers the 'dark side' of celebrity fandom in the form of stalking behaviours. Both expressions towards celebrities are related to the ways in which social media technologies have changed the relationship between fans and celebrities and the ways by which individuals can become intimately engaged with celebrity figures via media coverage, extensive media information, and the creation of creative digital fan spaces dedicated to the objects of fandom and celebrity. Such activity will be linked to Howard Becker's classic communal 'art world' to illustrate the modes in which fandom is an active process in a direct sense with individuals routinely commenting, defending (as in the case of Chris Crocker), or even acting as 'antifans' and denigrating individual celebrities on sites.

Chapter 6 explores the connections between celebrity, journalism, and media representation. The chapter will look at early twentieth-century developments in journalism that saw increasing news space specifically devoted to biographies of famous industrialists and royalty, the development of 'muck raking' for scandalous stories about the rich and famous, and the establishment of the gossip column. The chapter will then examine key journalistic representations of celebrity and celebrity discourse within contemporary celebrity magazines' websites (*Hello*, *OK!*, Perez Hilton), and newspapers to critically evaluate the claim that celebrity has initiated a process dubbed 'tabloidization' within mainstream journalism to the extent that it now devotes more coverage to the exploits and lifestyles of celebrities than to 'hard' news. However, this chapter will extend this analysis and relate it to further issues regarding journalistic practice and celebrity, such as citizen journalism and the ways in which digital technologies (mobile telephones to social networking technologies) enable scandals and celebrity moments of public embarrassment (or simply candid/private moments). In this instance, such mobile technologies have enabled members of the public to become 'paparazzi', primed to capture images of celebrity figures in candid moments and, via online platforms such as *YouTube* and transmit them rapidly across the world and beyond the control of celebrity handlers and agents. The key theoretical and conceptual approaches to be explored within the chapter will be: journalistic history, the tabloidization debate, and journalism law – principally privacy laws and the rise of celebrity-initiated 'superinjunctions'. However, the chapter will also discuss the comparatively recent development and proliferation of how Internet social networking sites such as Facebook and Twitter which have arguably altered the spatial relationship between celebrity and the public. This is so because many celebrity figures are using such networks to communicate to the world, sometimes directly, and frequently revealing personal and emotional information. As such, the traditional distance and protection that once dominated the celebrity/public nexus is, via technology at least, changing and in many instances diminishing, and celebrities themselves are now commonly contributing to the media discourses that surround them.

Chapter 7 examines celebrity within a global context, but from two distinctive perspectives. A traditional approach with regard to media has been to view global media culture as Western culture, or more commonly, American culture. From this position, the world consumes media (film, music, television) produced within the Western world and as such, according to critical theorists, is subject to Western consumer capitalist ideology in addition to purchasing Western cultural products, including celebrities. However, just as the one-way model of Western media transmission is, according to numerous critics, over-exaggerated, so, arguably, is the consumption of celebrity. As such, the chapter will consider non-Western celebrity systems which are arguably consumed predominantly in Western countries within a specific diaspora. While there are globally famous Western celebrity figures (David Beckham, Brad Pitt, Angelina Jolie), there are numerous celebrity figures who are heavily mediated within specific parts of the world and who equal (if not surpass) their Western counterparts. For instance, the Indian actor Shah Rukh Khan and K-pop singer Psy will act as case studies. Consequently, the chapter will assess the degree to which celebrity demonstrates both the extent of globalization and its limitations, which in this regard will be related to Indonesian religious groups protesting against a Lady Gaga pop concert. However, the chapter will also consider differences in social reactions to celebrity lifestyles, with reference to a case study of the 'sex tape scandal' involving the rock star Nazril Irham (famous with the band Peterpan) filmed with a woman believed to be the television presenter Luna Maya, in Indonesia in 2010. While sex tape exposés can represent an extension of the fame and celebrity portfolio of Western celebrities embroiled in similar situations (such as Pamela Anderson and Paris Hilton), Irham was sentenced to three and a half years in prison in 2011. Thus, social and cultural reactions to celebrity culture and lifestyles are not globally uniform.

Having established the origins of fame and celebrity in relation to the historical figures Alexander the Great and Julius Caesar, Chapter 8 points to a major source of transformation within celebrity and how celebrity is articulated and received, from Reality TV to Internet social networking sites. In terms of the former, these include 'ordinary people' having the chance to become celebrities via Reality TV shows such as *Big Brother*, MTV's *The Hills, Jersey Shore, The Real Housewives* series, *Keeping Up With The Kardashians, Here Comes Honey Boo Boo*, and *Duck Dynasty*. In other instances, Reality TV has been perceived as a means by which faded celebrities can potentially revitalize their careers, to varying degrees of success and in numerous formats (*The Osbournes, Hogan Knows Best, Celebrity Rehab, The Simple Life, I'm a Celebrity . . . Get Me Out of Here!*). Therefore, new broadcast technologies and television formats that developed throughout the 2000s have enabled more individuals to access media spaces and gain crucial visibility (however short-lived), and have transformed the nature of celebrity to an extent. Although a range of illustrative examples will be cited, the key case study will be Britney Spears, a pop star and globally recognized celebrity figure who has dramatically moved from a career scrupulously controlled in terms of image, to one increasingly marked by self-initiated, but short-lived, Reality TV-based visibility. The key theoretical and conceptual approaches explored and applied within the chapter will be: Erving Goffman's dramaturgical analysis of the presentation of self. This theoretical approach will be supplemented by critical readings of television technology and Reality TV, and the social, cultural, and personal impact of social networking technologies. The chapter will also re-examine Rojek's expression of the traditional celebrity 'veridical "I" and public "Me"', and the ways in which technology is potentially effacing the long-established distance between the public gaze and celebrity lives to give access to 'backstage' private spaces.

The focus of Chapter 9 is upon the cultural links between celebrity and body aesthetics. The chapter considers the ways in which celebrity body types are represented as 'ideal-types' and as role models for wider society, referring to Bourdieu's concept of habitus and applications of it to the modes by which dominant expressions of femininity and masculinity can be read off from specific celebrity bodies. In relation to the major mediums of celebrity culture (specialist and general 'glossy' magazines), the chapter critically discusses the primary ways in which celebrity bodies are presented as role models, sources of imitation, and 'somatic' inspiration, and as objects of fantasy and desire. As such, the chapter will revisit arguments made by commentators such as Naomi Wolf, Mary Rogers, and feminist theorists such as Susan Bordo. The chapter will also consider the issue of body modification and cosmetic surgery, the issue of 'hyperreal' celebrity bodies within media discourses created via technological manipulation of photographic imagery ('airbrushing') techniques which raise problematic issues concerning apparent pressures to 'imitate', and the issue of ageing celebrity bodies. However, the chapter also considers the degree to which celebrities themselves are subject to critical bodily evaluation, and looks at the ways in which celebrities who experience health issues can positively influence fellow suffers, a factor illustrated by Angelina Jolie and her decision to undergo a preventative double mastectomy.

Chapter 10 ends the book with a focus upon extreme examples of celebrity. The chapter examines the ways in which the lines between fame and notoriety have arguably blurred to the extent that there is little to no difference between 'good' and 'bad' fame. The chapter surveys instances of celebrities engaging in scandalous or illegal activity, but also looks to the ways in which, historically, certain criminal figures have been represented in a 'heroic' manner to garner public appeal (and the figures themselves recognizing their 'celebrity'). To illustrate this point, the chapter briefly examines the example of the 1930s American outlaws, Bonnie and Clyde. However, the major focus of the chapter is a revisitation of the figure of the serial killer as the ultimate extreme candidate for the status of celebrity, and assesses the degree to which there, given the 'adulation' that some serial killers became acutely aware of their media fame and courted it (David Berkowitz and Dennis Rader, for example), are few limits to who can enter into celebrity culture.

Celebrity Cultures: An Introduction connects key works within the now fully-established body of work that represents celebrity studies with a range of key sociological ideas, combined with numerous examples of celebrities to fully explore the phenomenon that constitutes a major cultural force in twenty-first-century society. However, as the next chapter demonstrates, the roots of contemporary celebrity culture lie way back in ancient societies.

1
THE ANCIENT ART OF SELF-PUBLICITY

CHAPTER OVERVIEW

This chapter sets out the historical foundations of fame, a crucial place to start in evaluating the cultural impact of celebrity, as it stresses the ways in which common assumptions that celebrity is a contemporary social phenomena is not so clear-cut. While celebrity is closely associated with the rise of technologies of mass communication, the desire for fame, to stand out from the social mass, is deeply embedded within human civilizations, and has been for thousands of years. To fully articulate this view the chapter will focus upon:

- Alexander the Great and Julius Caesar's personal quests for enduring fame and the techniques that they developed to ensure that their 'celebrity' was recognized in their own time and throughout subsequent history (for example, conveying their own history, making use of images to circulate their images), and effectively engaging in Public Relations
- The reign of Louis XIV with regard to means by which he saturated France with images of himself and indulged in publicity stunts that Daniel Boorstin would later famously dub 'pseudo-events')
- Fame, publicity, and image manipulation in early Hollywood

ANCIENT ATTITUDES TO CELEBRITY

Within *Illusions of Immortality*, David Giles states that the 'ultimate modern celebrity is the member of the public who becomes famous solely through media involvement' (2000: 25). Similarly, Barry King (cited in Dyer, 1982) also suggests his own set of preconditions for stardom that (in addition to industrialization and a rigid separation of work and leisure) stress that the development of technologies of mass communication were an essential component. Furthermore, P. David Marshall (1997) argues that the 'audiences' of these technologies emerged in the twentieth century (from large-scale social masses) as the power-givers to celebrities, as the sustainers of celebrity power and cultural influence. Moving through cinema, radio, and television to multi-channel TV, movies on demand, Internet blogs, and social networking sites, the means with which the public 'consumes' celebrity has only seemingly confirmed that the pantheon of celebrities that currently fill the cultural landscape are the product of a media-technology society. Be it via traditional 'mass communication' mediums such as cinema and television, or through 'new media age' forms that are more individually controlled and accessed, such as YouTube (Iezzi, 2010), celebrity is perceived to be a phenomenon of the modern world. So, from the early silent cinematic romances of Rudolf Valentino and the drama and glamour of later Hollywood, to the Reality TV antics of the denizens of *Jersey Shore* or the TV exploits of the Kardashian family, we can see how central the role of media/mass communication technologies have been and continue to be in the transmission of celebrity personalities, and the public construction of celebrity identities. However, although the existence of a celebrity culture is deemed to be a modern social phenomenon, the desire for fame and the resultant public adulation that fame bestows upon an individual is not limited to modern media-saturated societies; far from it. Here are the musings of Leo Braudy:

> Gazing back from a world in which the production and multiplication of images
> is in the hands of many, we might wonder what it meant to be famous when
> the means of communication were slow and the methods primitive. (1986: 15)

Actually, there are discernible connections between the media-constructed/consumed celebrities of contemporary society and the pursuit of renown in the distant past. Indeed, on analysis it quickly becomes clear that even in pre-media ancient civilizations the intense desire for individual fame was manifest, if not, as Robert Garland states, already displaying pathological levels of obsession. To illustrate, Garland cites the example of the arsonist Herostratus who, in 348 BCE Turkey, set fire to the great temple of Artemis simply because of the fame and renown that the act would bestow upon him, suggesting that 'something approximating to a celebrity culture was already alive and well over two thousand years ago' (2010: 485).

Herostratus' pursuit of fame is also striking with regard to the parallels that it has with more extreme forms of contemporary celebrity, primarily that of the ascent to celebrity status of multiple murders and, most dramatically, the 'serial killer' (as will be discussed in Chapter 10). However, there were other individuals in antiquity who also sought fame effectively through violence, albeit on a grander, military scale, and who combined acts of supreme achievement with a knowing awareness of the ways in which a famous public image can be cultivated and communicated. And the exemplar of this process is unquestionably Alexander the Great.

ALEXANDER THE GREAT: HISTORY'S FIRST CELEBRITY?

The cultural theorist Chris Rojek (2001), author of the book *Celebrity*, one of the first major and highly influential evaluations of celebrity culture, argues that Alexander the Great (born in 356 BCE and died in 323 BCE) possesses the status of being the first 'pre-figurative' celebrity in history, an individual who achieved global fame in an age that lacked any means of the mechanical reproduction and widespread dissemination of information and images. Alexander was granted the status of 'ascribed celebrity' during the lifetime of his father, Philip, King of the Macedonians (fame bestowed through monarchical lineage), but that was too restrictive, so Alexander alternatively sought fame achieved by his own means. Thus, 'Alexander aimed to become a universal, unquestionable "presence" in everyday life. He sought to inscribe himself on public consciousness as a man apart, a person without precedent' (2001: 30). As such, Alexander would ultimately constitute a key early possessor of the four key qualifications of fame: 'a person and an accomplishment, their immediate publicity, and what posterity has thought about them ever since' (Braudy, 1986: 15). But how did a man achieve such fame without the stock communicative technologies and agents that have characterized the acquisition, communication, and 'selling' of celebrity that have become the defining factors of the culture of fame from the early twentieth century? How did Alexander ensure that his name would be immortal?

For the Christian philosopher, St Augustine, Alexander the Great was nothing more than a roguish pirate 'infesting the earth!' (1984: 139); however, Alexander is conventionally read in far grander ways. For instance, the novelist Mary Butts (author of the 1931 novel, *The Macedonian*) encapsulated his achievements in life and his legacy since his death in the following, distinguished fashion: 'There are men who sum up an epoch, and men who begin another. Alexander did both' (cited in Cartledge, 2004: 4–5). Consequently, the dominant perception of Alexander the Great is that he is not merely a figure from history, but that he is a *history maker*. Therefore, at one level the answer appears to be quite simple: Alexander achieved his fame via acts of military conquest that saw him leave Macedonia in 335 BCE to initiate his military campaign against Darius III of Persia and continue through Asia to ultimately invade India. Therefore, Alexander was one of the ancient world's greatest military leaders who literally stamped his mark on the world. But there is more to the story than that. History is replete with highly successful conquerors (from Hannibal, Attila, Charlemagne, Genghis Khan, and Tamerlane, to Napoleon and Hitler), and while they are all certainly famous (if not often infamous) in a historical sense, nevertheless they are not routinely regarded as being celebrity-like. And yet, Alexander the Great is.

This is because Alexander provides a blueprint for some subsequent rulers who *did* wish to be seen as extraordinary and who *did* wish to actively cultivate their fame in their own lifetimes, and beyond. And this is why, although an oft-told tale within academic accounts of celebrity, Alexander needs to be looked on as a key architect of the 'rules' of celebrity and the acquisition of fame because, as Paul Cartledge notes,

'Alexander had a clear perception of himself, driven by a desire for recognition by others, to be seen as more than merely mortal, but rather, as in some way superhuman or divine' (2004: 17). And how he did this is why the history of celebrity *must* begin with Alexander the Great.

In addition to Alexander's extraordinary military achievements, he 'was one of the first Greeks . . . to be worshipped as a god in his lifetime' (Cartledge, 2004: 215). Significantly, though, this perception was the result of deliberate design by Alexander as the early historian Plutarch's assessment of Alexander's lineage concludes: 'It is certain that Alexander was descended from Hercules' (Plutarch, 1998: 385). Thus, Alexander arguably knew exactly what he was doing with regard to the perception of his image but how was a 'globally' recognized name established in a world without a mass communication system or any mechanical means with which to reproduce text and images? To answer this question, we turn again to the work of Giles, because in his view, the conspicuous pursuit of fame by Alexander coincided with both social and psychological developments within human societies of the time to the extent that 'the history of fame is about nothing less than the history of *Western* civilization. It is also about the history of the *individual*, and therefore it is about the history of human psychology, too' (2000: 12).

The development of individual consciousness within human society, argues Giles, arose with the practice of naming (argued to have begun in the Mesolithic period), and the emergence of mourning and ceremonial burial and the worship of certain individuals (invariably royalty) as gods. Of the latter, stories of venerated individuals were told orally until more widely facilitated by the development of writing. However, alongside the dissemination of stories concerning particular individuals, writing also established the development of a distinctive form of literature; fictional accounts that not only had a considerable impact on early 'audiences', but which also began to actually influence human behaviour and thought. The most influential examples of this early literature (and its distinctive and dramatic social and cultural impact) were Homer's epic works *The Iliad* and *The Odyssey*, two texts which Giles argues not only communicated the concept of 'everlasting fame', but also, most importantly, valorized it. It was these two texts, argues Braudy, which crystallized the idea of the meaning of heroism, and it was Homer's articulation of the figure of the hero that influenced Alexander the Great's self-conscious quest for fame.

ANCIENT STRATEGIES FOR GAINING FAME

Within his now-classic and influential study of fame, *The Frenzy of Renown*, Leo Braudy articulates why Alexander the Great deserves to be called the genuinely first famous person in human history, and charts the particular pattern that he followed in his deliberate attempt to achieve this status. In essence, it was in reaction to the heroic exploits found within the pages of the *Iliad*, and most notably in imitation of the epic's central figure, Achilles. Like Achilles, Alexander sought fame through prowess in battle and through the conquest of armies and territories, and 'was impelled by an urge to see and do more than any Macedonian or Greek had before' (1986: 32).

Indeed, while the ancient world had no shortage of rulers who were engaged in the process of accruing wealth and land, waging war, and destroying enemies, Alexander the Great (while engaging in all of those exploits) significantly differed from them. As Braudy states, it would be Alexander who would stay fixed in the world's imagination, and not, crucially, merely for the magnitude of his military achievements, but for something else: for what was 'immaterial' about his achievements. Thus, when Alexander was analysed by early historians, the perception that his drive for conquest was more than simply for the spoils of war was a constant refrain; it was also characterized by the belief that Alexander was driven by something internal and mystical in nature. Therefore Braudy believes that:

> In his short life of thirty-three years, Alexander constantly posed, fulfilled, and then went far beyond a series of new roles and new challenges until he himself was the only standard by which he could be measured. At the head of his army, his eyes forever on the horizon, he stood self-sufficient but never self-satisfied. Unlike the time-and-role-bound rulers of the more ancient civilizations, who believed that their greatest achievement was to come into accord with the rhythms of dynastic history, he sought to be beyond time, to be superior to calendars, in essence to be remembered not for his place in an eternal descent but for himself. (1986: 32)

In 334 BCE, Alexander and his army left Macedonia to invade the Persian Empire in order to initiate the first of the challenges that he believed would fix his name in history, and it was within this military campaign that Alexander truly differentiated himself from previous conquerors; this revealed why it is that Alexander is such a central figure in the story of fame, and ultimately, celebrity – because, not only was Alexander influenced by the literary exploits of Achilles, but, via his mother, Olympias of Molossia, Alexander actually considered himself to be a direct genealogical descendant of Achilles, embodying all of Achilles' traits as both a heroic and fearless warrior and a military leader. Consequently, the campaign against Persia was not simply an act of war and a means for territorial conquest, but it assumed a potent *symbolic* character in that Alexander likened it to the Greek siege and ultimate destruction of the city of Troy. Therefore, in the midst of invasion and battle, Alexander began to weave a story of his own, complete with what can only be described as carefully staged 'publicity' events. And the most memorable and significant of these occurred in the city of Gordium. This is because on Alexander's arrival in the city:

> Word reached him of a local curiosity, a chariot in the palace of the former kings of Phrygia which was linked by legend to king Midas's accession at Gordium four hundred years before. It had been dedicated to a Phrygian god to whom the officers identified with Zeus the king, Alexander's royal ancestor and guardian, and it was bound to its yoke by a knot of cornel-bark which no man had ever been able to undo. (Lane Fox, 1997: 137)

Expanding on the tale, Braudy notes that the Gordian knot was akin to the Arthurian legend of the sword in the stone: a test that only the true king could succeed in.

The symbolic value was clear: whoever untied the knot would rule Persia. Initially, Alexander attempted to undo the knot by hand, but it would not yield. But rather than admit defeat (and face public humiliation in the eyes of his senior soldiers), Alexander effectively and audaciously 'rewrote the rules of the game' by cutting the knot apart with his sword in order to reveal the secret of the knot and thus untie it. The significance of this act was that rather than representing simply a face-saving act (or even being an aggressive fit of kingly pique), the cutting of the Gordian knot represented, arguably, a unique precursor to the modern publicity stunt. This is because what Alexander did in Gordium ostensibly represented what Daniel Boorstin, within his seminal work on fame, *The Image* (first published in the early 1960s), would dub a 'pseudo-event'.

HISTORICAL PSEUDO-EVENTS

Boorstin's argument within *The Image* is quintessentially a pessimistic one. His central argument is that since 1900 Western culture has witnessed the transformation of the 'hero' into the 'celebrity', a process initiated by the 'Graphic Revolution', the products of the mass communication system consisting of magazines, television, cinema, radio, and newspapers. The major cultural impact of the Graphic Revolution was its ability to create famous people 'overnight', and to effectively fabricate 'well-knownness' (1992: 47). From a litany of classical heroes, such as Jesus, Joan of Arc, Shakespeare, George Washington, Napoleon, and Abraham Lincoln – individuals marked by achievements of 'greatness' – the prevalence of individuals promoted by the media system constitutes Boorstin's now-classic definition of the 'celebrity' as the individual 'who is well-known for their well-knownness' (1992: 57). In Boorstin's view, the contemporary landscape of fame (Hollywood, for example) is one characterized not so much by genuine achievement, but rather by superficial media-created diversions sustained by a series of 'pseudo-events' – purposefully produced publicity-seeking episodes initiated by studios or public relations professionals and representatives. Pseudo-events are deliberately planned and staged 'for the immediate purpose of being reported or reproduced' and arranged 'for the convenience of the reporting media' (1992: 40). Although clearly a man of considerable military and material achievement, Alexander nevertheless recognized that to imprint his identity onto the culture of his time (and ultimately beyond it), something else was required: that his image needed to be communicated in a dramatic fashion, and manipulated.

Thus, although the pseudo-event is habitually seen as a comparatively new addition to the celebrity arsenal, the point of events that are purposely designed to be perceived by the wider community is applicable to Alexander, and it is why he is such an important figure within the history of fame – because, as Braudy states, the fact that Alexander cut the Gordian knot meant that he went beyond the traditional stipulations of the puzzle, to solve it by untying it. Instead, Alexander created his own solution, and by doing so, he set himself apart from all others who had failed in the endeavour. So, while there was no media system to report his deed, it still had a similar effect: it became the subject of talk. But the cutting of the knot was also a key moment in the differentiation of Alexander from his royal and military forerunners and peers because it was a decisive 'act that propelled him once again beyond the usual triumphs of kings and conquerors into the realm of imagination' (Braudy, 1986: 35). This was Alexander's ultimate goal. Accordingly, when the Persian Empire was defeated and Darius put to flight (and subsequently murdered by his own generals as a means with which to appease the unstoppable Alexander), Alexander continued on his quest to effectively conquer the world and pushed out across Asia (establishing at least 18 cities which he named after himself in the process).

ALEXANDER'S PUBLICITY-PRODUCING GENIUS

In Braudy's analysis, then, Alexander represents an individual who was never content with the ascribed fame (Rojek, 2001) that was his by dint of his royal lineage as the son of Philip II of Macedon. Alternatively, Alexander also sought a fame that was based upon his own achievement rather than simply resting upon his predetermined royal status; he actively set about creating 'Alexander the Great' from Alexander III of Macedonia, and he did this in two distinctive ways: by attaining a level of achievement far beyond those accomplished in the past, and, most significantly, by performing achievements *unheard of* in the past. These factors were both unquestionably realized through the geographical scope of Alexander's empire, but there was a further crucial layer to Alexander's quest that was the key to perceptions of him in his own lifetime, and also, crucially, in a way that has resonated into the present time and contemporary celebrity culture. This dimension was explicitly linked not to what Alexander's real character was like, but how he wished to be seen by the world.

For Alexander, his image to the outside world, how he was perceived by the culture of his time, was far more important than who he really was as a human being. As such, he actively projected a specific image of himself to his world, an image that consciously and carefully drew upon the heroes and divine figures of his time which he utilized as sources of inspiration and emulation. The most pertinent of these models was that drawn from the works of Homer. On all of his military campaigns it was rumoured that he carried with him a copy of the *Iliad* given to him by his childhood tutor, Aristotle. Therefore, argues Braudy, Alexander was driven by a very specific 'programme': the quest for fame. And here Alexander demonstrated particular genius because he acutely comprehended that he had to *control* the way he was seen within his world. In this manner, not only did he go further militarily than any leader before him, he desired that this drive would ensure that he was an individual to be talked about, to be interpreted in various ways, to mystify those who sought to understand his extraordinary success at so young an age.

One clear tactic in this regard was to deliberately manipulate the extent of his heroic lineage. Hence, he would not merely cite the great Achilles as a direct ancestor, but he also constructed a family tree that included such incredible figures as Dionysus, Perseus, and Hercules: 'all heroic adventurers in whom the line between god and man was uncertainly drawn' (in Marshall, 2006: 44). But heroics needed one more essential ingredient: to be recorded and immortalized. Therefore, in addition to his military personnel, a further vital member of Alexander's invasion force into Persia was Callisthenes – Alexander's official historian (and the nephew of Aristotle). The motivation for Callisthenes' presence was precise:

> Empires have risen through the military and political ability of powerful kings only to vanish, leaving behind crumbling monuments and the dust of a few anecdotes. But Alexander's urge was for cultural and imaginative domination as well. (Marshall, 2006: 46)

Therefore, Callisthenes possessed a very specific role within Alexander's army, but also an especially prescient one. Given that Alexander had left Macedonia behind, he nevertheless wished to transmit accounts of both his empire building and his Homeric status to the Greek city-states. Thus, Callisthenes' function was not simply that of official historian, but as Alexander's 'press agent', or publicist. As such, given that the contemporary nature of the public relations industry is predicated upon the protection and communication of 'reputation' (Franklin et al., 2009), Callisthenes and his precise function effectively made him history's first official PR man. Even more presciently, the contemporary Western public relations industry has increasingly become synonymous with the concept of 'spin' in relation to the conscious, planned process of 'image-polishing', a process of particular relevance to PR company work with politician clients (Miller and Dinan, 2008: 2). As such, Callisthenes's job was to enhance Alexander's public reputation, and one of his primary roles was to record the various indications of divine favour shown to Alexander in his quest, to underline the parallels between Alexander's actions and those of the past (especially Homeric) heroes (for instance, Callisthenes calculated for Alexander that it was exactly a thousand years to the month between the attack on Troy and Alexander's campaign against Persia). In essence, then, Callisthenes was Alexander's political 'spin doctor' as he established Alexander's personal mythology and cemented his 'living god' status. Furthermore, Callisthenes was purportedly fully aware of his importance in the construction of Alexander's public persona as he is said to have pronounced that 'Alexander's fame . . . depends on me and my history' (Lane Fox, 1997: 84). However, unfortunately for Callisthenes, it is alleged that he was ultimately executed by Alexander for not working hard enough to 'sell' his divine nature to the ancient world.

It was not only the written accounts of Callisthenes that projected Alexander's image into the consciousness of his world, however, as the conqueror also astutely recognized the need for people not simply to hear of his exploits and superhuman abilities, but to *see* him. Consequently, as Alexander enjoyed significant military victories across Asia Minor, he also began to employ visual artists to paint, and thus preserve, his visage. As Giles (2000) states, Alexander's appearance in these artworks and mosaics typically portrayed him with a flowing mane of hair and eyes cast towards the sky, a dramatic stance and image imitated by actors and rock stars centuries later (think of the Doors vocalist Jim Morrison's iconic 'Young Lion' photographs shot by Joel Brodsky, as a good example). Therefore, Alexander recognized that a good story needed pictures.

Nevertheless, his genius for self-publicity extended beyond artistic representations to a mode by which his image was guaranteed to be seen on a daily basis by the stamping of his likeness upon coins, and pictorial representations that served not merely to 'advertise' his appearance, but that also cleverly reinforced his 'divine' and superhuman lineage. Thus, in addition to establishing cities, Alexander also created a number of minting centres that stretched across Asia in order to deliberately circulate coins that featured his face merged with mythic figures such as Hercules and Dionysus. And it was a successful venture, as the maintenance of his name and legend was helped by the fact that these coins were circulated years after his death (Braudy, 1986: 104).

THE QUEST FOR FAME GROWS: JULIUS CAESAR AND ANCIENT ROME

Alexander's tactics to ensure his fame worked, as numerous successors similarly driven by the desire for fame adopted his style, from military leaders such as Hannibal, Pompey, and Mark Anthony – who considered themselves to be the 'new Alexander' – to Mithridates, king of Asia Minor, who modelled his image explicitly on the dress and hairstyle of Alexander. Furthermore, Alexander's use of coins as a means by which to broadcast his image throughout the ancient world was enthusiastically and expertly adopted by the Roman Emperor Augustus. And it was within ancient Rome, with its own expanding and seemingly all-conquering military empire, that the means for the securing of fame initiated and mastered by Alexander found fertile ground and blossomed.

In Braudy's view, Alexander's techniques resonated strongly within Rome, as military expansion and personal honour were both connected and public conduct was highly prized, to the extent that 'Rome would infect the world with the desire for personal recognition' (1986: 57). Indeed, it is from Rome that the Latin words 'fama', 'ambitio', and 'celebritas' were created to articulate the centrality of the search for individual recognition from the urban Roman public: words that would resonate down through the ages. Therefore, Roman society created an increasing dynamic for individuals to seek out opportunities to display public distinction, and seek them out in ever grander ways, because 'When all distinction comes from public action, the stakes of fame get higher, the actions more grandiose, and the players look for theatres larger than the normal round of public office' (1986: 58). Within this context of a military-based society, a key successor to Alexander would be Julius Caesar, a historical figure who, like the Macedonian king before him, recognized that acts of very real military achievement also needed to be augmented with a supreme and deliberate process of personal stage management. A key part of this strategy was to project an image to the Roman public that was predicated upon convincing them that he was more than a mortal man. To do this (with a clear homage to Alexander's tactics), Caesar asserted that his family lineage was traceable back to the Julian founders of Rome, therefore establishing a quality of the divine to his nature and his subsequent drive to become the ruler of Rome. But, although he communicated 'intangible' quasi-supernatural elements of his identity to the Roman public, his main drive towards fame was through successful military achievement, and his platform for this was the Gallic War (58–51 BCE). Hence, Julius Caesar would closely follow the Alexander model, and to the extent that he recognized that his conduct during the Gallic War must be communicated back to Rome, that the people must continue to be apprised of his achievements in his absence.

So, akin to Alexander, his exploits and achievements were recorded and transmitted back to Rome. However, there is a keen distinction from Alexander in that Caesar did not appoint a Callisthenes; instead, he became his own historian and publicist, and by extension, his own propagandist. And he set out his story in a very deliberate style; as Braudy states, the language of his account is 'in the third person – presented in the spare, plain style of the Roman soldier and good citizen doing his job, without the rhetorical or personal flourishes of the aristocratic oratorical tradition' (1986: 84).

In what has become known as *The Conquest of Gaul* (1982) Caesar created his own history (in book form), and set it out in thrilling fashion. Thus, the people of Rome would read and hear of Caesar's marches (and assured military success) against the warlike Helvetii and Belgic tribes, the triumphant invasions of Britain and Germany, and, most significantly, the war against the Gauls and their rebellious leader, Vercingetorix. Although there are accounts of temporary military setbacks, the tone of *The Conquest of Gaul* is one of triumph of Roman courage against often overwhelming odds, and the narrative is characterized by persistent references to the display of superior military strategic acumen by Caesar, a skill which ultimately saw not only Gaul pacified and the reach of Rome extended, but the absolute rout of Vercingetorix, with Caesar at the centre of battle. This is what this extract unambiguously communicates, setting out as it does Caesar dramatically joining his beleaguered legions, and, in quintessential *deus ex machina* style, turning the tide in Rome's favour:

> The enemy knew that he was coming by the scarlet cloak which he always wore in action to mark his identity; and when they saw the cavalry squadrons and cohorts following him down the slopes, which were plainly visible from the heights on which they stand, they joined battle. Both sides raised a cheer, which was answered by the men on the rampart and all along the entrenchments. The Romans dropped their spears and fought with their swords. Suddenly the Gauls saw the cavalry in their rear and fresh cohorts coming up in front. They broke and fled, but found their retreat cut off by the cavalry and were mown down. (Caesar, 1982: 199)

It is clear that *The Conquest of Gaul* is no work of objective history, but an account that constantly emphasizes Caesar's extraordinary achievements, and it is a text that simultaneously glorifies Rome and its unimpeded sweep across the known world (and Julius Caesar is not reluctant to spell out the ruthless march of his army as evidenced by the total annihilation of the town of Avaricum – an act identical to Alexander's razing of the rebellious city of Thebes) and which also exalts Caesar himself. At the conclusion of *The Conquest of Gaul*, the reader is in no doubt that it was *Caesar* who conquered Vercingetorix and his forces. In Garland's view, although Caesar's adopted son, Augustus, would ultimately become more politically successful as Rome's first emperor, and he also instituted a particular means by which public attention was cast upon him, establishing himself as the First Citizen and encouraging the view that he was 'society's benefactor', Julius Caesar's career, by contrast, can be interpreted as 'a very public bid to satisfy a giant-sized, out-of-control ego' (2010: 485). But fame in ancient Rome could be achieved without recourse to military achievement, as demonstrated by Marcus Tullius Cicero.

CICERO

Cicero, who lived from 106 BCE to 43 BC, unlike Julius Caesar did not come from an aristocratic family nor carve out a career with the Roman army, but like Caesar possessed an appetite for fame and recognized the means to get it: oratory and the written word. As Braudy explains, much of Roman history remains unknown because oratory was predominant over written records. However, Cicero, who rose to prominence through the law and politics, comprehended the need to record his words, client defences, and political speeches in order for the world of the future to recognize him, and became 'his own Callisthenes' (1986: 72). But Cicero was not merely an orator, he was an orator of consummate and acerbic skill, the principal factors that elevated him to fame within Roman society, especially with regard to his deft 'ability to attack his enemies, flatter his friends, and magnify himself' (1986: 75). The persistent theme of Cicero's self-magnification was his own achievements and their importance, but, as the historian Plutarch observes, his biting abilities to 'taunt' and 'gird' his political adversaries 'won him the great ill will of many' (1998), not the least of whom was Mark Antony, on whose orders Cicero was murdered.

THE ANCIENT WORLD AND THE RULES OF FAME

Garland's assessment of ancient celebrity distinctly chimes with the critical appraisal of fame mooted by Boorstin, but identifies such characteristics centuries earlier than Boorstin's analysis does. Ancient Rome saw the principles of fame-seeking 'invented' by Alexander become a conspicuous component of society and individual psychology, and a distinctly negative one, too. For instance, at the opposite end of the social spectrum from military leaders, Rome possessed a number of 'celebrities' who held dubious statuses as role models, the most conspicuous of which were the gladiators. Recruited from the convict and slave population, and although coerced into performing acts of combat to the death, many of the successful fighters achieved widespread fame and 'performed' before crowds of up to 50,000. Furthermore, emperors who did not prove themselves in battle (nor have any discernible abilities) nevertheless sought fame, such as Emperor Nero, who had designs upon being equally famous as an entertainer and athlete; so much so that he 'even went so far as to hire claques of supposed fans, who were paid to applaud his musical performances and no doubt as well boo those of his rivals. Anachronistically speaking, Nero clearly saw himself as antiquity's answer to Michael Jackson' (Garland, 2010: 488). Rome, therefore, was 'a whole society animated by the urge for fame' (Braudy, 1986: 17) – a charge more conventionally levelled at (principally) the Western world and Western culture.

Having established the pursuit of fame as a pervasive desire that united brutal gladiators with orators such as Cicero, however, the pursuit of celebrity did not intensify, but conversely, it faded away. As Giles (2000) explains, for hundreds of years, fame became an inconsequential factor within Western society. But why should this occur given the avowed desire for fame (and the invention of pre-media mechanisms to achieve it)? How could a social and psychological force that defined an entire empire lose its potency? The answer was within the changing culture of Western society itself, and from the Judeo-Christian religious doctrine that developed from within Roman society and which increasingly attacked the Roman preoccupation with public and private glory. As such, in the wake of the fall of the Roman Empire and the increasing control of the Church throughout Europe, the veneration of the individual was suppressed in place of the adoration and glorification of the divine. Still, during the Middle Ages, a number of cultural and technological factors emerged and combined to steadily undermine religious control, such as the invention of the printing press, the use of engraving, and later, portraiture, to portray the human face rather than religious imagery, and the population explosion leading to migration from rural areas and to increasing urbanization with dense populations. Furthermore, in the Renaissance, the rise of popular theatre also contributed to new forms of fame, and the theatre attracted crowds the size of which had not been apparent since the days of Rome (Giles, 2000: 16–17). As Rojek (2001) points out, although godlike qualities are often attributed to celebrities (and in the case of Alexander, actively encouraged), the contemporary meaning of the word celebrity in fact springs from the 'fall of the gods', and is attributed to the rise of democratic governments and societies that have experienced processes of secularization, that process of the decline of the social influence of religion and levels of religious belief that many societies have experienced (Brown, 2009). The importance of democracy, argues Alberoni (1972), is that a star system requires a society characterized by a clear structure facilitating social mobility for citizens, so that, in theory, anyone can become a 'star' and a famous personality. Therefore, improved technologies for the reproduction of images, secularization (or at least the retreat of total religious authority), democracy, and urbanization were all social factors that would result in the 'return of celebrity', as it were, as a social and cultural presence.

THE RISE OF 'CELEBRITY'

As Fred Inglis (2010) argues in his *A Short History of Celebrity*, the development of urban democracy, increasing individualism, and the development of communication media would, from the mid-eighteenth century, see the specific concept of 'celebrity' replace a more general process of 'renown' – a status typically linked with acts of 'high accomplishment' and civic acts which brought honour not to an individual, but to the role which they inhabited. Thus, within eighteenth-century London, individuals such as the actor, producer, and theatre owner, David Garrick, emerged as 'the first late eighteenth-century celebrity' as he clearly demarcated the theatre as possessing a line between the actor and the public. Furthermore, the actors and actresses in his employ (most famously the marvellously named Colley Cibber and Peg Woffington) inspired the audience to seek out information concerning their off-stage lives, particularly with regard to the fashions they sported and any potentially scandalous sexual transgressions they might be involved in. In other artistic contexts, the Romantic poet George Gordon Byron, or, as he would be more commonly referred to, Lord Byron, would emerge as a celebrity 'idol', a poet of genius and a 'lord of the realm, a well-known libertine, amazingly handsome, darkling curly-haired, dazzling and dashing' and ultimately 'that rarest of creature, a celebrity worth celebrating' (Inglis, 2010: 63–70).

For Inglis, the emergence of celebrities within this period was also strongly related to the visibility of specific individuals within public leisure spaces in major metropolitan areas such as London, Paris, and later New York. Within concert halls, cafes, and gardens designed for promenading, the famous faces of the day would be noted and recognized by the public: a process facilitated by the numerous portraits of famous individuals produced by notable artists such as Joshua Reynolds.

The centrality of visibility, however, brings me to my third and final substantive example of the chapter, Louis XIV, the 'Sun King'. He was a figure who straddled the seventeenth and eighteenth centuries, but who, in addition to being directly influenced by both Alexander the Great and Julius Caesar, acutely understood the ways in which image would become central to fame, and who fully and expertly comprehended the importance of self-publicity. The relevance of Louis XIV is that, although an absolute monarch who presided over a France that contained no avenue for democratic political expression, his mode of securing and transmitting his fame, and for ensuring its longevity, resonated keenly with the celebrity system that would soon follow in the years after his death in 1715. This is what Peter Burke observed in his book, *The Fabrication of Louis XIV*:

> As early as 1912, the 'glory enterprise' of Louis XIV reminded a French scholar of contemporary publicity. The parallel is even more obvious in the late twentieth century when heads of state from Richard Nixon to Margaret Thatcher have confided their image to advertising agencies. (1992: 4)

Just as Alexander recognized the potency of images to cement his eternal fame, so too did Louis, but on a far grander scale through the production of hundreds of images that charted his life from infancy to old age. So numerous were the portraits and artistic representations of Louis that a visual and continuous narrative of his life and achievements was created. As such, Louis' history was pictorially established as his reign unfolded (and he reigned for 72 years, having ascended to the French throne at the age of four). However, these images were not confined to single artistic works, but were reproduced in the form of tapestries and engravings for further dissemination and transmission of Louis' image. In effect, a media system was established which predates Walter Benjamin's conception of art in what he dubbed the 'age of mechanical reproduction'. Although a process linked back to the Greeks and developing through the Middle Ages and perfected in the 1900s with the widespread development of photography (Benjamin, 2008), the reproductions of Louis' portraits represented an effective earlier example of this process in which artworks were reproduced in numerous ways and in differing media, but the motivation had little to do with art and everything to do with maximizing his public fame. This is Burke's explanation:

> Reproductions magnified the king's visibility. Medals, which were relatively expensive, might be struck in hundreds of copies. 'Prints', on the other hand (woodcuts, etchings, copperplates, steel engravings, and even mezzotints), were cheap. They could be reproduced in thousands of copies and could therefore make a major contribution to spreading views of Louis as well as news about him. (1992: 16)

However, it was not only visual means that were employed to circulate Louis' likeness; his royal image was also reliant upon 'oral media' of his day in the form of poetry, prose, and histories dedicated to his divine status and achievements. Even monuments of Louis and medals bearing his image contained inscriptions written by writers of the stature of the dramatist Jean Racine, and the inscriptions were not merely descriptive text, but rather instructions to readers that positioned them to interpret the monuments in a narrowly proscribed way. This strategy was specifically in place because the function of these images and monuments was not to simulate artistically the king's likeness, nor were the manifold texts created to objectively document his history. Instead, the aim of the images was 'to celebrate Louis, to glorify him, in other words to persuade viewers, listeners and readers of his greatness' (1992: 19). And in order to visually convey this desired public perception, the artists who visualized Louis' demands drew upon Roman equestrian statues. Thus, France would ultimately contain numerous statues of the king attired in Roman armour and transfixed in a suitably heroic pose. However, there was nothing accidental about the influence of the past, as it was key heroic figures of antiquity that Louis' public images were based upon, to the extent that Louis was frequently described as being a 'new Alexander', and one of Louis' heroes was indeed the Macedonian conqueror and master of self-publicity.

Given the scale of Louis' publicity machine throughout his reign, Burke also draws attention to the approach of Boorstin, and he identifies France's seventeenth-century 'media' as a distinctive forerunner of the Graphic Revolution that characterized the early twentieth century. Given that the scale of media included professionals such as artists, sculptors, engravers, poets and dramatists, tailors, and even the choreographers who meticulously planned the form of court ballets, a clear and potent precursor to the Graphic Revolution existed and was expertly executed. Furthermore, Louis' 'publicity agents' also staged distinctly Boorstin-like pseudo-events through the organization of seemingly spontaneous events which 'were in fact staged with some care, such as the public rejoicings on the news of

French victories' (Evans, 2004: 21). And Louis's main palace, that of Versailles, was designed to be, as Nancy Mitford describes, 'the outward and visible sign of [France's] ascendency over surrounding nations' (1966: 32). But Versailles was more than a monument to national achievement; it was, as one would expect, an expression of representations of Louis XIV himself. Consequently:

> Versailles could be regarded as a permanent exhibition of images of the King. Louis saw himself everywhere, even on the ceiling. When the clock installed in 1706 struck the hours, a statue of Louis appeared and Fame descended to crown him with laurel. (Burke, 1992: 17–18)

While far from being a subtle enterprise, seventeenth- and early eighteenth-century media were pressed into the service of a king intent upon linking himself with the heroes of the past and ensuring that his image (represented in exactly the way he wished to be 'read') and fame were secured for posterity. Yet Boorstin's standpoint is that prior to the Graphic Revolution, the achievement of the status of being publicly well-known was an inexorable and gradual process, even for those who commissioned vast monuments to themselves (the Egyptian Pharaohs and the Roman Emperor Augustus, for example). It would be after 1900 that the technological processes would be substantially developed to facilitate the rapid manufacture of fame. There is little to argue with here as the development of cinema as a popular form of public entertainment within the first two decades of the twentieth century was a driving force in the creation of a celebrity class.

As Giles states, one of the most important features facilitators in the creation of individual fame in early Hollywood was the invention of the close-up shot (pioneered by the director D.W. Griffith in *The Birth of a Nation*). The importance of this technique was that it 'enabled audiences not only to see the facial features of the actors but also their portrayal of emotions, thus intensifying the intimacy between star and spectator. The advent of sound served to further strengthen the star-fan relationship' (2000: 24). As the Hollywood cinematic industry developed, so too did its star system: the establishment, from approximately 1917, of a number of 'studio-fashioned' film 'stars' who resonated with the public and, in addition to constituting economic assets to the studios and serving as audience attractors to specific films featuring them, rapidly served as pathways of escapism for audience members. Consequently, such was the allure of film stars, that cinema admission could 'melt away strain, pain, misery, and desperate tiredness in the delicious dark below the shining silver screen' (Inglis, 2010: 188).

FAME AND IMAGE MANIPULATION

Furthermore, the first age of cinema illustrated the speed (and methods) by which anonymous individuals could be catapulted from obscurity to fame in a matter of days, but effectively, as Joshua Gamson argues within *Claims To Fame* (1994), with a tight system of control of name and image. The most often-cited example of the creation of fame is still one of the most potent to underscore Boorstin's assessment of the power of the Graphic Revolution, and the manipulative means film studios employed to imprint 'stars' unto the public consciousness, that of Florence Lawrence, or the 'Biograph Girl'. Signed to the producer Carl Laemmle's Imp film company in 1909, Laemmle implemented a publicity campaign to publicize the actress in 1910, but in a very innovative form. There was a report in the *St. Louis Post-Dispatch* that Florence Lawrence had been killed in a streetcar accident in New York, complete with a photograph of the then unknown actress. However, days later an advert appeared in *Moving Picture World* that strenuously denied the event and claimed that the story had been perpetrated by 'enemies' of the Imp company, and that Florence Lawrence was alive and well. However, the entire story was the product of the Imp company publicists (deCordova, 2001), and it not only demonstrated the methods by which publicity could be utilized to create almost instant fame, but also that the manipulation of star images and personas (exaggerated 'discovery stories', hints at romance, etc.) would become a central feature of the Hollywood star system as a means via which to connect with audiences (Dyer, 1982). Thus, for Boorstin, since 'the Graphic Revolution much of our thinking about human greatness has changed. Two centuries ago when a great man appeared, people looked for God's purpose in him; today we look for his press agent' (2006: 72).

And yet, although what Boorstin dubs the Graphic Revolution – consisting of cinema, radio, newspapers, magazines, and television, but contemporaneously augmented by celebrity websites, blogs, multiple TV channels, and forums such as YouTube (Lawrence, 2009) – has undeniably enabled the fabrication of fame and celebrity to become culturally widespread, the historical juncture at which this occurred is perhaps more blurred than Boorstin acknowledges. While the contemporary 'celebrity industry' is centrally supported by 'sub-industries' such as the promotional efforts of the publicity industry, which chiefly consists of public relations firms and publicists (Turner, 2004) (although obviously not professionally formalized as it is today), the ethos of PR did exist. Thus, Louis XIV was a figure at the heart of an extensive publicity machine that was focused exclusively upon the creation of a specifically idealized image of him as king and as the divinely-ordained 'Viceroy of God'.

Yet centuries earlier, Julius Caesar recognized the necessity of carefully controlling his image in Rome as he marched across Europe to pacify Gaul and extend Rome's frontiers. In writing *The Conquest of Gaul*, Caesar created his own history to communicate his actions and frame his reputation with the goal of a triumphant return to Rome and the acquisition of sole power (the necessity of civil war against his co-ruler, Pompey, is set out in his records). Indeed, as the Roman historian Suetonius recorded, at the moment of his assassination in the Senate (that saw him stabbed 23 times), 'Caesar fell, arranging his toga so that even in death he would have control over his image' (Braudy, 1986: 89).

Nevertheless, the foundation of fame, within his own time and in contemporary celebrity culture, lies with Alexander the Great. While Alexander's military achievements were extraordinary, his recognition of the need to control public perception of these achievements, to construct and communicate a specific image of him that deftly blurred the lines between fact and fiction, the human and superhuman was also crucial. And of course, to establish his reputation within his lifetime and guarantee his legacy beyond his death, he employed an expert in image-making. Thus, while political 'spin' has been identified as a PR function that fully emerged in the late twentieth century, Alexander employed Callithenes to perform this task in 334 BCE, and established that fame is a status that must, even if built upon achievement of the highest level, be fabricated and manipulated – factors that are key characteristics of contemporary celebrity culture.

CONCLUSION

While the development of a specific 'celebrity culture' as we recognize it within contemporary society is, according to Inglis, located some 260 years ago, its foundations are ancient. The individual drive for fame, to stand out from the mass, is a longstanding human drive. That Alexander could achieve this in a society lacking any form of mass communication is all the more extraordinary, and the key reason why any discussion of celebrity must begin with an analysis of his methods. Indeed, while modern celebrity is predicated upon modes of publicity (visual images, publicity stunts, idealized public personas, etc.) that have their roots back in Alexander's innovations, his fame-seeking attitude resonated and inspired even within the ancient world itself. Earlier in the chapter, I referred to the example of Herostratus, but what was especially significant was that he burnt down the Temple at Ephesus on the day of Alexander the Great's birth, and as a result secured fame for himself but also aligned himself with one of the great architects of fame-securing itself. Therefore, while the means of attaining celebrity have been transformed extensively throughout human history, some factors seemingly remain the same.

FURTHER READING

To further explore the history of fame, readers should engage with:

- Braudy, L. (1986) *The Frenzy of Renown*. New York: Vintage Books.
- Inglis, F. (2010) *A Short History of Celebrity*. Princeton, NJ: Princeton University Press.

To complement the analysis of fame in direct relation to the historical rise of celebrity and with regard to direct ancient historical examples of the quest for fame and self-publicity, readers should consult:

- Caesar, J. (1982) *The Conquest of Gaul* (translated by S.A. Handford). London: Penguin.
- Cicero, M.T. (2009) *Political Speeches*. Oxford: Oxford University Press.

2

THEORIZING CELEBRITY

CHAPTER OVERVIEW

This chapter looks at key ways in which the rise and proliferation of celebrity has been and can be theorized sociologically, but more importantly the ways in which celebrity culture mirrors social and cultural forces and how people effectively *use* celebrity. Although the tone of some of these approaches is critical (Adorno in particular), classic and contemporary sociological theories can illustrate the ways in which individuals *use* celebrity culture, as a religious practice, a source of solidarity (from the deaths of celebrities to everyday 'celebrity talk' with other social actors), to the ways in which the rapid turnover of celebrity culture reflects wider unstable, fluid, or 'liquid' social and cultural structures. Therefore, to articulate these theoretical and conceptual approaches to understanding celebrity culture the chapter will examine:

- Max Weber's notion of charisma and status
- Theodor Adorno's mass culture thesis
- Émile Durkheim's concept of social solidarity
- Zygmunt Bauman's theory of liquid modernity
- Donald Horton and R. Richard Wohl's idea of the para-social relation
- Celebrity, religious practice, and death

To illustrate these ideas, a range of celebrity examples such as Steve Jobs, Britney Spears, Princess Diana, Michael Jackson, Barack Obama, and Miley Cyrus will be discussed.

THEORIZING CELEBRITY

Although the roots of fame and, more significantly, the active desire for fame, are traceable back to ancient civilizations, as explored in the previous chapter, the contemporary concept of celebrity emerged (in Europe, at least) in the middle of the eighteenth century. More importantly, it developed and was shaped by the dominant forces of modernity, industrialization, and urbanization. According to Inglis (2010), as the great metropolises of Europe arose, so too did the primacy of being seen (from professional actors on the theatrical stage, to famous individuals promenading in public spaces). These processes were then accelerated and intensified by the mass circulation of newspapers (with an increasing focus on the lives of the famous – from achievements to scandals) and the major modes of mass communication that would subsequently follow. However, while the social and technological dimensions of modernity explain the process by which specific individuals have gained public prominence and recognition from the 'mass', that still leaves the issue of what explains the nature of why some people achieve fame, and why the rest of society recognizes them as being famous and as being worthy of admiration, if not devotion. To put it another way, what is the effect of celebrity on society?

CELEBRITY, MODERNITY, AND CHARISMA

Given that the celebrity system comes of age within the process of modernity, a development that was characterized by social and technological upheaval and 'a ruthless break with any or all preceding historical conditions' (Harvey, 1989: 12), it is unsurprising that many of the key examinations of the power and influence of celebrity relate to key sociological thinkers concerned with the process of modernity, the most common of whom is the German sociologist, Max Weber (1864–1920) and his concept of charisma. Although not writing about celebrity, Weber's work is incisive as a means with which to understand how human history is replete with charismatic individuals who have achieved considerable political, cultural, and religious sway, and whose power has been perceived to be almost 'mystical', 'spiritual', or, as Laurence Rees (2012) describes it, to possess a 'missionary' quality. In many regards, Weber and charisma is a 'usual suspect' within celebrity studies, but it is an interesting starting point to sociologically and culturally understand why specific individuals can attain potent levels of devotion within the contemporary cultural landscape – because, as we will see in this chapter, celebrity can and does exert considerable influence at times at an individual level, but on occasion, when certain celebrities die, at a mass social level.

One aspect of Weber's sociology was his consideration of different forms of social authority, and he analysed charisma as a very significant type of authority. Moreover, charismatic leadership conventionally stands outside routine models of leadership and economic behaviour. Therefore, instead of bureaucratically-structured leadership, charismatic authority is historically the preserve of 'heroes and sorcerers'. Indeed, charismatic authority is the antithesis to bureaucratic, rationally-organized authority as the 'holders of charisma' typically are not connected with social conventions and routine occupations. As Weber states within *Economy and Society* (Vol. 1), the term 'charisma' is 'applied to a certain quality of an individual personality by virtue of which he is set apart from ordinary men and treated as endowed with supernatural, superhuman, or at least specifically exceptional powers or qualities' (Weber, 1978: 241). Therefore, charismatic authority is unlike rule-bound bureaucratic authority, or traditional social modes of leadership which are connected with customs and processes handed down from the past. In terms of recognizing charismatic authority, what 'alone is important is how the individual is actually regarded by those subject to charismatic authority, by [their] "followers" or "disciples"' (1978: 242).

As Ian Kershaw notes, the concept of charisma has seemingly contemporaneously fallen from favour as an explanatory factor for political leadership. But, in charting Adolf Hitler's rise to power in 1930s Germany (and the destructive aftermath), Kershaw asserts that Hitler's influence over Nazi Germany epitomized the essence of charismatic authority, because Hitler

> did not base his claim to power (except in a most formal sense) on his position as a party leader, or on any functional position. He derived it from what he saw as his historic mission to save Germany. His power, in other words, was 'charismatic', not institutional. It depended upon the readiness of others to see 'heroic' qualities in him. (1998: xxvi)

The issue of charisma within modern political leadership is certainly a crucial factor, particularly in terms of appeal to electorates and contemporary politicians such as former President of the US, Bill Clinton; and the former British Prime Minister Tony Blair combined charismatic qualities with political leadership and rhetoric to usher in a new image and identity for the Labour Party (New Labour). His ultimate successor, Gordon Brown, notably lacked such charismatic prowess and failed to beat his Conservative opponent, David Cameron in the 2010 British General Election. And such is the importance of a charismatic edge within contemporary political campaigning that in the 2012 US presidential election between incumbent Barrack Obama and Republican challenger Mitt Romney, Obama's charismatic appeal would be decisive in his securing of a second term in office (Taylor, 2012). In Weber's analysis, the possessors of charismatic authority ranged from kings and religious leaders (such as Joseph Smith, the founder of Mormonism), to the warrior class of the 'berserker' and the magical shaman.

THE CELEBRITY AS 'SHAMAN'

Of the latter figure, Rojek states that the shamans, or the 'medicine men', of many tribal societies were figures 'distinguished by extraordinary qualities' and individuals who were 'singled out by the spirits' (2001: 55) in the form of spirit possession (Mauss, 1972). However, the spirit of the shamanic charismatic is an essence that Rojek identifies within later Western celebrity culture as the source of their appeal. For instance, he cites Robert Johnson, the 'bluesman' who, legend has it, sold his soul to acquire musical talent, as a prime example. Certainly, Johnson's blues guitar prowess has resonated with numerous later players, and his technical approach constitutes him as a proto-guitar hero of the type typified by later rock and heavy metal music. But it is the 'magical' aura that surrounds Johnson due to the pact legend that renders him 'shamanic', argues Rojek; and he is not alone. Throughout the 1960s, iconic performers such as Jimi Hendrix, Jim Morrison, Mick Jagger, and David Bowie were rock shamans in possession of potent charismatic spiritual power, but of a distinctly modern form. As Rojek explains:

> The rock shaman produces excitement and mass hysteria rather than religious salvation. The ability to act as a conducting rod of mass desire, and to precipitate semi-orgiastic emotions in the crowd are the most obvious features of this form of shamanic power. (2001: 69)

A potential issue with the idea of charisma as an explanatory factor for the allure of celebrity is that the figures that Weber speaks of are invariably rare. For example, soon after the death of Apple's Chief Executive Officer (CEO) and driving force, Steve Jobs, the journalist John Arlidge wrote a piece that unequivocally linked his visionary business success to his possession of charisma (Dutton, 2013). While not on the level of kings and social authority, the issue and (perceived) possession of charisma is a readily identifiable quality within celebrity culture, from latter-day rock star 'shaman' who commands the attention of arenas of fans, to the charismatic appeal of Hollywood actors, from Cary Grant and Jack Nicholson, to Tom Cruise, Brad Pitt, Chow Yun-Fat, Hrithik Roshan, Shah Rukh Khan, Johnny Depp, George Clooney, or Robert Downey Jr. Therefore, the issue of the possession of charisma (or the skill with which to convince an audience that they possess it) and its 'magical' or 'magnetic' quality remains an interesting and significant sociological approach to explain why certain individuals become celebrity figures and emerge to prominence within contemporary cultures, and how they attract public attention and adulation. Of course, as explored in the Introduction, film stars are arguably closer to the kinds of examples cited by Weber in their comparative rarity.

The qualities of talent or uncommon physical attractiveness are primary elements, but performances by film stars are also frequently lauded for being 'magnetic' or 'sublime', that principle Edmund Burke described as 'the strongest emotion which the mind is capable of feeling' (2008: 36). However, there are those who are perceived to be utterly without charisma, yet this has proven to be no impediment to global success, for example Kim Kardashian (who will be discussed in more detail in Chapter 3), whom actors of the stature of Daniel Craig and Jon Hamm have publicly dismissed in *Elle* and *GQ* for possessing only a public persona and displaying little foundation for her success and cultural celebrity visibility (Brockes, 2012). And yet, although lacking the 'supernatural' qualities of Weber's historical leaders, or the rare gifts of acting talent (and the work ethic and tenacity that propelled them to fame) that mark many of the world's premier film stars, the concept of charisma is still frequently linked as at least a contributing factor to explain the allure of celebrities. P. David Marshall stated that charismatic leadership would decline in the wake of the rise of bureaucratic modes of rational organization and governance, which renders charismatic modes of leadership irrational. It is in this regard, argues Marshall, that charisma retains its ability to explain the nature of celebrity, because like 'the charismatic figure, the celebrity demarcates an area of social life and identification that is fundamentally irrational' (1997: 22).

Returning to Robin D. Barnes' definition of the celebrity as (compared with the possessors of fame) a fleeting status that is based upon marketing, being in the right place at the right time, and instant appeal, then the seemingly 'irrational' appeal of celebrities who have no immediately identifiable locus of talent or achievement bar marketability of personality (or controversy), suggests the currency of charisma in relation to celebrity. Thus, rather than a leadership quality, charisma can be translated into the possession (or spun perception) of an 'X factor' or particular image/lifestyle in relation to celebrity culture and its seemingly 'irrational' nature (that merit is irrelevant and notoriety can be as valuable as talent or achievement in gaining public attention).

CELEBRITY, WEBER, AND STATUS

In addition to the concept of charisma, there is a further aspect of Weber's sociology that also can be drawn upon to theorize the nature of celebrity: his articulation of the concept of status. As Kurzman et al. (2007) note, the conflation of Weber with theorizing celebrity is a pertinent one as, while a distinctive celebrity system was developing in America (principally in Hollywood and its emergent star system), Weber was simultaneously devising his conception of status in Germany. Weber (1978), in his short essay 'Class, Status, Party', accounted for the ways in which certain societies were socially stratified in multiple forms, and that there was a distinctive difference between class stratification and social divisions established along the lines of status differences:

> With some over-simplification, one might thus say that 'classes' are stratified according to their relations to the production and acquisition of goods; whereas 'status groups' are stratified according to the principles of their consumption of goods as represented by special 'styles of life'. (cited in Gerth and Wright Mills, 1961: 193)

Yet a distinctive facet of status groups' practice is that they frequently use strict measures to control or limit access into their enclaves, but among industrial, ethnic, religious, and power status groups, celebrity has emerged as a distinctive, modern status group within contemporary cultures. Thus, even though, as Kurzman et al. note, Weber believed that status differences would fade from societies, as its 'maverick' quality would ultimately be routinized into traditional or rational-legal forms of social authority (van Krieken, 2012), celebrity represents a potent, fresh development of the concept and social position. At one level, celebrity constitutes a distinctive (employing C. Wright Mills' classic concept) 'power elite' who (generally) live lives marked by remarkable life chances, high levels of financial wealth, and various privileges (from complementary designer clothing from top fashion houses to preferential treatment and personal security in hotels and public spaces). Typically, therefore, celebrity equates with a distinguishing 'superior' social status position and enables celebrities to exist within privatized social spaces (gated communities and private travel) that establish networks that habitually include interaction and discourse with other celebrities. Therefore:

> Through these social settings, celebrities develop a form of endogamy: they tend to enter into romantic relationships with other celebrities. The ultimate celebrity couple of the late 20th century, Posh and Becks, admitted as much. English soccer star David Beckham writes about his wife, singer Victoria Adams Beckham: 'I'd be lying if I didn't admit that being a pop star was part of the attraction. That did it for me and likewise, the fact that I was good at my job was part of the attraction for her. We were both successful and could relate to each other as equals".' (Kurzman et al., 2007: 356)

However, Kurzman et al. conclude that this status is a direct result of the prevailing capitalist economic system and that the status position of celebrity is a 'product' of a 'culture industry', as well as that celebrity is effectively a capitalist product conveyed via the technologies of mass communication and media: effectively the position of Daniel Boorstin. Certainly, Boorstin sees the development of fame throughout the twentieth century as the steady but increasing decline of 'heroic' figures. Thus, whereas human culture has produced heroic types ranging from Moses, Jesus, Julius Caesar, or George Washington, individuals who demonstrated greatness though acts of significant achievement, the Graphic Revolution has eroded this through the sheer preponderance of images it transmits. Therefore, in the wake of the rise of mass communication technologies, Boorstin argues that the American public

> encounters a vastly larger number of names, faces, and voices than at any earlier period or in any other country. Newspapers, magazines, second-class mail, books, radio, television, telephone, phonograph records – these and other vehicles confront us with thousands of names, people, or fragments of people. In our always more overpopulated consciousness, the hero every year becomes less significant. (2006: 77)

Of course, Boorstin's analysis predates the additional impact of the Internet, blogs, digital music downloads, Reality TV and social networking sites within this media proliferation of famous images. But even without these latter media which have intensified the proliferation of celebrity images, the pre-digital Graphic Revolution established a new form of renown: persons of 'celebrity'; individuals who lack distinctive qualities and who effectively represent the 'human pseudo-event'. Furthermore, entry into the 'democratic' sphere of celebrity is ostensibly less onerous than in the past (whereby fame rested upon an act of great achievement or substance), with the only challenge and effort required being that of staying within the public eye and within the media system. As such, images predominate over achievement in modern celebrity culture.

MASS CULTURE AND CELEBRITIES FOR THE MASSES

Not surprisingly, the pessimism of the effects of the 'Graphic Revolution' upon the nature and acquisition of fame presented by Boorstin has been connected with the equally cynical appraisal of the culture industries put forth by two of the key members of a collective of thinkers dubbed the Frankfurt School: Theodor Adorno and Max Horkheimer (Evans, 2004). Within their classic text *The Dialectic of Enlightenment* (1973), Horkheimer and Adorno argue that the key defining characteristic of mass culture in the twentieth century is its over-riding sense of sameness. The role of culture in Western capitalistic societies is to impose a pervasive brand of uniformity through its primary modes of mass communication products such as cinema, radio, and magazines. The result is that beneath this monopolistic control:

> All mass culture is identical. The technology of the culture industry results in standardization and mass production. The need which might resist central control has already been suppressed by the control of the individual consciousness. (Horkheimer and Adorno, 1973: 121)

The major forms of the mass communication system impose themselves on the consciousness of individuals and act to define what can be consumed. Indeed, the dominant forms of mass communication consumed in leisure time are exclusively defined and set by the mass culture industries, shutting off opportunities for alternative or amateur media production and viewing individuals as nothing more than customers. But the effect of this is not only articulated in terms of a financial nexus (individuals pay for mass communication products), but it also serves a key ideological function because, as Horkheimer and Adorno state, 'culture has always played its part in taming revolutionary instincts' (1973: 152). Thus, mass culture products are both a source of capitalist revenue and also, due to their function as entertainment, an alternative 'opium of the people' – a means through which to transmit and instil a conservative message.

As Adorno argues in *The Culture Industry* (2006), mass culture should be the culture that develops from the masses themselves, but this is not the contemporary meaning and operation of the term. Rather than some form of organic, spontaneous cultural art form arising from below, mass culture is systematically imposed from above. As such, not only are the masses a proletariat within industry, but, in their private leisure spheres, they are intimately connected with the capitalist machine in terms of the entertainment they consume via mass communication. Therefore, argues Adorno, the new within the culture industry is actually nothing but a disguise for an eternal sameness. The result is not merely a wider source of profit generation, but also a distinctive and cultural effect on cultural forms and the individuals who consume them. A key illustrative example cited by Adorno whereby the effacement of the division between high and low culture can be readily identified is popular music – a form that, according to Adorno, explicitly and demonstrably illustrates the extent of the decline of cultural taste throughout mass culture. In Adorno's analysis, the message of mass culture can be found in all forms of music that are marketed for consumption. Indeed, the act of music, far from being a cultural event or a source of emotional or bodily pleasure, is intrinsically ideological. Thus, when a particular individual listens to a piece of music, 'the listener is converted, along his line of least resistance, into the acquiescent purchaser' (2006: 32). It does not matter if the form of music consumed is classical or popular, the underlining intent and effect is the same: the listener is exposed to a commodity and is being manipulated purely for reasons of marketability. The net effect is a widespread erosion of individuality, in which everyone does what everyone else does because the same cultural products are marketed to all members of society in a manner governed by the standardized production of consumer goods, products which are, for Adorno, simply 'trash'. The overarching premise of Adorno's critique of mass culture is that, whether it is music, television, or sport, there is no neutrality. Even the most seemingly benign forms of cultural industry product not only are commodities to be consumed for leisure and entertainment purposes, but they possess messages that are geared towards the conservation of the prevailing capitalist system.

With reference to cinematic celebrity, the Hollywood film star is not the natural possessor of charisma, but alternatively a key representative of the 'cult of personality': a figure positioned to 'epitomize the potential of everyone in American society'; an ideological enterprise predicated, argue Horkheimer and Adorno, upon the perception that the 'masses are by their very nature psychologically immature and thus are drawn to the magic of these larger-than-life personalities in the same way that children identify with and implicitly trust their parents' (Marshall, 1997: 9). In a more practical sense, film stars also function to frame the content and expectation of standardized cinematic 'product'. Applying Adorno and Horkheimer's cultural critique to the predictable quality of contemporary Hollywood films and the ways in which many film stars' public identities predictably confirm audience expectation of narrative content, theme, and plot, Alan How argues that within much of mainstream cinema:

> We know pretty much what will happen in a film within the first five minutes, in fact if we know *who* is starring in it we can equally predict much of its content. At the present time, if Clint Eastwood is in it, it will be a 'tough guy' movie, if Kim Basinger or Brad Pitt are in it [it] will be 'sexy', if Hugh Grant is in it, it will be a comedy of errors. (2003: 69)

If we add a few more contemporary examples such as Will Smith, George Clooney, Anne Hathaway, Hugh Jackman, Christian Bale, Bradley Cooper, Michael Fassbender, or Jennifer Lawrence, then we might see an extension of the point: by and large, the kinds of star fronting a film will typically determine its content from the outset, irrespective of plot, and establish the conventions of its genre (Action, Romcom, Teen, Musical, Crime Thriller, etc.). And yet, although Anne Hathaway might be typically associated with the romantic comedy genre (*The Princess Diaries*, *The Devil Wears Prada*, or *Valentine's Day*), she portrays very different characters (and gives very different performances) within *Love and Other Drugs*, *The Dark Knight Rises*, and *Les Misérables*.

COMPLEX CELEBRITY IMAGES

This relates to Dyer's (1982) classic critique of Boorstin (and by extension the culture industry manipulation critique) that asserts that it does not examine the content of star images. Rather, Boorstin's argument rests upon the idea that there is no content to star images, only surface differences of appearance. But these differences of appearance are not, argues Dyer, necessarily superficial, and stars need also to be seen in the context of both their roles and their filmic presentation. This is because the examination of stars' images frequently reveals complexity, contradiction, and difference. For example, in analysing the career of the American actress Jane Fonda, Dyer argues that a range of conflicting images emerge: the 1960s 'sex symbol' of *Barbarella*, the serious and Oscar-winning actress (for *Klute* in 1971 and *Coming Home* in 1978), and her activities as an anti-Vietnam political campaigner (for which she was dubbed 'Hanoi Jane'); and one could also add her 'Fitness Queen' status in the 1980s via her release of Jane Fonda home workout fitness videos. A similar, but more contemporary, argument could be made of the actress Angelina Jolie, whose public persona has ranged from Hollywood 'wild child', to Oscar-winning actress, to admired film director and political activist through her involvement with the United Nations. Consequently, pinning down a decisive 'star image' is more complex and unpredictable than Boorstin concedes.

Furthermore (and a critique equally applicable to Adorno), Boorstin treats society as a monolithic mechanism in which human consciousness apparently plays little part, other than as a force to be stimulated and exploited by the rapacious and cunning capitalist 'culture industry'. However, as Dyer argues, semiotic analysis frequently suggests that humans engage in the practices of encoding and decoding (Hall, 1980), that audiences work with meanings in a 'polysemic' manner, negotiating their own readings and often rejecting meanings. This lies at the heart of fan studies (Grossberg, 1992; Jenkins, 1992; Hills, 2002; Brooker, 2002; Bailey, 2005; Parke and Wilson, 2011) which have long since explored and exposed (and continue to do so) the often sophisticated ways in which fans deconstruct their favoured texts, debate them (from traditional fanzines to online discussion boards), and in some instances rewrite texts in the form of fan or online 'slash fiction' (for example, the origins of E.L. James' *Fifty Shades of Grey* novel trilogy, a publishing sensation in 2012, emerged from *Twilight* fan fiction and which, interestingly, made James a celebrity). The important issue to emerge from this analysis is that individuals derive pleasure from the artefacts of the culture industries, and, more importantly, they can *use* texts to *enrich* their lives: a relationship and process that can be extended to the fandom of celebrities.

CELEBRITY AND SOCIAL SOLIDARITY

As Ellis Cashmore (2006) notes in *Celebrity/Culture*, within a study published in 1991 and conducted by Neil Alperstein, he discovered the distinctive 'imaginary social relations' many people reported they had with celebrities appearing in television commercials. Although respondents had never physically met the celebrities they ostensibly 'connected' with, there was nevertheless a distinctive quality of 'artificial involvement' between them to the extent that these people used them to help them 'make sense of reality.' Thus, television viewers reported the experience of feeling close to celebrity figures; even though the only contact that they had with them was via television. For example, one viewer disclosed how she regarded Joan Lunden, the host of *Good Morning America*, as 'a trusted friend', stating that: 'When she happens to be sick or on vacation, I miss her' (Cashmore, 2006: 81). The important issue to acknowledge here, in response to critics such as Boorstin and Adorno, is that far from considering his subjects as being obsessive due to their avowed loyalties to inspirational and reliable television 'friends', Alperstein credited them with possessing intelligence and wit, and asserted that they were not pathologically obsessed fans. But how can such strong connections exist between viewers and mediated celebrities? The answer to this question is seemingly explainable with relation to a now-classic concept, the para-social relationship.

THE PARA-SOCIAL RELATIONSHIP

The term was conceptualized by Donald Horton and R. Richard Wohl in 1956, and explained, from a psychological perspective, the impact mass-media forms such as radio, cinema, and television were having on viewers and listeners. What they concluded was striking, because a key characteristic of these mediums was that:

> They give the illusion of face-to-face relationship with the performer. The conditions of response to the performer are analogous to those in a primary group. The most remote and illustrious men are met *as if they* were in the circle of one's peers; the same is true of a character in a story who comes to life in an especially vivid and arresting way. We propose to call this seeming face-to-face relationship between spectator and performer a *para-social relationship*. (1956: 215)

The para-social relationship describes relations of intimacy that are established through the mass media rather than through direct experiences and face-to-face meetings in real-world settings. In Rojek's view, this constitutes a form of 'second-order intimacy' because it stems from representations of a celebrity rather than actual physical contact. But, it is still contact. As Horton and Wohl state of the ways in which actors address the audience within television shows, they frequently face the spectator and speak directly to them, as if they were 'conversing personally and privately' (ibid.). Therefore, as Rojek explains, within societies in which many people affirm that they experience sub-clinical feelings of isolation and loneliness, the para-social relationship is a significant component within their explorations for some kind of social recognition and sense of personal belonging and engagement, and celebrities can provide such belonging. And this goes beyond interaction via the television/cinema/computer screen, as the obvious physical and social remoteness of the celebrity, who belongs, after all, to a distinctive socially and culturally privatized status group, is compensated for by the excess of mass-media information fanzines, press stories, TV documentaries, interviews, biographies (and also Internet gossip sites, celebrity Twitter accounts), which act to dynamically 'personalize the celebrity', and thus transform 'a distant figure from a stranger into a significant other' (Rojek, 2001: 52–3).

In addition to the para-social relationship fulfilling individual needs, it also has a distinctive social function because it has undeniable analogies with acts of religious worship, as fans frequently project extraordinary powers and attributes onto chosen celebrities. To explore this, Rojek turns to the classical sociologist, Émile Durkheim, who, within his study of religion, proposed that the religious ceremony both consecrates the sacred belief system of a community and provides an outlet for 'collective effervescence'. This latter condition refers to a state of popular excitement, frenzy, even ecstasy. However, Durkheim argued that the growth of individualism would inevitably reduce the significance of organized religion, but since social equilibrium requires formalized interruptions from routine, the state would need to organize regular holidays in which collective effervescence could be harmlessly released, and the bonds of collective life be routinely reaffirmed. However, although Durkheim's prediction about the decline in the social influence of organized religion has proven to be accurate, his proposition that state policy should increase the number of secular holidays has not. Furthermore, while the secularization debate has illustrated the extent of the de-institutionalization of state religion (particularly in the Western world), nevertheless, it exaggerates the degree to which religion has been substituted by scientific ideas and institutions and legal-rational bureaucratic systems. At one level, religious belief has been commuted into widespread belief in alternative modes of religion – New Age beliefs or Scientology (Saliba, 1995; Heelas, 1996), and the belief in the supernatural – such as ghosts and angels (Davies, 2009), but it has also, argues Rojek, been restructured around cultural activities such as sport (the release of emotion at the soccer game, the tennis match, or the NFL clash), and, significantly, is linked to celebrity.

This is so because 'celebrity culture' is now so ubiquitous, and 'establishes the main scripts, presentational props, conversational codes and other source materials through which cultural relations are constructed' (Rojek, 2001: 57). However, Rojek's use of Durkheim enables us to deepen the applicability of Durkheim to celebrity, because, while celebrity clearly does afford moments of public effervescence (the film premiere, the concert, the celebrity personal appearance), the pervasiveness of celebrity (given its global scale and significance) means that it could also, arguably, represent a means with which contemporary cultures come together. In essence, celebrity can be argued to represent a modern contributing factor to social solidarity or how societies knit together coherently.

MECHANICAL AND ORGANIC SOLIDARITY

Durkheim sets out his conception of how societies, from simple and small-scale to more complex and industrial, operate, in *The Division of Labour in Society*, arguing that the division of labour is a necessary condition for both the intellectual and material development of societies; indeed, it is the very source of civilization itself. Although there are clear and necessary economic outcomes from the existence and operation of a social division of labour, any economic service is secondary to its true function: 'to create between two or more people a feeling of solidarity' (1984: 17). Hence, the division of labour is a key source of the 'social glue' that binds individuals together to form a functional and integrated society.

However, the division of labour applies to only one of Durkheim's conceptions of solidarity, *organic*, but there is a primary form, and one that tends to explain the ways in which integrative social 'networks' have been established in smaller-scale societies, a form of solidarity called *mechanical* solidarity. Mechanical solidarity is illustrated by what Durkheim refers to as 'solidarity by similarities' and manifests itself in the form of feelings shared by the majority of a social group, for example, etiquette, ritual, and ceremonial or religious practices – what Durkheim calls the collective, common or the 'conscious collective': 'the set of beliefs and sentiments common to the average members of a single society [which] forms a determinate system that has its own life' (cited in Lukes, 1973: 4). That it has a 'life of its own' is explained in terms of its detachment from specific social conditions and specific individuals because it outlives them; it persists as generations come and go.

Consequently, it represents something quite different from the consciousness of individuals, existing above and beyond them as a common social consciousness that influences the morality and social behaviour of individuals to instil social cohesion. This sense of a collective, shared conscious way of acting, and set of beliefs, is spread throughout an entire society. The force of religion was a key means with which solidarity was achieved, and Durkheim set out his argument within *The Elementary Forms of Religious Life*, based on the analysis of 'elementary', 'primitive', or 'humble' religious and ceremonial practices, specifically those practised by Australian Aboriginal tribal societies in relation to 'totemic' religious rituals. A totemic object typically took the form of a plant/vegetable, an animal, or rocks, and had exclusive, emblematic significance for a particular clan, representing the collective ideals that the group bestowed upon such objects. It is a sacred object, regarded with veneration and surrounded by various ritual activities. Totemic objects are endowed with the value of being *sacred* to the group, and they are segregated from alternative *profane* plants, vegetables, animals, or objects. The latter serve as food, while it is prohibited to eat those objects which have been sanctified as sacred. In Durkheim's view, more importantly, the totem becomes a symbol of the clan/tribe, and in the course of collective ceremonies that surround the totemic object, the social group is bound together. Therefore, religion upholds and reaffirms collective sentiments and collective ideas, reinforcing unity and cementing mechanical solidarity. However, the shift to larger-scale social formations necessitated a different form of solidarity: organic.

Organic solidarity is the unifying force of the secular world. Where everything social was religious, the power of religion is a diminishing force in industrialized societies, argues Durkheim. In the place of religious functions, political, economic, and scientific functions have established themselves as powerful social forces, and the means by which a common consciousness is instilled in a large number of individuals is achieved through differentiation. The structural nature of an 'organic' society is entirely different from a 'mechanical' one, which is why it is called 'organic'. Instead of homogenous values, organic solidarity is characterized by a system of difference, of different 'organs' which act – as organs do within a living body – in a coordinated fashion, each possessing a specialized function. Each 'organ' is different, but vitally interrelated to the 'body' as a whole. Within increasingly urban and industrial societies, social groupings that are not bound by close-knit blood relations, or specific sacred practices, the socially solidifying forces come from specialized, but differing, employment roles – what Durkheim calls 'the division of labour'.

As such, in densely populated spaces, urban centres that necessitate constant social contact, individuals – despite their numerousness and lack of emotional or family connections – form a society through industrial interdependence and co-operation. Hence, the differing roles serve to knit industrial societies together. Within a condition of organic solidarity, social actors have a specific role or form of employment that is entirely specific to them. The same is true for other social actors in the given society, who come together through their mutual interdependence. Durkheim's vision of society is that of an interconnected network of social dependencies coming together to form a cohesive social whole: a harmonious collective. Although individuals meet each other in terms of their differing jobs, the outcome is far more significant, argues Durkheim. What is actually occurring is a process whereby individuals meet as differing 'social functions'; as such, 'society has an interest in the interplay of these functions and the actual function of the division of labour', as with religious or sacred practices before it, 'is to create between two or more people a feeling of solidarity' (1984: 17).

CELEBRITY AND RELIGIOSITY

Within contemporary societies, there are alternative social 'facts' that also perform a socially solidifying role, and celebrity, arguably, is distinctively one of them. This is because celebrity points to the ways in which the shift from mechanical to organic was perhaps never absolute because there has always been a degree of slippage between them. On the one hand, the various discussions of new religious movements that developed from the second half of the twentieth century have already pointed to this slippage. The case for the need for some form of spirituality in the face of an anomic world has been persuasively made by a number of sociologists. On the other hand, however, celebrity has increasingly been seen to represent something akin to a new religious movement, albeit a secular one.

For many commentators, celebrity can be read in a religious manner due to the ways in which many are perceived to be figures worthy of worship, and, although offering no salvation, are nevertheless approached in a religious manner (Maltby et al., 2002). At one level, this can be by association, or even the endorsement of particular religious belief systems, such as Tom Cruise and Scientology, or Madonna and Kabbalah, or simply celebrity figures who openly discuss their particular religious identities and incorporate them into their professional lives. A prime example of the latter would be the American film and television actor, Jim Caviezel (most famous for his lead roles in the film *The Passion of the Christ* and the television series, *Person of Interest*) and his much-acknowledged Catholic faith.

CELEBRITY, RELIGIOUS PRACTICE, AND DEATH

Celebrity as a 'social fact', however, also has numerous parallels with religious practice and religious worship in a more widespread social and cultural sense. Rojek (2001) identifies a number of conspicuous parallels between religious belief and approaches to celebrity which clearly point to the amalgamation of religion and celebrity in numerous contemporary societies. One example is the construction of 'reliquaries of celebrity culture', a secular version of the church reliquary, or receptacle for holy relics. From the standpoint of celebrity, 'totemic' relics range from personalized autographs to 'film stars' soap, chewed pieces of gum, lipstick tissues and even a blade of grass from a star's lawn' (2001: 58), but they take on a particularly 'sacred' quality. Defining celebrity as a form of 'neopaganism', Marche argues that the owners of Esther's Haircutting, the salon in which Britney Spears notoriously shaved herself bald in 2006, 'knew immediately that the relics of her breakdown were sacred. The sweepings from their floor along with a blue lighter and the half can of Red Bull the star left behind went on auction a few days later with a reserve of a million dollars' (2010: 10). A further example of the disproportionate value placed on mundane items rendered 'sacred' because they were discarded by celebrities is illustrated by the selling on the electronic auction site eBay, for $6,600, of the Hollywood actress Scarlett Johansson's used handkerchief. Similarly, the globally famous pop star Justin Bieber donated a lock of his hair to the talk-show host Ellen DeGeneres housed in a box he also signed. The hair was subsequently auctioned for $40,668, with the money going to the Gentle Barn Foundation, an animal-rights organization.

Although the concept of 'media pilgrims' is a long-established concept referring to fans who visit the production sites of their favourite films/TV shows, and so on (Couldry, 2000), celebrity-themed religiosity is palpable with regard to the phenomenon of film and popular music fans engaging in 'pilgrimages' to sites associated with a celebrity's life, such as Graceland, Elvis Presley's Tennessee home. Also, cemeteries where celebrity figures are interred have become much-frequented tourist locations, such as Père Lachaise in Paris, which 'houses' an assortment of famous remains from Balzac, Isadora Duncan, and Oscar Wilde to Edith Piaf and Jim Morrison. Similarly, Levitt (2010) cites sources that estimate that in the twenty-first century around 350 people visit the Los Angeles grave of Marilyn Monroe (who died in 1962) every day, while the actor Heath Ledger's apartment rapidly became the site of numerous objects of commemoration left by fans, as did Apple stores in the wake of the death of Steve Jobs, the company's visionary CEO, in 2011. The effect that celebrity deaths have on the public is due, argues Levitt, to the unremitting stream of information concerning celebrity lives provided by the media, a flow that establishes a strong sense of familiarity and identification, even though any kind of immediate or personal connection is absent, which, for most members of the public, is the norm in relation to celebrities.

It is this secondhand, media-created proximity that is put forward to account for the often highly emotional reaction that can accompany news of the death of a particular celebrity and which underscores the potency and depth of feeling established through the para-social relationship. Thus, while celebrity elicits practices analogous to religious worship, the deaths of some celebrity figures have produced extraordinary moments of social and cultural cohesion, in effect, incidents of social solidarity, but relating to social and individual reactions to the deaths of celebrity figures, which have been extensively mediated.

With reference to the subject of dying and bereavement, Clive Seale (1998) argues that a common feature within social and cultural life consists of the rejection of the inevitability of death and the denial of death. However, with reference to the history of the figure of the corpse within culture, John Sutton Baglow stresses that while the mechanisms and social processes by which death and the corpse became increasingly physically invisible (through the hospital as the principal site of dying and silence about death in social discourse), popular culture has brought the figure of the corpse to the public fore to the extent that (with reference to 'New Age' books and TV shows such as *Six Feet Under*) 'death imbues our culture. Far from denying it, we imbibe it, talk about it, and (thanks to a plentiful supply of foreign wars and sensational homicides at home) experience it, if in mediated form' (2007: 227). But in addition to television (and we can add further examples such as *C.S.I.* and *Body of Proof*), the extensive mediation of celebrity deaths has enhanced this visibility further.

PRINCESS DIANA

The social significance and power of celebrity death was perhaps first vividly illustrated as early as 1926 in the case of the silent-film era actor, Rudolf Valentino, when 100,000 people attended the funeral home to view his body and thousands more gathered to watch his funeral procession. But the most telling example of the social influence of a celebrity in the wake of their death was that of Diana, Princess of Wales. Following her death on 31 August 1997 as the result of a car crash in the Pont de l'Alma tunnel in Paris, Diana became the focus of pervasive public mourning, a process intensified on the day of her funeral, 6 September 1997. The social impact of this event is ably illustrated by Brown et al. (2003) in their report that over 1 million people lined the three-mile funeral procession route, while approximately 2.5 billion people watched the worldwide satellite broadcast. Although such public outpouring of grief was critically assessed by some commentators as the result of either a form of mass hysteria or simply media representation and manipulation (Turnock, 2000), for Brown et al. the reason was the intense degree to which many individuals had forged a potent para-social relation with Diana. This is their explanation:

> Princess Diana embodied the archetype of the princess myth. She was a relatively unknown, beautiful young woman, discovered by the heir apparent prince, who became the 'people's princess'. Despite her personal moral failures, psychological struggles, and clashes with the house of Windsor, Diana

was seen as one who reached out to help those less fortunate. These actions made her a heroine to many admirers who sought to protect her reputation. (2003: 588)

The mourning process was such that it seemingly created what Richard Johnson refers to as the 'Dianized nation': a definitive period in which Britain was a state that was 'in a state of shock' (2006: 525). The reason for this, argues Johnson, stems from Diana's apparent 'availability' when she was alive, her modification of traditional royal protocols of distance from the public to one of connection (frequently physical at official engagements and charity events). Thus, the keen sense of emotional connection with Diana as a famous figure manifested in clear examples of social 'solidarity' at the time of her death, as one commentator stated of the individuals who had come to publicly mourn her: 'the waiting crowd seemed as near as it was possible to get to a cross-section of the country: young and old, men and women, rich and poor, black and white' (2006: 526).

PUBLIC REACTION TO CELEBRITY DEATH

In consequence, as C.W. Watson concurs, the death of Diana gave rise to widespread and authentic expressions of public grief, a distinctly Durkheimian example of the articulation of collective emotions and a collective ritual that constituted 'a uniform emotion that was common to all' and 'which created a sense of communion which encouraged a belief in shared values' (1997: 4). Similarly, shortly after the news that the iconic and globally famous pop singer Michael Jackson had died on 25 June 2009, the 'grassroots' user-created Internet encyclopaedia *Wikipedia* had to be momentarily shut down due to the surge of individuals attempting to edit the Jackson entry (Whannel, 2010), and his death overwhelmed social networking sites such as Twitter and Facebook. While not all of the posts expressed feelings of grief or condolence (there were also jokes, rumours, and spam), millions did (Hoe-Lian Goh and Sian Lee, 2011). As Paul Hollander (2010a) states, Jackson's death dominated news media and, as with Diana, more than 1 million people attended Jackson's memorial service, held in Los Angeles. However, as a controversial addendum, the visibility issue transcended coverage of the funeral as numerous newspapers and magazines ran images of Jackson's dead body in a hospital bed, and it continued with the trial of his physician, Dr Conrad Murray, and the extensive media coverage that followed. Similarly, the death of the singers Amy Winehouse in 2011 and Whitney Houston in 2012 were global news events, but with regard to Houston, her funeral – which included numerous celebrity mourners, as one would expect – also enabled the wider public to watch via online coverage. Similarly, the actor Robin Williams' death in 2014 garnered global news coverage and widespread professional and fan media tributes.

Hollander's appraisal of the *public* reaction to Jackson's death highlights an alternative perception of celebrity 'worship' that identifies its status and influence as an intrinsically *pathological* component of contemporary societies. Hollander turns to Boorstin's *The Image* (1992) for reference and he echoes Boorstin's cynical view of the trajectory of fame throughout the twentieth century as one in which celebrity and achievement have increasingly become mutually exclusive forces. Yet, as Hollander concedes, although there is an economic, or 'power', dimension with regard to an entertainment industry that has progressively become an integral component of global economies (from Hollywood and Bollywood to Nigeria's Nollywood) which are strongly motivated to promote the celebrity system (creating entirely new industries such as public relations), this is not simply a case of capitalist ideological domination and manufactured desire. Rather, there is an authentic genuine demand for celebrity in contemporary society. And it reflects Durkheim's sociology perfectly: Hollander articulates this sense of need in terms of a celebrity 'worship' that acts as a substitute for some form of collective belief that has diminished. Thus, the 'cults' devoted to celebrities act in a manner akin to devotion to football, baseball, or soccer teams serving as 'ersatz communities and sources of solidarity' (2010a: 151).

CELEBRITY AS A SOCIABLE TOOL

Yet the 'cult of celebrity' need not be pathological, as Hollander suggests, but rather could serve as a key vehicle for day-to-day social solidarity. Indeed, 'celebrity worship' need not be viewed as an aberrant form of behaviour, as it often is. Rather, an interest in celebrity coincides with a prevalent form of social interaction – gossip. As Carol Brooks states, within her article 'What celebrity worship says about us', although frequently dismissed, gossip, or rather 'pointless conversation', is a 'powerfully healthy social elixir' (2004: 1) and the use of other people's lives, their problems and positives, can help individuals to define what they value as a culture. This is especially valuable, if not essential, in societies that have developed beyond small-scale settlements with close social proximity to industrialized 'multiple villages' – domestic spaces, work spaces, leisure sites – that individuals constantly move in and out of, with limited social contacts. As such, gossip about individuals who are located within an individual's home area is of no relevance to work colleagues. This is where the value of celebrity lies; because celebrity, argues Brooks, acts as a 'universal cultural currency' that can cover every social location within an individual's life.

So, talking about celebrities, their fashions, professional achievements, but especially their scandals, romances, or flopped projects act as a 'social bridge' and one of the few that can successfully cut through class, ethnic, religious, sexual, and myriad other cultural barriers. A prime example of a celebrity inspiring enormous degrees of conversation, debate, support, disgust, and criticism was Miley Cyrus' 2013 VMA award performance of her hit song 'We Can't Stop', involving her 'trademark' tongue poking, risqué outfit, and sexually provocative posturing with singer Robin Thicke, which dominated media discourses the following day and became a key source of public debate, much expressed on social media platforms and behaviour reflected upon by other celebrity figures (most notably, Drake, Taylor Swift, and Kelly Clarkson who tweeted responses to Cyrus' controversial performance). But, if a proportion of daily discourse invokes the critical views of Boorstin et al., Brooks suggests otherwise because:

The truth is, celebrity chat is not about them; it's about us. Far from being victimized by information about celebrities, we're using it for our own positive social ends. Far from worshipping the stars in a simplistic way, we're dissecting their lifestyle choices and their love lives to help us define who we are, to learn and reinforce our shared values, to build support networks and to reach out to people with whom we have little in common. (2004: 2)

In other words, it is a means to attain and reinforce a potent sense of solidarity in complex societies which have transcended the mechanical, small-scale ritual-istic/religious sources of social cohesion. While the division of labour may be the primary and structural solidifying force in 'organic' societies, celebrity can be argued to act as a further form of 'social glue' because it is, whether people admire or hate it, a universal cultural presence and a dominant force within the media system. This is all the more so in cultures that follow a celebrity's every move and thought via social networking sites such as Facebook, Twitter, or Instagram (as we will see in Chapter 5). This, then, is why Brown et al. (2003) argue that para-social relationships are not aberrant but socially common, due to the degree to which individuals are exposed to celebrity figures via the media with such regularity that they can be considered as 'friends' and as such acutely mourned when they die.

LIQUID TIMES, LIQUID CELEBRITY

I have suggested, via classic sociologists such as Durkheim, that celebrities have distinctive individual and social uses and keen significances for many people, and the issue of celebrity-inspired solidarity is all the more interesting when the nature of modernity post-Durkheim is considered. Although modernity was supposedly eclipsed in the late 1970s and throughout the 1980s by the rise of a 'postmodern condition' (Lyotard, 1984), many sociologists kept faith with the spirit and pro-cesses of modernity and produced a range of accounts that convincingly charted its transformations of time and space, and its unpredictability (Giddens, 1991; Beck, 1992). However, it is with reference to the sociologist Zygmunt Bauman's 'liquid modernity' concept that the link between Durkheim's solidarity and the relevance of celebrity as a source of social cohesiveness in the twenty-first century can be further mapped.

In Bauman's (2000) analysis of contemporary Western societies, he argues that the ideal metaphor with which to conceptualize social and economic conditions is that of 'fluidity: a world characterized by the dissolution of social networks, the collapse of institutions of collectivity, and the intensification of individualization. It is a social and cultural landscape marked by uncertainty and rapid change: a system charac-terized by social forms that constantly 'decompose and melt' (Bauman, 2007: 1). As Redmond (2010) explains, Bauman broadly presents a portrait of modern Western life in which the central components of individual and social lives (work, interper-sonal relationships, politics, national identities, citizenship, community, production systems) have become ever more fluid, unstable, and subject to continual change: a society of 'togetherness dismantled' (Bauman, 2003: 119). However, in focusing upon Barack Obama's 2008 presidential election campaign, Redmond argues that celebrity culture acutely reflects this social condition as it is also a world of fleeting spectacle and rapid bombardment by images. But the charismatic appeal of Obama offered a distinctive moment of 'solidity' within a liquid, spectacle-dominated culture. Indeed, Redmond views Obama within this multimedia campaign (notable for its extensive use of social networking platforms such as Facebook and Twitter) as an example of both 'charismatic authority and collective effervescence' – thus combining Weber and Durkheim within the context of 'liquid celebrity' (2010: 89). Celebrity, in this instance entwined with mediated politics, demonstrates the ways in which celebrity can represent a potent 'sense of shared belonging lost in the liquid age' (2010: 90). Although Obama's diminished popularity in his second term demonstrates how transient thia states can be.

While Jock Young, within his book *The Vertigo of Late Modernity*, makes a similar point, suggesting that celebrities constitute 'guiding narratives for a shifting world' (2007: 184), Bauman himself also identifies celebrities as key figures within the liquid society, and the perfect reflection and emblem of its key qualities. This is due to

> the abundance of their images and the frequency with which their names are mentioned in public broadcasts and the private conversations that follow them. Celebrities are on everybody's tongue; they are *every* household's household names. Like martyrs and heroes, they provide a sort of glue that brings and holds together otherwise diffuse and scattered aggregates of people. (2005: 49–50)

The suggestion here, then, is that there is a social quality inherent to celebrity that accords with Brook's gossip function, and by extension, the solidarity-like social glue function linked with Durkheim. Therefore, celebrity is a cultural phenomenon that is applicable to individual lives and also operative and explainable at a structural social level. On the one hand, celebrities are the human face of a rapacious and cynical culture industry, the shallow residue left behind following the 'fall of heroes'. But on the other hand, celebrities resonate keenly in people's lives: they fulfil personal needs and inspire very real feelings of grief to the extent that the deaths of celebrities can unite communities. Thus, from the late nineteenth-century/early twentieth-century modernity mapped by Durkheim and Weber, to the 'liquid' conditions of contemporary Western societies, celebrities can be seen in a more profound light than simply as the 'manufactured and managed' products within a 'world of media spectacle' (Kellner, 2003: 4).

CELEBRITY THEORISTS AS CELEBRITIES

Given that Bauman argues that celebrities represent the liquidity of modern life so well due to the frequently short-lived 'episodic' nature of their careers, however, a view of cultures knitted together in a succession of solidarities by awareness of and devotion to celebrities is a culture not only articulated by Adorno and Boorstin, but arguably predicted by them. And such critics would no doubt stress the extent to which societies that have recourse to celebrities and celebrity lifestyles as their source of cultural solidarity, or must navigate their social lives by the positions of film stars, pop stars, and Reality TV personalities, is a culture that is still firmly in the grip of the culture industries. Indeed, even the social theorists who analyse celebrity are now becoming celebrities themselves. For example, Hollander argues in relation to Slavoj Žižek, author of influential texts such as *Enjoy your Symptom!* (2001), *In Defense of Lost Causes* (2008), *Violence* (2008), and *Living in the End Times* (2011), that he courts a celebrity intellectual status through the expression of obscure academic jargon that is read by his audience as evidence of profundity. Thus, just as celebrity represents cultural decline and limited media industrial output, the celebrity of Žižek, Hollander argues, is 'among the reliable indicators of the decline of the quality of academic-intellectual life in the North America and Europe' (2010b: 1).

CONCLUSION

While once those who achieved the status of fame did so because of acts of significant, singular distinction, the contemporary cultural landscape is one in which the basis of celebrity gossip concerns the law-enforcement woes of Lindsay Lohan, or the latest brand enterprise unleashed by the Kardashian family. And, as we shall see in the next chapter, when considering the close relationship between economics and celebrity, there is much to suggest that celebrities are an inherent element within the contemporary culture and media industries – not only enhancing profitability for established brands, but also, increasingly, establishing themselves as brands available for purchase.

FURTHER READING

To further explore the theoretical ideas that underpin this chapter, readers should consult:

- Couldry, N. (2003) *Media Rituals: A Critical Approach*. London: Routledge.

- Durkheim, É. (1984) *The Division of Labour in Society*. Basingstoke: Macmillan.

- Horkheimer, M. and Adorno, T.W. (1973) *The Dialectic of Enlightenment* (translated by John Cumming). London: Allen Lane.

- Weber, M. (1978) *Economy and Society: An Outline of Interpretive Sociology, Vol. 1*. Berkeley, CA and London: University of California Press.

To further explore the ways in which the key theoretical ideas explored within this chapter relate to celebrity culture readers should engage with:

- Boorstin, D. (1992) *The Image: A Guide to Pseudo-Events in America.* Harmondsworth: Penguin.
- Marshall, P.D. (1997) *Celebrity and Power: Fame in Contemporary Culture.* Minneapolis and London: University of Minneapolis Press.
- Rojek, C. (2001) *Celebrity.* London: Reaktion.

3

THE BUSINESS OF CELEBRITY

CHAPTER OVERVIEW

A significant aspect of the economic and consumer landscape is the degree to which celebrity images are aligned with products and services and thus animating brands and enhancing their opportunities to reach out to consumers. So, from Nicole Sherzinger advertising Herbal Essences shampoo, Cate Blanchett endorsing Armani fragrances, and Uma Thurman advertising Louis Vuitton, to Kareena Kapoor promoting Vivel Di Wills Soaps and George Clooney, Daniel Craig, and Nicole Kidman marketing Omega watches, celebrities have become part of big business. Furthermore, many have graduated from selling the wares of existing brands to marketing their own, such as Beyoncé, Jennifer Lopez, and Justin Timberlake. This chapter, then, examines the economic aspects of celebrity culture and the intimate and growing connections that have been established between the business world and celebrity. In terms of topics for discussion, the chapter includes:

- The rise of the film star as an attraction for cinema audiences
- Celebrities taking economic control over their careers
- Celebrity product endorsements
- Celebrity brands such as clothing and fragrance lines
- Celebrities as entrepreneurs and business figures acquiring celebrity status

To illustrate the ways in which celebrities are economically active from the perspective of selling products for leading brands to becoming brands in their own right, the chapter will refer to celebrity examples such as, Paris Hilton, David Beckham, Justin Timberlake, Gwyneth Paltrow, Jennifer Lopez, and the Kardashians.

SELLING STARDOM

This is so because the development of film stars rapidly came to have a specific function as their visibility grew among spectators, and interest developed in their roles, lives, relationships, and images. And while a distinctive celebrity class consolidated as Hollywood film production flourished, a unique economic nexus was established between the agencies of 'talent' and production. A major factor that fostered this connection was, as Richard Schickel observes within his survey of the history of stardom, that public demand for film stars was promptly recognized by studios as an element that could play a stabilizing role within early film production as this demand was predictable. The result of such dependable public interest was that star names became a key source of collateral when producers approached banks for loans to finance feature-length films (cited in Dyer, 1982).

Hence, the early film stars soon became recognized as an essential constituent of the economics of Hollywood in terms of studio capital, components of film budgets, forms of investment, and a means with which to market film products. As such, investing in a star name to feature within a film project would act as a guarantor of success (invariably) and as an attractor for fans of that star name, with a consequent end result of profitability. And it is clear why film stars were rapidly utilized in this regard, as Hortense Powdermaker explains:

> From a business point of view, there are many advantages in the star system. The star has tangible features which can be advertised and marketed – a face, a body, a pair of legs, a voice, a certain kind of personality, real or synthetic – and can be typed as the wicked villain, the honest hero, the fatal siren, the sweet young girl etc. The system provides a formula which is easy to understand and has made the production of movies seem like just another business. The use of this formula may serve to protect executives from having to pay too much attention to such intangibles as the quality of a story or of acting. Here is a standardised product which can be advertised and sold, and which not only they, but also banks and exhibitors, regarded as insurance for large profits. (cited in Dyer, 1982: 11)

Yet while casting a successful star within a film could never be an absolute guarantee of box office success (film stars move in and out of popularity, and sometimes the project may simply be unattractive, regardless of who takes top-billing – the 2003 Jennifer Lopez/Ben Affleck-starring crime comedy *Gigli* serves as a good example of this, as do Bruce Willis' 1991 comedy *Hudson Hawk* and Johnny Depp's 2013 $225 million budget *The Lone Ranger*), Dyer argues that the economic importance of stars can be highlighted by a number of key instances within film history that do demonstrate the efficacy of star-power. For example, the comic actress Mae West 'saved' Paramount from receivership in the early 1930s, and Marilyn Monroe had a decisive film presence that countered the emergent challenge of television against cinema-going in the 1950s. What such examples demonstrate is that the essence of celebrity, combined with a fashionable star persona, image, or body, can be translated into a material economic outcome that contributes to the financial success of media industries. Consequently, celebrity culture is very much part of the capitalist economic system, and, as Barry King argues, although celebrities may appear to exist in a fantasy world of glamour, wealth, and freedom from the mundane routines of the wider public, they also fall within its system and are key expressions of its values.

CELEBRITIES TAKING ECONOMIC CONTROL

In essence, King articulates the economic function of celebrity within the context of political economy and its Marxist underpinning. Within the context of Marx's writings, human industrial systems have consistently been structured in a dualistic structure between an oppressing ruling class and an oppressed labouring class that finds its most potent and combative form in the era of capitalism (emerging from the sixteenth century and maturing in nineteenth-century Europe), and represented by the means of production-owning bourgeoisie and the labouring, exploited proletariat. For Marx, the economic system is predicated upon the exploitative extraction of profit and value from the labouring class, who must not merely sell themselves to the capitalists (their labour power is the only productive possession that they own), but they are also just as much a commodity as the commodities that they produce (Marx and Engels, 1985). And in lieu of the social revolution initiated by the proletariat that would place the means of production into their hands and abolish economic and class inequalities with the establishment of a communist state, the political economic view still operates within the context of ongoing exploitation and the persistent commoditization of human labour. And so it is, argues King, with the film star or celebrity because 'he or she is a paid impostor, assuming a persona for the purposes of delivering a live or recorded performance' (2010: 11) and as such, they are a commodity used for the production of profits.

The nature of their commoditized status is one that has developed and transformed throughout the twentieth century, and beyond. As King argues, the Hollywood studio era, or 'star system', that dominated from the 1920s until the 1960s did render film actors as employees 'exchanging their labour power for a fee and working under fixed-term contracts that bound them to particular studios and required them to appear in films as assigned and undertake loan-outs as directed' (2010: 12). But as Richard deCordova, in his history of the star system, points out, although film stars within the star system can be read as the 'products' of the studio machinery, the star system did not produce stars in a manner akin to the ways in which factories produce goods. This was because the outcome is not a standardized product, but something 'highly individuated – the individual star' (2001: 9). And this sense of individualization, with stars possessing 'an undeniable specificity' (ibid.), would ultimately evolve (for many stars) into a business sensibility that broke away from studio control and contractual obligations (which included earnings caps) and which led to stars becoming distinctive 'stakeholders' within their business. Thus, stars such as James Stewart and Elvis Presley:

received shares of profits as defined by their respective positions in a legally fixed cascade of disbursements – back- and front-end money, gross or net points, and so on. This change, which signalled the shift in the status of the stars from employees to free-lancers and ultimately entrepreneurs, led to the superstardom context possible in contemporary Hollywood. (King, 2010: 12)

While the economic 'superstardom' stakeholder clique typically includes stars such as Tom Cruise, Johnny Depp, Leonardo DiCaprio, Adam Sandler, Jennifer Lawrence, Angelina Jolie, and Will Smith, King chooses an unlikely example to demonstrate the entrepreneurial quality of contemporary celebrity economic accumulation: Paris Hilton. King selects Hilton, whose initial fame derives from her status as the great-granddaughter of the founder of the Hilton hotel chain, Conrad Hilton, because she perfectly epitomizes the ways in which a human being can operate as a commodity. And Paris Hilton is significant because she is a prime example of a celebrity who has effectively sold her 'presence' rather than any discernible talent. Indeed, Paris Hilton arguably epitomizes Boorstin's category of 'famous for being famous' designation of celebrity. Ostensibly famous for being an heiress to the Hilton fortune and a visible socialite, Paris Hilton would rapidly become 'a carnal entrepreneur' who was able to charge 'somewhere between $150,000 and $200,000 for a twenty-minute appearance at an upscale party' (King, 2010: 13). This lucrative use of her socialite status would be rapidly complemented with a series of ventures tied exclusively to her celebrity name. And yet, the catalyst for her emergence as an internationally-known figure came via an event that in previous eras might have ended a media career: a sexual scandal in the form of a private sex tape (featuring her then-boyfriend, Rick Salomon) that was leaked and then commercially released by an adult entertainment company. Yet, far from closing doors to public attention, what would ultimately be called *One Night In Paris* became a huge-selling/downloaded commodity that perfectly advertised a celebrity brand that was predicated on Hilton's 'license to simply be in the public eye, to be in her body, to be visible' (Hillyer, 2010: 20). And so it was that the publicity that flowered from the video became the basis for new streams of income.

As Jerry Oppenheimer describes it, suddenly 'she possessed an aggressive management team that included numbers crunchers, marketing experts, branding geniuses, shrewd New York literary agents, cut-throat Hollywood film and TV talent agents, and high-priced lawyers negotiating a portfolio of lucrative deals for her' (2006: 4). The material economic outputs of *One Night In Paris* took the form of makeup products, a jewellery line marketed on Amazon, and a nightclub chain; media ventures such as the Reality TV series *The Simple Life*, Paris Hilton's 'My New BFF', and 'The World According To Paris'; roles in films such as *House of Wax* (2005) and *The Hottie and the Nottie* (2008); and the 2006 release of a music album, entitled Paris. Hilton also released a series of books, the most notable of which was *Confessions of an Heiress*, a glossy guide to Hilton's fashion tastes, celebrity friends, the dos and don'ts of being an heiress, a professional portfolio and merchandise range, and a glimpse into her 'jet set' life. All of which effectively establishes what Oppenheimer dubbed 'Paris Inc.'.

PARIS HILTON INC.

Paris Hilton constitutes a potent early 2000s example of the processes Graeme Turner identifies within his book, *Understanding Celebrity*: that celebrities are strategically developed to make money and their names and images are used to market and sanction a range of media. Thus media producers and agencies seek celebrity involvement with their products and projects because of the perception that a celebrity presence will play a decisive role in attracting potential audiences. Consequently, from the days of the star system to contemporary Hollywood (and beyond), studios and producers employ established stars as a key means with which to attract investment to film (or television) projects. But the use of celebrities and their images extends beyond professional outputs to wider markets as companies employ celebrities to brand their products and bestow upon them glamour, chic, and a 'star aura' that will make them stand out from crowded marketplaces and abundant competitors. But, at the heart of the investment/endorsement nexus, Turner stresses the essential point that

> Celebrity also makes money for the individual concerned ... The celebrity can develop their public persona as a commercial asset and their career choices, in principle, should be devoted to that objective. As the asset appreciates – as the celebrity's fame spreads – so does its earning capacity. (2004: 34–5)

Paris Hilton's rise to international celebrity status (and the myriad commercial opportunities and offers that resulted) clearly illustrates this dynamic, and Turner's point also demonstrates the ways with which visibility and popularity act as a beacon to attract the financial interests of alternative industries. However, visibility and cultural currency is not the only attractor to companies seeking to sign celebrity figures to endorse and advertise products. Achievement is still a potent issue, and as such it is little surprise that it is individuals who have attained celebrity status though sporting prowess that constitute some of the most lucrative contracts in this regard. In Barry Smart's view, the connection between sport and business is a clear one: not only is sport itself an industry of immense economic, but crucially, cultural importance, the essence of sport is a quality that corporations wish to imbue their brand images with. As Smart argues, 'the cultural form that has been identified as most readily exemplifying authenticity has been sport' (2005: 104). In some instances, the relationship between brands and sports has been close, for instance that of Nike and a range of iconic sports stars. Formed in 1964 by Phil Knight and Bill Bowerman, Nike, signified by its *swoosh* logotype, is one of the most recognizable brand names in the world, and rapidly became one of the highest earning global brands (Goldman and Papson, 1998). And the company very quickly recognized that in order to attain eminence in the sports shoe industry (against rivals such as Adidas), links with sportspeople of great achievement were key to development. The first of these, in the early 1970s, was with the American distance runner, Steve Prefontaine, whose attitude to sporting performance mirrored the brand credentials Nike was striving for: 'attitude' and 'rebellion' – the themes that would underpin and inform the brand's tagline: 'Just do it' – and was followed by sporting stars such as Andre

Lester Hayes, Bo Jackson, Eric Cantona, and, most famously, Michael Jordan
d by Tiger Woods, Cristiano Ronaldo, and Wayne Rooney, among others).

BRANDED CELEBRITY AND CELEBRITY BRANDS

Matt Haig (2011) describes NBA star Michael Jordan as a 'superbrand' in his own right as he stands not so much as a professional sportsman, but has a legacy as a 'basketball phenomenon', and represented a synergy that was the result of his outstanding playing abilities and inspirational performances on court combined with the central values of the Nike brand – to mutually beneficial effect. This is what Smart states:

> Jordan had fulfilled the hopes of *Nike* CEO Phil Knight by capturing the imagination of the sporting public with his superior athletic ability and, by becoming so closely associated with the company and all it stood for the cultural and commercial figure of Jordan came to signify that great athletic performances were articulated with great products. Jordan's fans became customers and *Nike's* customers joined his legions of fans. (2005: 118)

Celebrities, then, can act as a potent beacon to fans and transform them, due to attraction and emotional connection to the celebrity, into consumers. And there is a very sound economic reason for signing up celebrities to endorse products, even though it will incur considerable costs in terms of the fees paid to the celebrity. This is because the consensus is that the initial outlay will be repaid in the form of increased profits. As Cashmore (2006) states, recent years have seen a demonstrative intensification in the relationship between the worlds of advertising and celebrity, and for very good reason. For instance, on signing up star England footballer David Beckham to endorse their razor lines, Cashmore reports that Gillette saw a sharp increase in sales throughout 2005, and thus evidence of the footballer's consumer appeal. This was followed by endorsement deals with Brylcreem, Pepsi (who have an extensive history of celebrity connections from Michael Jackson to Beyoncé Knowles), Adidas, Marks & Spencer, and Police eyewear, and the latter company explicitly linked their success to Beckham's advertising presence (Beckham's effect lead to Silvia Nanni, the managing director of Police, tripling his fee). Additionally, on signing with Real Madrid in 2003, club merchandise, and especially replica football shirts, increased 67 per cent in Beckham's first season with the club (Vincent et al., 2009). As such, Cashmore (2006) argues that although expensive to companies, the investment in celebrities is worth it as celebrity-endorsed advertisements are frequently seen by consumers as being far more convincing than advertisements endorsed by non-celebrities. This is because, as Mark Tungate concurs, the 'benefits are as blinding as the spotlight: stars give brands a well-defined personality for the minimum of effort, and bring with them a rich fantasy world to which consumers aspire . . . It's not a theory. When a celebrity wears something, it has a direct impact on sales' (2008: 120).

The association among celebrities, endorsement, and fashion is, not surprisingly, a key commercial area in which the figure of the celebrity looms large, and is highly lucrative for both celebrities and fashion houses. As Bronwyn Cosgrave (2008) observes, in terms of Hollywood and fashion, designers have long since courted stars to parade their creations at the annual Oscars ceremony. Ranging from Mary Pickford, Bette Davis, Vivien Leigh, and Jennifer Jones, through to Grace Kelly, Elizabeth Taylor, Katherine Hepburn, Barbra Streisand, Jane Fonda, Cher, Sharon Stone, Gwyneth Paltrow, Hilary Swank, and Anne Hathaway, designers such as Adrian, Christian Dior, Cartier, Yves Saint Laurent, Bob Mackie, Vera Wang, Valentino, and Armani Privé have strenuously sought endorsement on the most prestigious and globally mediated event in the Hollywood calendar. It is not of course only prestigious events like the Oscars that have seen a cash nexus forged between celebrity and fashion, as any trip to a mall will testify: celebrity images in association with fashionable clothing, fragrances, and accessories now proliferate, and for good reasons.

CELEBRITY AND THE CONSUMER IMAGINATION

Celebrities, argue Tim Jackson and David Shaw (2009), stimulate consumers' imaginations in ways that alternative public figures (politicians and royalty) do not. As such, luxury brands have recognized the value of celebrity marketing power, such as Victoria Beckham's endorsement of Gucci, Versace, and Dolce & Gabbana; Kylie Minogue's marketing of Julien Macdonald and Chanel; and Jennifer Lopez's advertising of Valentino and Yves Saint Laurent. For instance, Uche Okonkwo (2007) stresses that celebrities wield considerable power in the marketing of luxury fashion brands. Although the link goes back to the use of Princess von Metternich as an advertising patron for Charles Worth's Parisian fashion house, La Maison Worth, in the nineteenth century, a key moment was Marilyn Monroe's announcement that she wore only Chanel No. 5 in bed – a pronouncement that immortalized the fragrance's association with Monroe, and which made it an icon in the pantheon of luxury fashion perfume brands. While this association might have been spontaneous, luxury fashion houses have subsequently sought out the benefaction of celebrities to sell their products, and it is a process that has accelerated rapidly since the 1990s (with Chanel employing Nicole Kidman, Keira Knightley, Blake Lively, and Brad Pitt). The concept and practice of branding is an integral aspect for market success because branding 'is essential as a recognized sign of value in a business world where customers have multiple choices, and where investors need a symbol of acknowledged capacity for value creation' (Castells, 2001: 76), and is an essential component to delineate corporate personalities (Olins, 2003) from others. This is what Jean Baudrillard, the influential French thinker, stated in *The System of Objects*:

> The concept of 'brand', which is advertising's prime concept, sums up the prospects for a 'language' of consumption rather well. All products . . . are now offered under brand names. Every product 'worthy of the name' has a brand . . . The brand's primary function is to designate a product; its secondary function is to mobilise emotional connotations. (2005: 209)

Brands, therefore, are not merely products, but are the key means with which companies and service providers attract and keep customers by promoting value, image, prestige, and lifestyle in association with their products and services (Rooney, 1995). In David Aaker's view, the construction, maintenance, and development of brand equity – the intrinsic value of a brand – is facilitated through processes such as communicating brand name awareness, forging links of consumer loyalty, and establishing potent brand associations with customers and guiding the mental images customers have with brands, and a potent strategy is to associate brands with celebrity spokespeople. Thus, as Okonkwo notes, luxury brands such as the handbag and accessories company Louis Vuitton have employed Uma Thurman, Jennifer Lopez, and Scarlet Johansson to serve as the fashionable 'faces' of the brand, as well as venerable iconic male stars such as Keith Richards and Sean Connery. Given the efficacy of this approach, premium brand fashion names such as H&M have engaged in this associative process, with celebrities ranging from the quirky and cult (the indie American actor, Vincent Gallo and the singer, Lana Del Rey), to the iconic (Madonna, Kylie Minogue, and David Beckham). In other instances, companies employ celebrities not as endorsers, but as high-profile 'brand ambassadors' – the term employed by the Swiss watchmaker, Longines, whose ambassadors include the actresses Chi Ling Lin, Aishwarya Rai Bachchan, and Kate Winslet – all of whom visually embody the principle of elegance that underpins the brand's personality.

While the demise of a famous figure may suggest an obvious obstacle to product endorsements, death, Okonkwo notes, is no impediment to luxury brands establishing associations with celebrity icons. This is evidenced by Montblanc marking the hundredth anniversary of the birth of the classic Hollywood actress Greta Garbo with a pen dedicated to her. Indeed, deceased celebrities have become increasingly of great value to advertisers in recent years. This is what Ross Petty and Denver D'Rozario (2009) argue, due to the expense of celebrity endorsers and the risk that a brand runs in the advent of unexpected scandal, or mediated acts of controversial behaviour by contracted celebrities (as occurred when the golfer Tiger Woods' marital infidelities became global news – a scandal that resulted in Woods being dropped by brands such as Accenture and TagHeuer and losing millions of dollars). Similarly, the iconic model, Kate Moss, in the wake of a video that allegedly depicted her taking cocaine in 2005, was dropped from campaigns for the fashion brands Chanel, Burberry, and H&M. As such, the images of iconic actors and musicians such as Humphrey Bogart, Louis Armstrong, Jimmy Cagney, and John Wayne have been utilized to market Diet Coke and Coors beer, while Audrey Hepburn has been digitally reanimated in her *Roman Holiday* Princess Ann role to front a campaign for Galaxy chocolate. Similarly, TagHeuer has added the image of the classic Hollywood actor Steve McQueen (who died in 1980), whose onscreen persona epitomized 'cool masculinity' (and who engaged in motor sports off-screen) to its roster of sporting and acting endorsers that includes Maria Sharapova, Uma Thurman, Brad Pitt, Cameron Diaz, Leonardo DiCaprio, Shah Rukh Khan, and Chen Doaming. Aside from some of the critiques of the practice of using dead celebrity images (the issue of taste and decorum) or legal issues relating to celebrity rights, the majority of brand use of the famous involves living celebrities; and, in Okonkwo's view, there are a number of reasons why brands utilize celebrities, regardless of expense and risk:

- Celebrity endorsement is a great brand-awareness creation tool for new brands.

- Endorsement by celebrities helps to position and re-position existing brands.

- Celebrities contribute to sustaining a brand's aura.

- Celebrities generate extensive PR leverage and opportunities for brands.

- Celebrities are used to reach a global market.

- Celebrities promote a brand's products and appeal. (2007: 158)

To illustrate the last point, this was the exact rationale of the cosmetics brand, Rimmel, when they employed the supermodel Kate Moss in their advertising campaign for their lines in the United Kingdom, called 'Reclaiming the streets of London', because Moss was considered to represent 'the ultimate London girl: cool, experimental and edgy . . . Which fits perfectly with the experimental, fun side of Rimmel' (Lim, 2005: 85). In this regard, celebrities function as 'Identity Brands' as they make 'consumers feel empowered and enlivened [and] generate and evoke . . . intense emotional attachments' (Hewer and Hamilton, 2012: 416); they provide, as Paul McDonald argues, 'shortcuts' for companies to give their products distinctive identities, a factor that underpinned Nespresso's coffee makers to forge a potent brand 'fit' between their endorser, the actor George Clooney, and the company that yielded a $1.7 billion sales figure (2013: 62). Therefore, the association between brands and celebrity endorsers, spokespeople, and 'faces' has mutually beneficial financial outcomes (raised brand awareness and desirability and (ideally) increased profits), and a substantial fee for the celebrity (that usually runs into millions of dollars). Furthermore, alongside the proliferation of fashion brands employing celebrities to endorse them is the trend of an increasing number of media figures who are increasingly diversifying into the productive aspects of the fashion industry for themselves.

For instance, numerous pop performers have augmented endorsement work for established brands with forging their own brands. Choosing the fashion industry as an example, the market is now complemented with a range of celebrity-owned/designed clothing and accessory ranges, such as Gwen Stefani's L.A.M.B. (Love, Angel, Music, Baby) fashion range; P Diddy's 'Sean John' menswear/womenswear fashion label; Jay-Z's Rocawear label; Beyoncé Knowles' House of Dereon; Kylie Minogue's Love Kylie lingerie range; Elizabeth Hurley's Elizabeth Hurley Beach bikini and beachwear line; Justin Timberlake's William Rast clothing products; Milla Jovovich's Jovovich-Hawk fashion line; Rihanna's NSFW collection (released with River Island); and the Kardashian sisters' Dash clothing stores and their Kardashian Kollection (produced in association with the clothing brand Dorothy Perkins). But why is this 'celebrity labour' in diverse fields occurring and what is the primary motivation?

CELEBRITIES AND FLEXIBLE ECONOMICS

Summing up the extent of Justin Timberlake's celebrity activities, *Vogue*'s Vicki Woods defined him as 'singer, songwriter, actor, scriptwriter, commercials producer, record mogul, fashion-company owner, living brand' (2008: 1) and the list needs to be completed with a media entrepreneur to include Timberlake's investment in Myspace as a music social media network in 2011. At one level, the motivation for this recent explosion in celebrity brand activity, to the extent that they represent a distinctive 'human brand' category (Lawrence, 2009), is explainable due to the nature of both celebrity and contemporary capitalist economic production. As such, if an individual achieves stardom, then a rational process will be to consolidate this position and reflect the transformation of the Western economic system from the 'Fordist' production system (typified by the factory production lines producing standard goods for mass consumption) to a system based upon 'flexible accumulation' which is distinguished by greatly intensified rates of innovation and production and faster product turnover times (Harvey, 1989).

The idea of consumers becoming jaded more quickly and demanding new products ensuring that producers must have diverse portfolios and be constantly changing is relatable to celebrity culture because the world of celebrity is 'inherently transitory' (Gray, 2004: 209) and public and industry interest is unstable. But, in a more immediate and business-oriented sense, if the presence of celebrity bestows positive, glamorous, and emotional associations with products, then a direct celebrity stamp cuts to the branding chase. A key factor in the investment of resources to sign up celebrities is that it is invaluable in standing out in a market saturated with competing brands (again, a wander through a shopping mall drastically and visually conveys the extent of this corporate battle), but the famous have the resources to engage in this process themselves. Consequently, many actors have established film production companies to ensure more production control (examples include Tom Cruise, Drew Barrymore, Adam Sandler, Nicholas Cage, Johnny Depp, Charlize Theron, Leonardo DiCaprio, and Zac Efron) and others have engaged in a similar process within the television industry (Oprah Winfrey, for example). But in many instances, the diversifications engaged in have little to do with the celebrities' primary 'job'.

Thus, as Hamish Pringle states within *Celebrity Sells* (2004), celebrity brand ownership is not necessarily a new process. For instance, the film director Francis Ford Coppola (famous for *The Godfather* and *Apocalypse Now*) has produced the Rubicon Californian wine range (Brad Pitt and Angelina Jolie have also developed in this area with Miraval by Jolie-Pitt), and the actor Paul Newman launched his salad dressing line 'Newman's Own' in 1982, but with a benevolent intention as all profits are donated to educational and charitable causes. And staying with culinary products, the ex-heavyweight boxer George Foreman progressed from endorsing the Salton grilling machine that led to the 'George Foreman Champ Grill' and the later (more health conscious) 'Lean Mean Fat Reducing Grilling Machine'. In other instances, celebrities have engaged in vertical and horizontal flexible role developments that have resulted in ventures outside their central professional identity. For example, the actress and model Elizabeth Hurley developed (with her then-partner Hugh Grant) a film company (Simian Films), and then established a beachwear and accessories fashion label, Elizabeth Hurley Beach, and subsequently an organic food range sold through Harrods. Similarly, the Oscar-winning actress Gwyneth Paltrow founded a lifestyle website, Goop.com, in 2008 to 'share all of life's positives', and which, in addition to a blog written by Paltrow, offers recipes and sells items such as jewellery, clothing, cosmetics, greeting cards, and purses. Alongside Goop.com, Paltrow has become notably associated with culinary skills and services, going so far as to release the cookbooks *Notes From My Kitchen Table* and *It's All Good: Delicious, Easy Recipes that Will Make You Look Good and Feel Great*, in which she declares, expressing the ways in which her professional portfolio has developed and expanded, that 'cooking has become my main ancillary passion' (2011: 12). Consequently, mirroring the transformations that have characterized wider economic development, contemporary celebrity is about using fame to widen portfolios, and the economic activity of the famous illustrates that many of them are flexible accumulators. Indeed, it is not only celebrities, but even their children who are endorsing products, such as David and Victoria Beckham's son, Romeo, advertising Burberry clothing, while Tom Cruise and Katie Holmes' daughter Suri launched a fashion range in 2013 at the age of seven.

SMELLS LIKE CELEBRITY SPIRIT

Lim (2005) cites the example of Jennifer Lopez, or 'J-Lo', as a further potent example of celebrity 'brand extension', who initially found fame as an actress achieving acclaim and commercial success in films such as *Selena* (1997), *Out Of Sight* (1998), and *Maid In Manhattan* (2002), before establishing a multimillion selling pop music career. Thus, having forged two distinctive professional identities, Lopez extended these into the fashion industry, initially in partnership with Andy Hilfiger to form the company Sweetface Fashion that reflected her 'sexy, fun and fashionable' brand persona. The enterprise began with a range of clothing and accessories that included sportswear, swimwear, sunglasses, and her Jennifer Lopez Collection adult and children's fashion range. A distinctive (and highly lucrative) further extension of the Lopez brand has been into the fragrance market. Although now associated with a variety of perfume products (*Still, Live, Deseo, Love and Glamour*, and *Love and Light*), it was her first fragrance, *Glow*, that established Lopez as a major player in the luxury perfume brand category. According to Lopez, the product expressed her identity and factors associated with her life and personality, as she explained: 'It represents everything I've loved ever since I was very young – fresh, clean, simple, sensual things. Things like fresh air, the breeze coming in through the window, the ocean, summer sunshine' (cited in Lim, 2005: 107).

The potency and appeal of Jennifer Lopez's Glow fragrance is that, as Lim further explains, the product serves to convey Lopez's 'essence' and by extension to 'animate' the product with her celebrity persona. Therefore, celebrity brands can rapidly and effectively achieve what all brand managers wish for their products: for them to possess a clearly defined and perceptible sense of identity, and to convey a distinctive personality with which to emotionally connect with consumers. With o celebrity brands, they are vividly personalized through their bond to a ecognizable celebrity. And the idea that consumers/fans can appropriate the of a favoured celebrity via the purchase of a branded fragrance is possibly a key reason why there are a number of celebrity fragrances now on the market to the extent that they represent a primary mode of brand extension. Consequently, a varied collection of celebrities have turned to fragrances to extend their brand portfolios, ranging from Bruce Willis, Tim McGraw, Celine Dion, and Antonio Banderas, to Heidi Klum, P. Diddy, Sarah Jessica Parker, Victoria and David Beckham, Kate Moss, Beyoncé Knowles, Gwen Stefani, Dita Von Teese, Cher Lloyd, Katy Perry, Taylor Swift, Arjun Rampal, and Justin Bieber.

As Julia Boorstin (2005) notes in her overview of the rise of celebrity-based fragrance lines, the proliferation of celebrity fragrances has rapidly become a significant and profitable component of the global perfume industry. Although traceable to the 1930s when the fashion designer Elsa Schiaparelli created a bottle that mimicked the comic actress Mae West's body, the celebrity fragrance came of age in 1987 when the Hollywood actress and fashion icon, Elizabeth Taylor, released a perfume called Passion, and then White Diamonds, with Elizabeth Arden, to ultimately achieve sales of $1 billion. But celebrity fragrances were sidelined in the 1990s by perfumes created by established fashion designers such as Giorgio Armani and Calvin Klein; although the link between celebrity and fragrance lines was re-established in the late 1990s when fashion houses such as Elizabeth Arden and Chanel employed Catherine Zeta Jones and Nicole Kidman to front their perfume campaigns, and then as the 2000s progressed, celebrity-branded perfumes became firmly established, spearheaded by companies such as Coty.

The rationale for branded fragrances is, from a business perspective, clear, as the retail consultant, Candace Corlett, explains: 'Building a fragrance brand name from start, without any affiliation, is a very expensive proposition . . . a much quicker route to sales is to borrow a star's identity' (Boorstin, 2005: 3). And given that Lady Gaga's debut perfume, 'Fame', reportedly sold 6 million bottles in the first week of its release, a celebrity name is a potent profitable force; and the development and release of fragrance lines represent a key contemporary means by which to 'monetize' celebrity (Burr, 2009: 29).

ENTREPRENEURIAL CELEBRITIES AND THE ENTREPRENEUR AS CELEBRITY

The prevalence of celebrities engaging in cross-platform economic activities underscores the degree to which flexible modes of capitalist accumulation are not only evident within wider structural levels of societies, but can be identified at the micro level of celebrity-led business engagement. Hollywood and beyond exhibits the synergistic behaviour of corporations manifested at the level of the individual and the crucial factors that all brands seek – identity, personality, and emotional engagement with consumers – are potently encapsulated within celebrities. Their fame, personality,

and fan bases enable celebrities to diversify from foundational career traje
(acting, music, modelling, etc.) into subsidiary lines, with brand-awareness a
ognition built in. From the perspective of political economy, contemporary celebrity
culture mirrors and exemplifies the mode of flexible accumulation which Harvey
argues capitalism has adopted from the 1980s onwards as celebrities spread out their
earning potential and capitalize on their fame by establishing footholds in numerous
industries. Furthermore, this practice is not restricted to those who have attained
dominance (and frequently critical acclaim) within their respective fields, as 'attributed' celebrity figures have similarly carved out commercial 'empires', and none arguably more effectively than the Kardashian family.

Consisting principally of the sisters Kim, Khloé, and Kourtney (with the addition of stepfather Bruce Jenner, brother Rob, and half-sisters Kylie and Kendall)
and their 'Momager', Kris Jenner, the Kardashians have emerged as, on the one
hand, a prime example of celebrity entrepreneurship, and on the other, a potent
example of Boorstin's 'famous for being famous' celebrity status. Although Bruce
Jenner acquired fame within sport and won the gold medal in the Decathlon event
at the 1976 Montreal Olympics, followed by acting roles in American television, and
Kris Kardashian was part of the O.J. Simpson murder trial (she was a friend of
one of the victims, Nicole Brown, and then wife of Simpson's defence lawyer, Robert
Kardashian), it was in 2007 that the Kardashian's celebrity status was established.
This came as a result of Kris Jenner pitching a Reality TV series based upon the
eccentric lifestyles of her blended family to the producer Ryan Seacrest for broadcast
on the American entertainment channel, E! On the basis of a pilot, the series was
commissioned and screened as *Keeping Up With The Kardashians*, which has run
into more than nine series in numerous countries, with a number of subsequent
spinoffs such as *Kourtney and Khloé Take Miami*, *Kourtney and Kim Take New York*,
and *Khloé and Lamar*.

Having resurrected Bruce Jenner's career, and utilized his 'heroic' status as
an Olympic athlete to becoming a successful motivational speaker with related
endorsement deals and fitness infomercials, Kris Jenner would ultimately mould her
family into a distinctive brand. This is what Jenner stated in her autobiography, *Kris
Jenner . . . And All Things Kardashian*:

> I knew we were onto something big. And I loved the business side of all of this.
> That's what drove me, that's what excited me: the possibility to make this into
> something so much more than a TV show. Every time we renewed for another
> season, I would think to myself: *how can I take these fifteen minutes of fame and
> turn them into thirty?* . . . So while I was producing that television series, I also
> had to find some time to think about what would come next. (2011: 270)

The result has been an entrepreneurial whirlwind of commercial activity that has,
in addition to the television series, encompassed clothing, makeup, fragrances, a
novel and the lifestyle book, *Kardashian Konfidential*, which fuses autobiographical material on the sisters with fashion tips and ruminations on their stardom and
celebrity lives. However, it has been Kim Kardashian who has emerged as the family

star, and whose life, from early Paris Hilton-type of sex tape, fashion choices, and relationships, to her pregnancy with the US rapper Kanye West, attracts maximum media attention and Internet discussion (based upon topics such as whether her famous posterior is natural or is the result of implants). In the view of the journalist Emma Brockes, all of these branded products actually 'act as window dressing for the business, merely, of being Kim Kardashian', and that she is the central brand (2012: 2). While at one level the Kardashians are castigated for their 'famous for being famous' status, and for a fame built on the foundation of attributed celebrity status (Rojek's Reality TV category by which celebrity is essentially 'thrust upon' individuals regardless of achievement or discernible talent), the Kardashians have ably demonstrated the degrees to which celebrity can be commoditized and individual identities globally branded, to huge financial and commercial gain. A key issue with the Kardashians is that within interviews they reflexively refer to themselves as a brand and their entire lives as branded experiences.

CELEBRITY CEOS

If celebrities have increasingly displayed entrepreneurial zeal and established themselves as potent business forces, however, individuals from the worlds of business and industry have also increasingly become famous to the extent that they have entered into the world of celebrity. This is perhaps not really surprising as the connection between celebrity and business is a longstanding one; indeed, it predates Hollywood. While contemporary celebrity culture now includes 'star CEOs', the key architects of American capitalism have always been a source of keen fascination with the public. As Patricia Sánchez Abril states, the self-made 'magnates' constituted a core part of the character of late nineteenth-century America, and the select group ultimately dubbed 'the robber barons' (Rockefeller, Carnegie, Vanderbilt, and Astor) became famous names intimately connected with their companies. Indeed, they 'were more than just actors in the business world: they were the founding fathers of American business and widely credited with changing the country from a mercantile-agrarian economy to a booming industrial society' (2011a: 184).

Inevitably, such distinction ensured that they were extensively covered by the by-now consolidated press (aided by developments in camera technology) and the focus of gossip, muckraking, and exposés of their elite lifestyles and business practices. But, while the nature of business leaders would transform as the twentieth century rolled on (professional managers and family-owned enterprises opened out to share-ownership), the prevalence of television in the 1960s ensured that this new business class would also become increasingly 'celebritized' through mass communication coverage – a factor that, although diminished during the 1970s in the wake of weakened American corporate performance, ineffectual management, and apparently decadent 'fat cat' behaviour (senior managers awarding themselves generous bonuses while rendering thousands of employees redundant), was re-galvanized in the 1980s. The reason for this was due to the ways in which individuals from the world of business interacted with ever more extensive forms of media, a process that would result in a fusion between the mediums of entertainment and business, and a particular type of business-celebrity. The result was that:

> A new type of business celebrity would emerge, created by the business pressures and media of the day. Unlike the robber barons, who were famous for creating American big business, the celebrity executive would become famous merely by participating in it – as the head of a corporation, an entrepreneur, or a business guru. (Sánchez Abril, 2011a: 192)

This process was also accelerated by the prevalence of investor capitalism within the American business culture, a process that resulted in more business-related people finding their way into business periodicals and becoming the focus of front-page cover images and emergent business news media forms that arose during the 1980s, such as CNN, CNBC, and the Financial News Network. The efficacy of such media interest was the emergence of 'corporate heroes', such as Lee Iacocca, the CEO of Chrysler Corporation, the car manufacturer. Voted into the position in 1979,

> Iacocca inherited what seemed to be a company doomed to bankruptcy. By the early 1980s, Iacocca had succeeded in convincing the government to grant Chrysler $1.2 billion in federally guaranteed loans. Soon after, Chrysler made a startling turnaround, with a strong line of new products and profits to match. The public's perception of Iacocca's single-handed revival of Chrysler made him a media darling. His influence expanded beyond business. His 1984 autobiography, entitled *Iacocca: An Autobiography*, became the best-selling biography of all time. (Sánchez Abril, 2011a: 195)

The 1990s saw the business-celebrity become even more entrenched and iconic, with a host of entrepreneurs similarly penning autobiographies and, in the examples of Donald Trump, Bill Gates, and Steve Jobs, emerging as 'paradigms of American success', having actively 'nurtured and cultivated their fame such that it has crossed the boundaries of their industries or the business world into the world at large' (Sánchez Abril, 2011a: 206–7). Furthermore, this process is not restricted to Western cultures; as van Krieken identifies in relation to contemporary China and increasing Chinese industrial and business dominance, CEOs constitute potent 'models' for admiration and emulation. For example, van Krieken cites the example of the entrepreneurial property developer, Wang Shi, who has acquired 'an especially heightened celebrity status, having climbed the highest mountains on all seven continents [and] constructing the accumulation of enormous wealth into a lifelong 'adventure' (2012: 128).

CELEBRITY BUSINESS PEOPLE AND TELEVISION PUBLICITY

In the view of Raymond Boyle and Lisa Kelly (2010), television formats that have turned to business and entrepreneurs for content have played a major role in propelling business figures into the public eye. At one level, of course, business figures have always been featured on television and in the news for economic com mentary; however, recent years have seen entrepreneurs take centre stage and become significant celebrity figures through business-oriented popular television formats. The most notable example of this genre was arguably *The Apprentice*, which centres on the opportunity for an entrepreneurial individual to win the opportunity to work for the 'self-made' American billionaire Donald Trump (the UK's version is fronted by Lord Alan Sugar) if they can prove their capitalist acu- men through a weekly series of profit-creating consumerist exercises (Ouellette and Hay, 2008). Other examples include *Dragons' Den*, which involves entrepreneurial individuals who judge would-be entrepreneurs' business ventures, and which has resulted in 'Dragons' such as Duncan Bannatyne, Peter Jones, and James Caan becoming notable television personalities. The result of this status is that their fame has granted them wider media exposure, in Caan's case providing commen- tary on current affairs and global business events on mediums such as *Sky News* and *Bloomberg* and the release of best-selling books such as *The Real Deal*, *Start Your Business in 7 Days*, and *Get The Job You Really Want*. Further examples of this process also include celebrity chefs such as Jamie Oliver, Gordon Ramsey, and Marco Pierre White, who run successful restaurant ventures, but who also extensively appear on television with regard to cookery formats (*The Naked Chef*, *Jamie At Home*, *Food Revolution*) and Reality TV and game show formats (*Kitchen Nightmares*, *The Chopping Block*, *Hell's Kitchen*).

CONCLUSION

Business and celebrity are synonymous, and the economics of celebrity reflects the dominant spirit of capitalism that established itself from the 1980s in the Western world, and beyond. From the early days of Hollywood, film stars acted as mecha- nisms to enhance the profitability of films, and as celebrity culture has developed, an entrepreneurial zeal that spans both companies and services seeking out celebrity names and faces to front products, and celebrities establishing themselves as brands, with diverse portfolios, has become firmly established. Thus, celebrity is a force that enhances consumerism as it maximizes the desired ends of all brands: to emotionally resonate and connect with would-be customers. Celebrity, therefore, is a potent force in this regard as it represents the aspirations and fantasies of many. Consequently, while purchasing fragrances or clothing from the likes of Jennifer Lopez, Lady Gaga, Justin Bieber, or Rihanna will not bring the object of desire closer to the fan, it does, on a symbolic level at least, evoke the 'essence' of the celebrity, or so the advertis- ing promises. And this is marketing gold. Critically, of course, this returns us once again to the critical stance of theorists such as Adorno. Indeed, the Frankfurt School regarded consumerism as nothing more than the purveyor of 'shallow fantasies' and false needs. However, with the presence of celebrity within economic activity, indeed, as a prime driver, as John Gray's analysis concludes, economics is now centrally fixed within the fantasy of the lives of the famous and taps into the aspirational attitude of consumers. As such, celebrity, whether it is loved or loathed, is big business and it is just getting bigger.

FURTHER READING

With regard to the economic issues of flexibility briefly covered in this chapter, readers wishing to understand the shift from stable production systems to flexible accumulation in greater detail should look at:

- Harvey, D. (1989) *The Condition of Postmodernity*. Oxford: Blackwell.

Similarly, readers wishing to learn more about brands and branding and how they relate to celebrity endorsement should consult:

- Aaker, D. (2010) *Building Strong Brands*. London: Pocket Books.
- Healey, M. (2008) *What Is Branding?* Hove: Rotovision.
- Okonkwo, U. (2007) *Luxury Fashion Branding: Trends, Tactics, Techniques*. Basingstoke: Palgrave Macmillan.

Finally, for a contemporary analysis of celebrity and business activity, see:

- Redmond, S. (2014) *Celebrity and the Media*. Basingstoke: Palgrave Macmillan.

CELEBRITY AND POLITICS

CELEBRITY POLITICS

From a cynical perspective, the British philosopher John Gray argues that the borders between politics and entertainment are fundamentally distorted to the extent that in 'the current media culture of revelatory diaries and confessional memoirs, kiss-and-tell journalism and voyeuristic television, ex-politicians are no different from anyone else in seeking to turn themselves into marketable commodities' (2004: 202–3). But in the view of John Street (2006), who has extensively examined the link between politics and celebrity, this is not really so unusual, as in recent years it certainly appears that the worlds of politics and popular culture have become indivisible as politicians have increasingly become more like celebrities.

To make sense of this development, Street turns to the thoughts of the economist Joseph Schumpeter and his work *Capitalism, Socialism and Democracy*, published in 1943. Within this seminal text Schumpeter focused attention on the similarity between the worlds of business and politics, arguing that the connection lay in the way in which the business person dealt in a particular commodity and the politician traded in votes. As such, both effectively were regulated by the operation of a distinctive market force: the law of supply and demand. Consequently, 'success in business and success in politics were just a matter of producing a product that customers wanted. Competition ensured that the best won' (2006: 359). The link between business and politics has intensified since the 1940s, with the ethos of business practice increasingly establishing itself as a central tenet within the political process. For instance, political parties and politicians evoke the language of market research as policies are invariably 'advertised' and voters strategically 'targeted', while parties have become branded 'products' characterized by the importance of maintaining an appropriate public image and competing for votes in a manner akin to the way in which businesses compete for customers. In line with the classic economic view of Schumpeter, Street points out that voters frequently make their choice between parties on the basis of the evaluation of competing policy content and promises and thus behave in a manner akin to consumers in a market. This rationale was proffered as a key reason why the British Labour Party's electoral campaigns continually resulted in defeat throughout the 1980s and early 1990s as they were judged by the electorate to lack a plausible 'product', even to voters who would have political sympathies (opposed to the right-sided political identity of the Conservative party) to their natural constituency.

Within a British context this changed in the 1990s with the rise to power of Tony Blair, a figure who moved away from the more overly leftist stance of previous Labour leaders (most notably Michael Foot and Neil Kinnock) and who possessed a professionalized and charismatic sense of political authority. Furthermore, Tony Blair represented the historic 'rebranding' of the classic Labour Party into a new identity, that of 'New Labour, defined by its left-of-centre stance, or its embrace of 'Third Way' politics with its fusion of welfare state commitment and focus upon social equality connected with the market economy and the ethos of 'no rights without responsibilities' (Giddens, 1998, 2000). Furthermore, Tony Blair's New Labour would also see the lines between politics and fame blur as a number of 'cool' celebrity figures of the stature of Noel Gallagher of the rock band Oasis were invited to 10 Downing Street (Street, 2001).

STAGED CELEBRITY AND THE POWERLESS ELITE

As Rojek argues, the linkages between politics and celebrity illustrate the central quality and nature of 'staged celebrity'. Staged celebrity refers to the calculated technologies and strategies of performance and self-projection designed to achieve a status of monumentality in public culture. Rojek cites Abraham Lincoln's iconic 'journey from a log cabin to the White House' narrative as a key historical example (2001: 121), arguing that Lincoln's 'plainsman oratory' style was a key factor in courting voters and was part of a process of skilful political calculation. Furthermore, as celebrity culture established itself as a distinctive social presence, it would progressively provide new opportunities for celebrity endorsement of political figures and parties. Consequently, presidents from the 1920s have sought to obtain voter allegiance through actively courting film entertainers. The most visible instance of this practice occurred in the 1960s and surrounded the presidency of John F. Kennedy. Hence, Kennedy, via his 'Ratpack' film actor brother-in-law Peter Lawford, was brought into contact with high-profile actors of the stature of Frank Sinatra, Sammy Davis Jnr, and most famously, Marilyn Monroe.

The combination of presidents (and would-be presidents) with celebrities would become a permanent fixture within the American political landscape. For instance, in the 1990s Bill Clinton was dubbed the first 'rock 'n' roll president' when he used film and pop stars to enhance his image, while his wife Hillary Clinton's bid for a seat in the Senate was supported by Nicole Kidman and Robert De Niro. But Barrack Obama's two successful presidential campaigns have seen a glittering array of Hollywood and music elites, from Barbra Streisand, Oprah Winfrey, and Bruce Springsteen, to Matt Damon, George Clooney, Anne Hathaway, Katy Perry (even sporting a Vote Obama dress at one pop performance), Lady Gaga, and Jay-Z and Beyoncé, show public support. And for commentators, the rationale for this association is clear from the perspective of politicians as the 'intention is to create an aura of "popularity", to borrow precisely from the relationship of trust and admiration that is associated with figures in popular culture' (Street, 2001: 191). But in some instances, for example Nicolas Sarkozy, the former President of France (from 2007 to 2012), his celebrity connection was forged through his marriage to the Italian singer-actress-model, Carla Bruni.

Arguably, a more striking facet of contemporary culture is not merely the instances of politicians transforming themselves into celebrities, but the ways in which the blurring of the line between politics and celebrity is resulting in ever-increasing numbers of celebrity figures entering into the political arena, either as activists, advocates, or elected figures. And yet, this should not be possible due to the very nature of celebrity itself. This position is conventionally related to Francesco Alberoni and his now-classic article *The Powerless Elite* (1972), in which he articulates an influential sociological account of the rise and nature of 'stardom'. For Alberoni, within every society there are individuals who, in the eyes of other members of their society, are considered to be remarkable and who, crucially, attract widespread social attention. Historically this is usually applied to individuals who held positions of political, economic, or religious power, such as kings, aristocrats, or priests – individuals who possessed the ability to influence their societies. But, while such individuals are also readily identifiable within modern Western societies, Alberoni identifies a further social group 'whose institutional power is very limited or non-existent, but whose doings and way of life arouse a considerable and sometimes even a maximum degree of interest' (1972: 75). These are the stars or cultural 'idols', the celebrity figures C. Wright Mills defines as 'The Names that need no further identification' (1959: 71–2), who may have cultural influence, but who are 'unimportant from a political point of view' (1972: 76) and who cannot occupy institutional positions of power. Thus, while stars (film, sport, etc.) are clearly a significant (adapting and re-formulating C. Wright Mills' famous sociological term) 'power elite', they cannot convert this status into institutional power that would see them direct or govern political decision making. And the principal reason why such influential individuals cannot assume political positions of power is very particular to their nature.

This is because the stars' sphere of influence is restricted to the level of culture and there is no possibility of their 'charisma' (Alberoni utilizes Weber's idea) of ever becoming significant from a political perspective. As such, stars represent a noteworthy social phenomenon, an elite and highly privileged group who do not instil social envy (because within open democratic states that are characterized by social mobility, anyone, in theory, could become a star) and who possess no real access to political power. But this does not fully explain exactly how powerful individuals who can excite fervent followings (as we saw in Chapter 2) seemingly cannot translate this into political power. The answer to this, for Alberoni, actually lies within the very nature of stardom itself. This is because for stardom to work, it requires a large number of spectators within a large-scale society, a mass audience, to render a minority of people into points of reference for the entire population – simply put, that they are recognizable to significant numbers of a given population. However, this visibility negates the 'true nature of power' because the genuine 'power elite', those who drive society and dictate its actions and future, are typically characterized by isolation.

A key reason why this is the case is that traditionally the powerful seek to ensure a degree of secrecy since their actions might not accord with those of the general, non-privileged population. Consequently, the power elite seek to reduce their observability. As such, any increase in observability is frequently a demonstration of the diminution of power and of the power elite never wishing to be exposed to a high degree of observability (we might think of Julian Assange's WikiLeaks organization as a contemporary example of the controversy in revealing the 'secrets' of the power elite, be they governmental or business). In the case of stars, the reverse is the case because for them 'observability is practically unlimited' (Alberoni, 1972: 82); indeed, it is the lifeblood of celebrity status. Therefore, because stars are always in the public eye, they are rendered politically powerless as their status contravenes the nature of institutional power.

CELEBRITY VISIBILITY, NEWSWORTHINESS, AND POLITICAL CAUSES

Alberoni is another of our 'usual suspects' in speaking of classical approaches to the study of celebrity, and his ideas are intriguing, but limited. Dyer (1982), points to the fact that in the 1950s and 1960s there were numerous Hollywood stars (Marlon Brando, John Wayne, and Jane Fonda) who, while possessing no institutional political positions of power, nevertheless transmitted very clearly-defined ideological positions and expressions of personal political views – views that had power directly because of their visibility as world-famous Hollywood film stars. Furthermore, the increasing celebrity status of many American political figures in 1960s America was a direct result, argues Todd Gitlin (2003), of media focus due to their newsworthiness and recognizable cultural status. Therefore, as Cashmore notes, Alberoni's approach has become progressively out of step with the contemporary celebrity/politics equation because the link between celebrity and politics is centrally based on the *overt* cultural visibility of such figures, a visibility/cultural power dynamic that can be transmuted into political currency. According to Jessica Evans (2004), global charitable organizations such as Oxfam have recognized the value of using celebrity figures to communicate and simplify potentially complex economic and political arguments. Celebrities can raise public awareness directly, due to their cultural visibility and fame. Consequently Oxfam campaigns have frequently featured international celebrity figures, such as Chris Martin, Youssou N'dour, Djimon Hounsou, Colin Firth, Thom Yorke, Gael Garcia Bernal, Angelique Kidjo, and Michael Stipe. Additionally, the charity has several further avowed celebrity supporters that include Alicia Keys, Ed Sheeran, Rooney Mara, Annie Lennox, Scarlett Johansson, Kanye West, Lady Gaga, Chris Martin, Bono, and Yoko Ono.

A crucial issue to explore is the degree to which the link between politics and celebrity stretches back further than Alberoni acknowledges. For example, in van Krieken's view, the celebrification of politics is traceable back to the sixteenth century and the strategies of self-presentation that were being enacted by monarchs.

Chapter 1 discusses the historical self-promoting exploits of Alexander the Great, Julius Caesar, and Louis XIV, but to this list we can also add Henry VIII of England, who similarly engaged in practices to win the 'hearts and minds' of the population while enhancing his own image in a strategic manner. And he did this by constructing a public persona that would, in contemporary terms, be viewed as 'an action-man celebrity identity, a combination of swashbuckling film idol, military hero and sports star' (van Krieken, 2012: 102). Here, then, was a king who wished, via public displays of prowess in sports such as jousting and archery, to transcend his ascribed monarchical status and did so by transforming himself into a publicly-recognized political celebrity figure.

Moving into the early twentieth century, the political power of celebrity influence was not lost upon social decision-makers. For instance, referring to American war leaders, Leo Braudy (1986) observes that such political figures turned to the emergent film industry, and more importantly to its new stars, within the period of the First World War to 'sell' the conflict to an American public who viewed it as a geographically remote European campaign. As a consequence, stars such as Douglas Fairbanks Jr., Charlie Chaplin, and Mary Pickford heavily promoted the selling of war bonds. Similarly, as the celebrity commenter Cooper Lawrence (2009) argues, the singer Kate Smith's weekly radio programme, *The Kate Smith Hour*, ended with her singing a rendition of Irving Berlin's 'God Bless America' in support of raising money for war bonds for the US military in the early 1940s, to considerable effect. The recognition that celebrities could indeed have potent political influence was developed in America in the 1960s by Alan R. Novak, a senior counsel to the Democratic Senator, Edward M. Kennedy, who identified that many Hollywood stars were openly Democrats and that a number of benefits would be reaped in recruiting them to endorse candidates, from substantial financial contributions, to the more influential issues of lending glamour to the party and ensuring maximum media coverage, factors that have been intrinsic, as pointed out earlier, to the Democratic party ever since.

Although such instances show that for decades celebrities have demonstrably had considerable persuasive powers, or at least political and military figures have believed them to have such abilities over public opinions (to the point of galvanizing an American population to support and join the First World War), we might still argue that Alberoni's analysis remains intact. The celebrity examples I have just cited have political significance, but still lack institutional power. They have powerful voices that many people did listen to, and still constitute a powerless elite. But there have been celebrities who have gained political office, and have wielded considerable institutional power and thus represent a critical evaluation of Alberoni's 'powerless elite' concept.

CELEBRITIES AS POLITICIANS

The most striking example of a 'star' attaining political power is that of the American actor Ronald Reagan, who moved from acting in films such as *Hellcats of the Navy*, *Cattle Queen of Montana*, and *Bedtime for Bonzo* in the 1940s, 1950s, and 1960s, to becoming the President of the United States from 1981 to 1989 (with his second election a landslide victory). And not only would he become an iconic president, but he would, via what would be dubbed 'Reaganomics', establish himself as one of the key political popularizers of neoliberalism, the economic doctrine based upon the principles that true human wellbeing must be achieved through enabling individuals to realize their entrepreneurial freedom within a social framework based upon private property rights, free markets, and free trade (Harvey, 2007: 2). Ronald Reagan attained a considerable level of institutional authority, and while his Hollywood career was long abandoned, Ellis Cashmore (2006) argues that Reagan's climb to the Presidency of the United States was based upon skills transferred from acting and his status as a film star. When he retired from acting in 1964 (the date of his last film, *The Killers*), Reagan's political experience was largely limited to his tenure as the President of the Screen Actors Guild between 1947 and 1952 and 1959 and 1960. However, switching political allegiance from the Democrats to the Republicans, he stood for the office of Governor of California in 1966 and was successfully elected. In the 1970s, on his third attempt, he successfully gained the presidential nomination and ran against Jimmy Carter, defeating him and becoming elected as President. With regard to his political success, Cashmore stresses that Reagan's acting skills were an invaluable asset, especially in debates with opponents, and for the changing American media landscape as supporters and rivals dubbed Reagan 'The Great Communicator: his expression of ideas in plain, easy-to-understand language was made for a culture in which the media was taking on greater importance' (2006: 214).

While Ronald Reagan had an apprenticeship in politics with the Screen Actors Guild, the next dramatic example of a Republican celebrity gaining political power relied instead on his globally recognized star image, and that was the election of action-film mega-star Arnold Schwarzenegger to the position of Governor of California in 2004. In a recall election against an unpopular Governor (Gray Davis) that gave him only 62 days of campaigning time, Freya Thimsen argues that Schwarzenegger drew upon the generic conventions of his film career (the heroic, physically imposing figure represented in films from *Pumping Iron*, *Conan the Barbarian*, and *The Terminator*, to *Total Recall* and *True Lies*) to enable him to ultimately 'metamorphose into 'The Governator' (2010: 49). And the play upon his iconic screen cyborg character was deliberate, as Cashmore states, because the rhetoric of his campaign was filled with slogans such as his promise to 'terminate taxes' for the people of California. As such, due to his communicable efficacy, his 'American dream' persona (a body-builder from Austria coming to America and making it big), but more importantly, his globally-recognizable image, Schwarzenegger drew far more public attention than his fellow aspiring politicians who lacked film star status, and easily eclipsed other candidates who did possess a cache of fame (including former child star Gary Coleman, pornography magnate Larry Flynt, and Arianna Huffington). In essence, then, *being* Arnold Schwarzenegger was a key factor in electoral success.

Furthermore, Ronald Reagan and Arnold Schwarzenegger are not alone in having gained political office. Clint Eastwood, Sonny Bono, and the wrestler-turned-actor Jesse 'The Body' Ventura have all been elected to mayoral positions. And in a wider global context, the Pakistan cricketer, Imran Khan, launched his own political party, the Pakistan Tehreek-e-Insaf, in 1996 and attained considerable political visibility in the 2013 elections. Consequently, Alberoni's view that stars do not have the capacity to make decisions that actually change society can be directly countered with reference to Reagan, Schwarzenegger, and so on – celebrity figures whose public visibility has been instrumental to their political success within positions of institutional power. And yet, it could be argued that these examples, significant though they may be, are still relatively rare and that, in the main, celebrities remain a powerless elite. But if we consider the issue of *unelected* political roles that are adopted by celebrity figures, then the inadequacy of Alberoni's view becomes an issue again.

CELEBRITY POLITICIANS-WITHOUT-OFFICE

The concept of the celebrity 'politician-without-office' is a term that has arisen, Cashmore argues, principally from the mid-1980s, a period in which the boundaries between the worlds of politics and celebrity became progressively indistinct, and an increasing number of celebrity figures began to become visibly associated with political causes. The key difference between these figures and the likes of Arnold Schwarzenegger is that, as Street states (referring to Bono), they speak out on political issues and claim 'the right to represent people or causes without seeking or acquiring elected office' (2004: 438). For example, issues such as conservation and environmentalism have attracted numerous celebrity figures, from Kit Chan Kit Yee, Robert Redford, Sylvester Stallone, Amitabh Bachchan, to Leonardo DiCaprio, Matt Damon, and Cate Blanchett, who 'take the authority to speak out as politicians on environmental matters' (Brockington, 2009: 29). Yet, for many commentators, it was the mid-1980s that saw a definitive rise in the political activist celebrity and which paved the way for the preponderance of contemporary celebrity voices. A key element was the process initiated principally by Bob Geldof and his activities relating to famine relief in Africa. Geldof's fame stemmed from his position as lead singer for the Irish band the Boomtown Rats, who rose to prominence in the British punk era and had a number of hit singles, most famously in 1979 with 'I Don't Like Mondays', which attained the number one chart position in the United Kingdom, before spliting up in the 1980s.

Although carving out a respectable musical career, as Cashmore observes, as the Boomtown Rats faded, Geldof's public persona would morph from rock singer to that of 'St Bob', due to his ascent to position of 'international statesman' through his initiation of the Band Aid project which resulted in the release of a song, 'Do They Know It's Christmas', that brought together a range of pop and rock musicians (Sting, George Michael, Bono, Simon le Bon, Midge Ure, Phil Collins, Geldof, and many others) to raise funds for Ethiopian famine relief. The single went to number one in 1984 and ultimately sold 3 million copies. Geldof then co-organized the globally-transmitted Live Aid concerts performed in July 1985 (which consisted of two concerts, one in London and the other in Philadelphia). Live Aid raised over $100 million for use to alleviate famine in various parts of Africa, and, in addition to representing a global media event (with an audience of 1.5 billion) and supremely successful charitable and humanitarian endeavour, also announced 'the entry of rock stars and celebrity figures into the realm of global politics' (Cashmore, 2006: 219).

CELEBRITY AND POLITICS: BONO

Within his book, *Celebrity Humanitarianism*, Ilan Kapoor (2013) argues that Live Aid constituted a whole new cultural category within the realm of celebrity politics: 'Charitainment', and from this period Geldof became more famous as a political leader. For example, in 2004, Geldof was appointed to the Commission for Africa to lead on global responses to tackling the issue of African debt, a position that saw Geldof assume a position of significant political power, but which also became the driving force for a second musically-based charity event: the Live 8 concerts held in 2005. And in this endeavour, Geldof was not alone as he was joined by fellow rock star singer Bono, on the global political stage. Unlike Geldof, Bono (real name Paul David Hewson) has juggled his increasing political interests with an ongoing position as the lead singer of the hugely successful rock band, U2. Bono's interest in political issues (aside from his presence within Band Aid and Live Aid) was linked to his role in the NGO (non-governmental organization) Jubilee 2000 in the 1990s, which was an organization dedicated to eradicating Third World debt. This was followed by Bono's formation of DATA (Debt AIDS Trade Africa) in the early 2000s, and the RED products, versions of Armani and Apple products that donate a percentage of sales to the Global Fund to fight against AIDS in Africa. Additionally, Bono's status as a globally-renowned rock star has enabled him to meet and debate with world leaders, and influence them. For instance, in relation to his role within the Commission for Africa, former President of the United States Bill Clinton identified Bono as 'the person most responsible for the passage of a bill on Third World debt relief through the US Congress' (Varga, quoted in Drake and Higgins, 2006: 90–1). For Rojek, Bono's success as a 'celanthropy advocate' is that, irrespective of his rock star status and estimated £400 million fortune, he presents a public image that normalizes his status to be just like the wider public in order to instil the message of 'Make Poverty History', that 'ordinary people have the power to make permanent change possible' (2013: 61). It must be acknowledged, though, that Bono's political activities are not always appreciated, as evidenced in 2013 when the singer was publicly pursued by a number of German anarchists who were chanting 'Make Bono history' (Anonymous, 2013, *Independent*).

As a result, the number of celebrities engaged in philanthropy and ambassadorial roles has sharply increased in the past two decades, to the extent that concepts such as 'celebrity diplomacy' (Cooper, 2008) have become commonplace to capture the degree to which international relations and goodwill missions increasingly contain celebrity presences, or, more importantly, celebrities are sought out to become the 'faces' of various political causes. However, while Bob Geldof and Bono have been long recognized as key (and highly influential) figures in this regard, others have joined them, most notably the Hollywood actress, Angelina Jolie.

ANGELINA JOLIE: CELEBRITY ACTIVIST

For a significant period during her early career, Angelina seemingly cultivated a media image that vacillated between her work as a progressively acclaimed actress and her off-screen, volatile, unpredictable, and potentially self-destructive personal behaviour which included tattoos, and numerous marriages. However, recent years have seen her assume an avowed and active commitment to 'global issues', a dedication that nominally was expressed via her film career in films such as *Beyond Borders* (Martin Campbell, 2003), her children (adopted and biological), and her highly publicized relationship with the American actor and fellow film star and political activist, Brad Pitt. However, Jolie's political engagement was effectively initiated in 2001, when she assumed the role of Goodwill Ambassador for the United Nations High Commissioner for Refugees (the UNHCR). Jolie was not the first celebrity to be used by the UN, and indeed the UN has a longstanding track record of engaging with Hollywood to raise awareness of its global work. The popular comedic actor and singer Danny Kaye was appointed in 1953 as UNICEF's inaugural Goodwill Ambassador. As Wheeler argues, Kaye was appointed because it was believed that his name and fame would overturn indifference to the plight of children in poverty throughout the world, attract publicity, and raise money for the organization:

Kaye agreed readily and was appointed officially as UNICEF's Ambassador-at-large. Shortly afterwards, Kaye toured UNICEF projects in Myanmar, India, Indonesia, Korea, Thailand and Japan to publicise its activities in alleviating the plight of children. His trip was filmed for a short documentary entitled *Assignment Children* (1954), which was underwritten by Paramount Pictures, shown to an estimated audience of 100 million and whose profits entered UNICEF's coffers. (Wheeler, 2010: 10)

As Lim (2005) notes, the United Nations would appoint people they knew would be heard as further 'Goodwill Ambassadors' – like the actresses Liv Ullman and Audrey Hepburn. Hepburn was the United Nations Goodwill Ambassador for UNICEF in 1987 and visited countries such as Bangladesh, Ethiopia, Sudan, and Vietnam. Therefore, Jolie represents a continuation of this practice, and like Kaye's excursions, as part of her work, she kept a diary to record her UNHCR experiences. These diaries were formally published in 2003 (with proceeds donated to the UNHCR) and were entitled *Notes from My Travels: Visits with Refugees in Africa, Cambodia, Pakistan, and Ecuador*. In these accounts, Jolie emerges not merely as a 'celebrity ambassador', but also as a diarist, and an observer of the human, social, cultural, and economic effects of war and genocide in which she therefore strives to characterize herself not as an 'icon' but rather as a person like any other, as her diaries strive to reveal.

Although not previously associated with any obvious political expression or ideological affiliation, her 'globalized' sensibility would become famous through her adoption of three children: Maddox, from Cambodia, Zahara, from Ethiopia, and Pax, from Vietnam. Moreover, Namibia was her chosen location for the birth of her first biological daughter (with Brad Pitt), Shiloh. Furthermore, Jolie would spend a significant proportion of 2001 volunteering on behalf of the UNHCR. As Jolie stated of her motivation for embracing this role: 'If I can use this celebrity thing in a positive way, that might mean young people get involved, it has to be worth it' (Mercer, 2007: 131). As such, *Notes from My Travels* begins at the very beginning of her political mission:

> I am on a plane to Africa. I will have a two-hour layover in the Paris airport, and then on to Abidjan in Cote d'Ivoire (Ivory Coast). This is the beginning of my trip and this journal [...] On the plane from Paris an African man wearing a nice blue suit and a warm smile asked me if I was a journalist. I said 'No, just an American who wants to learn about Africa'. He said, 'Good!' (2003: 5)

In this quote, Jolie seeks to portray herself as an example of an American culture that is critically uneducated about the political and humanitarian situations that exist in contemporary Africa. Moreover, at the outset of her journey, she alludes to an apparent 'anonymizing' process occurring. For instance, while still on the aeroplane on the first stage of her mission, Jolie's famous tattoo designs are noticed, and she is informed by an African fellow traveller that this will make her conspicuous to authorities, as visible tattoos are conventionally used by authorities as a primary reason to detain suspected rebels posing as refugees, since tattooing is a common tribal practice in Guinea and Sierra Leone. This idea that she could be mistaken for a rebel is a source of humour within Jolie's diary, and an acknowledgement that as a globally recognized film star such misunderstandings do not occur (nor indeed does she often have to state who she is due to her recognizable celebrity status). The incident leads to a reflexive musing by Jolie, about the nature of the world she is entering, the physical environment, but more crucially, the people she will meet and act as an advocate for. Thus, when she arrives at her first refugee settlement in Africa, she states:

> While standing in one place too long my ankles began to itch. They were being bitten by bugs so small I couldn't even see them. In some areas the smell was rancid. I felt sick. The strength of survival here is amazing to me. They don't complain. They don't even beg. Contrary to our image of this country, its people are civilized, strong, proud, stunning people. Any aggressive feeling is pure survival. There is no time for casual or lazy behaviour. As I wrote that, I realize I am writing as if I am studying people in a zoo. I feel stupid and arrogant to think that I know anything about these people and their struggles. But I am simply making observations of the people here in Cote d'Ivoire. (2003: 11)

In addition to reportage concerning her immediate experience, Jolie begins a process of actively diminishing and downplaying her 'iconic' public identity. This apparent freedom from her public 'celebrity' self subsequently leads her to act in ways that she would not in the West. For example, Jolie discloses her private American address to a young African girl so that the girl can write letters to her, an act that contravenes the culture of distance that conventionally characterizes the routine Western.celebrity–public relation in which the public are kept at a distance from personal contact, by gated communities and frequently security guards, and private details remain closely protected.

Therefore, the dominant tone of Jolie's *Notes From My Travels* consistently centres upon Jolie's attempts to 'anonymize' herself in favour of her 'missions', to downplay her celebrity status and fame to communicate instead the work of the UNHCR, its personnel, and its support to alleviate the conditions faced by refugees. Yet there are instances in which we are reminded that Jolie is very much a *celebrity* intermediary because she is a film star of status and her star-power is substantial. This is best exemplified in Jolie's accounts of the instance in which she is invited to an engagement with Kofi Annan, then Secretary-General of the United Nations, and other prominent UN figures, a political platform few UNHCR workers could engage with.

With regard to the effect that Jolie's political activism has, her relationship with Cambodia remains acute to the extent that, in 2005, she was awarded Cambodian citizenship for conservation work and for setting up two foundations, the Maddox Relief Project (named after her first adopted child) and the Jolie Foundation. Furthermore, Jolie's political activities with the UN have also continued because since her initial missions, Jolie has maintained her intermediary role with the UNHCR and has undertaken a series of further missions to countries such as Sudan, Thailand, Jordan, the Russian Federation, Lebanon, Sri Lanka, Kosovo, India, Egypt, Kenya, Costa Rica, Iraq, and Afghanistan. As with *Notes from My Travels*, Jolie has similarly documented her political work in the form of journal entries posted on the UNHCR official website documenting these missions. In terms of impact and efficacy, Roy Greenslade (2013) notes that while the issue of awareness-raising in relation to political issues and causes may sound clichéd, nonetheless, the celebrity factor is of considerable impact. As he observes in relation to Jolie's 2013 visit with British Foreign Secretary William Hague to the Democratic Republic of Congo to campaign against the use of rape within war zones, there would have been few mainstream media images contained within newspaper and media content had Hague undertaken the endeavour alone.

THE FUNCTIONS OF POLITICAL CELEBRITIES

It is not just Africa that has seen politicized celebrities becoming activists. For instance, in the wake of the devastation of New Orleans in the wake of Hurricane Katrina which struck in 2005, a number of celebrities became involved in relief work and financial support (such as Angelina Jolie, George Clooney, Oprah Winfrey, John Travolta, Jamie Foxx, Celine Dion, Nicolas Cage, and Jay-Z), and in relation to rebuilding projects, in which the most notable celebrity figure is the actor Brad Pitt. As Joy Fuqua observes in her study of Brad Pitt's political activism, Pitt's relationship with New Orleans was expressed through the Make It Right Foundation (MIR) that involved his interest in architecture with a project (initiated in 2007) that combined aid work with sustainable housing, infused with green approaches to house building designed to be resistant to adverse weather conditions. The project involved a competition that brought together architects, engineers, and designers to create new housing structures, with the actor taking a lead role in the process and fronting publicity images and articles that appeared in periodicals such as *Architectural Digest*. Therefore, Pitt acted as both a hands-on participant and 'an icon to direct attention toward MIR' (Fuqua, 2011: 199) and 'his image became the instrument of the reconstruction effort' (Figueiredo, 2009: 3). Thus, from Bob Geldof's impassioned pleas for aid relief in the 1980s, to post-Katrina New Orleans, the concept of the celebrity activist has been firmly established within the cultural landscape.

In the view of David Meyer and Joshua Gamson, one of the most important resources that celebrities have in relation to political issues and political movements is their visibility, because 'celebrities carry a spotlight with them' (1995: 185). As such, celebrities draw media attention and their participation or association with a political event can draw people to it who may otherwise have had no interest, or awareness, of the particular concern. For example, then, people 'with no previous interest in pesticides . . . may listen to a public service advertisement because Meryl Streep appears in it. Rock fans may attend an antinuclear power demonstration to see Bruce Springsteen, yet wind up hearing numerous speakers talk about alternative means of generating energy' (ibid.). Viewed from this perspective, then, the participation of celebrities in political events acts as an effective 'hook' to guarantee media coverage, and it also makes public attendance at events more likely if they include celebrity presences, and generates publicity that can attract wider awareness and support.

Alternatively, as Cashmore points out, celebrities can help in engaging the public in political issues through converting what could be highly complex economic, political, and historical arguments and data into much more easily understandable information that results in greater degrees of public awareness and public action, from the donating of funds to political pressure and activity. For example, Oxfam ran a campaign under the banner 'Ever felt dumped on?', which highlighted unfair trading relations between the West and the South with the message that 'If we all join together and make a big enough noise, politicians and corporate bosses will have to make trade fair' (http://www.oxfam.org.nz/what-we-do/issues/make-trade-fair/dumped-on-photo-shoot). Although obviously a complex issue with various economic and political dimensions (including the historical heritage of Western imperialism and colonialism), the campaign conveyed the central message of rectifying this relationship through a photography shoot that saw various actors and musicians, such as Colin Firth, Thom Yorke, Chris Martin, Michael Stipe, Youssou N'dour, Minnie Driver, Antonio Banderas, and Alanis Morrisette being 'dumped on' with materials and substances such as coffee, chocolate, rice, milk, cotton, maize, and wheat. Therefore, through a series of striking visual images including a stellar cast of celebrities, the issue is simplified, but the message is clear: that global trade is unequal and action must be taken. Such an example further fits into the perception that the engagement of celebrities with political issues, from the activities of the UN and Oxfam through to environmental conservation and Third World debt, ensures that such issues are firmly in the public arena. In this sense, then, celebrity status, with its prominent degree of visibility, is an effective vehicle to be utilized by political groups. Indeed, it is also a factor that is recognized by celebrities themselves, as the actress Susan Sarandon (who has spoken out against the war in Iraq, and been a visual Democrat supporter) stated of translating her celebrity status into political activism: 'If my privacy is going to be invaded and I'm going to be treated as a commodity, I might as well take advantage of it' (Meyer and Gamson, 1995: 185).

THE CONSEQUENCES OF THE 'CELEBRITOCRACY'

While the political roles of celebrities can ensure that political messages and causes receive maximum publicity, and thus raise awareness for key social issues and problems, there are a number of critiques of politically-inclined celebrity. At one level, argues Cashmore, the ways in which politics and celebrity have become intertwined is indicative of a culture in which media have altered the nature of politics and transformed it into a spectacle and a series of popularity contests in which political messages are secondary to slick images and performances on camera. Furthermore, the progressive presence of celebrities within the political arena, whether formally elected, invited to front organizations, or self-appointed commentators, has resulted in a 'dumbing down' of politics. Hence, on the one hand celebrities such as Arnold Schwarzenegger can run for office relying not on political expertise, but on sound bites that draw upon his star persona – he is electable because he is Arnold

Schwarzenegger; while on the other hand, there is the danger that complex issues can be reduced to simple photographic images that cut through what *are* complex debates and which require a deeper level of engagement than that afforded by slogans and photographic images of appealing celebrities. Related to this critique is the charge that celebrities, regardless of how sincere and committed they may be to their political cause and message, are not sufficiently informed on the crucial matters, and not qualified to speak out on intricate matters of geopolitical economics and national, religious, and ethnic conflicts.

For instance, Marina Hyde, within her acerbic book *Celebrity: How Entertainers Took Over the World and Why We Need an Exit Strategy*, cites the example of the actress Sharon Stone, and her peace mission to Israel which included meetings with Israeli President Shimon Peres. In Hyde's view, Stone's official statement explaining her presence in the country, and the degree to which she believed her celebrity status could act as an agent of change in the enduring conflict between Israel and Palestine, captures the lack of insight the famous have, and the degree to which they over-state their political influence while not fully understanding the actual politics of the situation. This is what Stone stated:

> I just think that because I have fame . . . I have the opportunity to sit here and reflect back to you anything that you have or desire to see happen. The only power that I have is the opportunity to be a mirror back to you of something that you may be thinking and need to be reminded of. So the only power that I have is to remind you of something that is alive in your own heart. If you want to have something change maybe I can remind you of that. (2009: 82)

Stone compounded these words with the additional statement that she 'would kiss just about anybody for peace in the Middle East' (2009: 83), further compounding Hyde's assessment that while the desire to use celebrity for good is frequently genuine, it is also just as frequently naive and demonstrates that the understanding of politics lacks firm foundation. Although Hyde's use of Stone points to the more eccentric example of the perception that celebrity can be a force for change (even if the celebrity in question is not entirely clear how it can be harnessed), there are commentators who point to more serious consequences of the celebrity politician. This is the concept of what Lawrence (2009) refers to as the 'rise of the celebritocracy', a social cultural condition in which, while they themselves are citizens entitled to political expression like any other citizen, nevertheless, their voices are far louder than the non-famous, an issue that could have serious implications for democratic processes.

This is the view of Kapoor, and he offers a sustained and frequently scathing perspective on the effects of celebrities within the world of politics. Indeed, he questions the motives of such celebrity activism and identifies insidious effects of the 'celebritization' of politics, as he states:

> Far from being altruistic, such activism is ideological: it is most often self-serving, helping to promote institutional aggrandizement and the celebrity

'brand'; it advances consumerism and corporate capitalism . . . and it contributes to a postdemocractic political landscape. (2013: 1)

What this implies is that celebrity figures have become part of a process within the Western world that has increasingly seen policy issues and decisions that have traditionally been the preserve of states taken over by private agencies who are unelected, but which wield considerable power. Therefore, Kapoor's approach to celebrity humanitarianism, advocacy, and diplomacy is deeply critical and is centrally informed by Slavoj Žižek's use of ideology which accords with the idea that it 'is that which attempts to obscure the Real, to cover . . . gaps, contradictions, or imperfections' (2013: 6). As such, far from representing acts of altruism and goodwill, celebrity political activities are ultimately conservative due to their complicity with the prevailing social and economic order because the various activities, from advocacy work to staging charity events, seldom question the causes of global poverty, debt, and so on, but rather address the symptoms – with maximum publicity for those involved (and, in the case of Live 8, resulting in huge increases in music sales for many of the key performers). Therefore, celebrities such as Geldof and Bono seek to address issues of global inequality without questioning the exploitative nature of Western economic structures, and assuming that these systems can rectify global inequalities. Consequently, celebrity advocacy is seldom anti-capitalist and sustains neoliberal ideology, and it frequently serves to silence the voices of peoples who experience economic inequalities as it is the celebrity who is the advocate, and the individual who garners media attention and political audience. As a result, commentators point to the ways in which celebrity diplomacy and humanitarianism actually serves to disempower the oppressed, or, as Nicholas Kristof caustically states of the relationship between poverty and celebrity charity, figures such as 'Bono and Angelina Jolie have made Africa almost sexy' through their celebrity sheen (2007: 1). In this sense, celebrity activism reduces politics to a media spectacle and, somewhat paradoxically, often renders the subjects of its advocacy invisible.

Consequently, contemporary culture depicts a very different celebrity relationship with politics than that articulated by Alberoni. While on the one hand the number of celebrities who attain actual institutional positions of power is still comparatively rare, on the other, the emergence and proliferation of celebrity 'politicians-without-office' has become a distinctive and pervasive feature of modern celebrity culture to the point that Kapoor argues that 'do-gooding is a virtual career requirement for the established or aspiring star' (2013: 13). Of course, as citizens within democratic states, celebrities, as well as any other member of the public, are perfectly entitled to either stand for political office or engage in political activism. The critical issue that surrounds the 'celebritocracy' is that, in line with Kapoor's critiques, celebrity voices are louder due to their status and a society that is fascinated with them. In this sense, although clearly many celebrities are associated with laudable causes (indeed, the American actress Jessica Alba and singer Christina Aguilera have fronted the Declare Yourself campaign which encourages young people to vote, thus enhancing democratic participation), the equation with political issues (many of which cannot be solved with donations) is reduced to a glamorous spectacle.

WHEN CELEBRITY POLITICS GOES WRONG

As a final point, and to provide a counterpoint to the bleak ideological function of politically-motivated celebrities outlined by Kapoor, activism, advocacy, and political endorsements do not always have the anticipated outcome. A recent example of this occurred at the 2012 Republican National Convention that concentrated upon supporting presidential candidate Mitt Romney's attempt to unseat Barack Obama. As part of the festivities, the Hollywood screen legend Clint Eastwood took to the stage to address the Party members and publicly endorse Romney. Although scheduled to deliver a rousing five-minute speech to close the Convention on a note of triumph, Eastwood proceeded to speak for just over 12 minutes in an improvised address to an empty chair that represented Obama 'in person' to mock his various failings as president since 2008. Although intended as a humorous act, the hesitant delivery and unscripted format resulted in widespread media coverage the next day, much of it derisive, with numerous pastiches and skits based upon it from comedians and talk-show hosts (such as Jon Stewart) and the public posting their own versions on social networking sites and YouTube. Thus, just because celebrity status can lead to political platforms, that does not mean that the outcome is a given, or that the public will react accordingly, regardless of ideological content or intent. Although, as Grant Cos and Kelly Norris Martin (2013) note, the event had a serious side, as in the wake of the Eastwood performance there were subsequent incidents of chairs found hanging from trees, and which were interpreted as racially offensive displays designed to symbolize the lynching of President Barack Obama.

CONCLUSION

This chapter has looked at the ways in which the worlds of politics and celebrity have progressively converged, and while Alberoni's view that celebrities conventionally do not acquire institutional power (there are still very few examples of celebrity figures winning political office), the number of celebrities speaking out on causes and acting as political advocates has intensified significantly. A prime (and perhaps surprising) example of this process is the example of the British comedian and actor, Russell Brand, who has emerged as an anarchistic political advocate for widespread social, economic and political change, a vision set out in his book (or 'manifesto'), *Revolution* (2014). However, for some critics, this raises questions concerning democratic representation and also raises the debate as to whether celebrities should communicate their political affiliations to the wider public with the intention of influencing them. Similarly, the issue of personal gain and brand enhancement, combined with the degree to which celebrities are qualified and knowledgeable enough to engage in political discourse, is a further crucial factor to consider. However, in the view of Jo Littler, and as this chapter has explored, although there are a number of issues that place the celebrity/politics/advocacy nexus in a problematical position, 'celebrity do-gooding is a response to suffering, and this should not be underestimated' (2011b: 137); such consciousness-raising can act as a stimulus for others to act to tackle issues of injustice. But whether we are cynical or supportive, the political world is now firmly entrenched within celebrity culture, and shows no signs of disengaging itself in the near future.

FURTHER READING

With regard to providing a historical and cultural context to the link between politics and celebrity, readers should consult:

- Street, J. (1997) *Politics and Popular Culture*. Cambridge: Polity.
- Todd, G. (2003*) The Whole World Is Watching: Mass Media in the Making and Unmaking of the New Left*. Berkeley, Los Angeles, CA and London: University of California Press.

Of further interest are texts produced by celebrities engaged in political advocacy, and three key ones are:

- Cheadle, D. and Prendergast, J. (2007) *Not On Our Watch: The Mission to End Genocide in Darfur and Beyond*. Dunshaughlin: Maverick House.
- Geldof, B. (2006) *Geldof in Africa*. London: Arrow Books.
- Jolie, A. (2003) *Notes from My Travels: Visits with Refugees in Africa, Cambodia, Pakistan, and Ecuador*. New York and London: Pocket Books.

For further reading concerning critical views of celebrity involvement with political causes see:

- Hague, S., Street, J., and Savigny, H. (2008) 'The voice of the people? Musicians as political actors. *Cultural Politics*, 4(1): 5–24.
- Kapoor, I. (2013) *Celebrity Humanitarianism: The Ideology of Global Charity*. London and New York: Routledge.

5
FANS AND CELEBRITY

CHAPTER OVERVIEW

Celebrity exists in a necessary relationship with the public and, more crucially, their fans. The concept of the fan refers broadly to individuals who are united in their interest in or devotion to the careers, professional outputs, or lives of particular celebrity figures and who derive myriad satisfactions and uses from their fan behaviour. This can range from purchasing the products of celebrity figures (for example, the music, concert tickets, fragrances, or clothing lines of Beyoncé); following their activities on social media networks such as Facebook, Twitter, or Instagram; or seeking out direct contact with celebrities, for example the extensive 'mobbing' that besets the members of One Direction by their fans (dubbed as 'Directioners') whenever they appear in public.

However, although fandom has long been analysed in ways that complicate its stereotypical view of obsessed individual or passive consumer, developments within media broadcasting have changed how fans relate to celebrities. As such, while Miley Cyrus' 2013 VMA music performance scandalized many due to her raunchy and scantily-clad routine with singer Robin Thicke (marked by her infamous 'twerking' dance), it represented on the one hand a decisive break with her previous young *Hannah Montana* TV fanbase, and on the other the acquisition of an older pop fan collective. However, even more significant was the degree to which fans commented via social media networks during and immediately after the performance (some of which were used by formal news agencies) to express condemnation or acclaim her new direction. This chapter, then, examines fandom in relation to:

- The nature of fandom
- YouTube fandom
- Para-social fan relations
- Stalking
- Social media and fandom

To illustrate the myriad relationships that exist between celebrities and political engagement, the chapter will discuss specific celebrity examples such as Chris Crocker and Britney Spears, Lady Gaga, and Kristen Stewart.

THE NATURE OF FANDOM

Although a concept that is open to numerous academic definitions and articulations and a varied tradition of differing approaches to it, a classic approach to the social phenomenon is that articulated by Lawrence Grossberg, who argues that the traditional conception of fandom and fan behaviour has been to approach it from two divergent perspectives: first, that (reflecting a Frankfurt School-type of assessment) they are merely 'cultural dopes' who passively consume the various texts and products manufactured by the popular culture industry; and second, that there is a segment of fans who actively and knowingly 'appropriate' the texts of specific popular cultures, and bestow upon them novel and innovative meanings. What these fans do is to take objects of popular culture and use them to express a sense of their lives and social experience. Alternatively, some fans may use popular cultural items and actively employ them in resisting the realities of their social position (in Lewis, '1992). In terms of more general perceptions of fandom, Matt Hills, whose work has extensively explored the nature of contemporary fandom, addresses the question of 'what a fan is' with the following overview:

> It's someone who is obsessed with a particular star, celebrity, film, TV programme, band; somebody who can produce reams of information on their object of fandom, and can quote their favoured lines or lyrics, chapter and verse. Fans are often highly articulate. Fans interpret media texts in a variety of interesting and perhaps unexpected ways. And fans participate in communal activities – they are not 'socially atomised' or isolated viewers/readers. (2002: ix)

With sympathy for the latter points, Grossberg argues that the relationship between an audience and a particular popular text (be it a band, a cultural product, or an individual) is an active and productive association. As such, individuals work to not only 'deconstruct' the meaning of a specific 'text', but work to ensure that its meaning is based upon something that closely connects to their own mode of living, their individual and social experiences, and even their desires. Consequently a text can have very different meanings for different people given their distinctive identities, social positions, and reading contexts. Thus, a text can represent a source of romance or sexual fantasy, influence identity, or even inspire rebellion. However, according to Henry Jenkins in *Textual Poachers* – the classic approach to the active process of reading texts and objects of fan interest – a pervasive perception of fans persists that is based upon the characterization of them as '"kooks" obsessed with trivia, celebrities, and collectables' (1992: 11). A major (and enduring) factor influencing such cultural and public perceptions is that one of the definitional meanings of the term 'fan' emerges from religious roots. This is how Jenkins explained the adverse undertones attached to the concept of the fan:

> Many of the stereotypes seem to have been attached to the term 'fan' from its very inception. 'Fan' is an abbreviated form of the word "fanatic", which has its roots in the Latin word 'Fanaticus'. In its most literal sense, 'fanaticus' simply

meant 'Of or belonging to the temple, a temple servant, a devotee', but it quickly assumed more negative connotations – frenzy, 'excessive and mistaken enthusiasm, even demonic possession'. (1992: 12)

Of course, the distinction between objects of fandom has long been split in terms of class (to like heavy metal, *Doctor Who*, *WWE wrestling*, or the Harry Potter novels and films is to be a fan, whereas to appreciate the operas of Richard Wagner is to be a connoisseur in possession of sophisticated levels of cultural capital and finesse), but from Jenkins' perspective, media fans, while clearly consumers of the products of popular culture, are also, crucially, 'consumers who also produce, readers who also write, spectators who also participate' (Jenkins, 1992: 208).

For example, Scott Duchesne, who investigated this concept of fandom in relation to fan conventions, and conducted ethnographic fieldwork at the Toronto Fan Expo convention, argues that such spaces represent, on the one hand, an economic space and a source for profit-creation for the celebrity professionals present (through merchandise and autographs that are provided for a fee), and on the other hand, highly creative spaces in which fans engage in masquerade events using hand-constructed costumes and accessories which are presented to a judging panel who award prizes based upon the passion evident in the quality and labour that has been expended to produce the costumes 'that act as a conduit for the human and corporate synergy between fan and celebrity, creating the myriad profits enjoyed by both' (2010: 22). Thus, while such fans could be seen as the classic 'dupes' who are a source of profit for the cultural industry, the level of creativity and engagement involved suggests otherwise, as does the *communal* aspect of such fan celebration. To explain this active mentality and *social* behaviour, Jenkins proposed a model which operates on a number of distinctive levels:

- Fans typically assume distinctive modes of reception in relation to cultural texts whereby fan viewing is characterized by a highly conscious selection of a specific programme which is consumed faithfully.

- Fandom constitutes a particular 'interpretative community'.

- Fan behaviour constitutes a specific 'artworld' which (drawn from the work of the sociologist Howard Becker) involves networks of fan artistic production, distribution, consumption, circulation, and exhibition networks (and more contemporaneously within Internet sites and social media platforms).

A particularly potent technological platform, which Jenkins argues in his book *Convergence Culture* (2008), is YouTube, which, launched in June 2005 to upload and stream videos without high levels of technical ability, has enabled grassroots media producers to gain far greater degrees of distribution, access, and audience visibility and thus effectively 'broadcast yourself' (Burgess and Green, 2009). In Jenkins' view, YouTube has been at the forefront of media convergence as it can be easily linked with alternative social media sites such as Facebook to embed or link videos and content so that 'amateur' producers have 'more routes into the marketplace of ideas'

(2008: 293). More importantly, the prominence of convergent technologies has further enhanced the active nature of fan culture, but has enhanced fan visibility with regard to favoured texts, and to express fan devotion to celebrities.

CHRIS CROCKER AND BRITNEY SPEARS

The pace by which digital convergent technologies could facilitate public expressions of celebrity fandom and, as a result, fans become a celebrity was demonstrated by Christopher Cunningham, better known as Chris Crocker. Already a blogger posting short self-based webcam films and conversations to camera that were streamed on the Internet and forums such as YouTube, Crocker gained global fame for his 'Leave Britney Alone' self-broadcast. At a time in which the pop singer Britney Spears was experiencing numerous personal issues (that were the staple of celebrity news reporting), epitomized by her infamous head shaving incident (captured on video and broadcast across the Internet) and crowned by a shambolic performance of her song 'Gimme Something More' at the prestigious 2007 MTV VMA awards. The routine garnered widespread Internet-based public/fan discussion, in addition to extensive criticism from media commentators. In response, the then-teenage Crocker produced a webcam video shot in his bedroom that emotionally (building to a state of near-hysteria) and tearfully defended Spears and castigated her critics. The result was that the video went 'viral' on YouTube and became one of the most watched videos on the network, with more than 40 million hits to become what Vanessa Thorpe describes as 'one of the most viewed rants in human history' (The Guardian.com, 2011). Indeed, as Thorpe states of the outcome of the broadcast:

> In that original Britney posting Crocker lashed out at those who had criticised her onstage performance at the 2007 MTV video music awards. Still one of the most discussed video blogs of all time on the YouTube site, the notoriety it brought Crocker saw him invited on to news networks such as CNN and Fox News and interviewed on the *Today Show* and *The Howard Stern Show*. He also earned mentions on top-rated chat shows and was satirised by actor Seth Green, who applied eyeliner and urged the public to 'Leave Chris Crocker alone!' (The Guardian.com, 2011)

Although a form of fame established thorough notoriety rather than talent, the speed of Crocker's ascent to fame was startling, and unprecedented through its establishment via YouTube. Furthermore, while Crocker may also seem to be the perfect example of Rojek's 'Celetoid' celebrity category, he has established himself post-Britney as an Internet performer, a documentary film-maker, and has released music though iTunes with the 'fame' established by his globally-viewed celebrity-based outburst. At one level, Crocker represents a singular (and eccentric) example of Hills' category of the 'subcultural fan' whereby 'media fans can become celebrated' (2006: 103) and become established as a Big Name Fan. And while the term is frequently associated with professional fan creators (Russell T. Davies, who went from fan to the writer/producer of *Doctor Who*, for example), Crocker's fan association with Britney Spears, regardless of parodies, cemented his rise to cultural visibility and his own particular brand of celebrity.

As Nick Salvato argues, reactions to the video from YouTube viewers and wider cultural commentators raised issues of authenticity as Crocker had produced a series of Internet-released videos which featured him as alternative characters. As such, 'the question of whether or not Crocker was acting arose extremely quickly on the heels of the video's posting. In his interview with Maury Povich, Crocker sought to distinguish "Leave Britney Alone!" from the stylizations of his previous performance pieces' (2009: 76). Thus, Crocker represents a face of Internet celebrity that demonstrates the rapidity of fame in the convergent landscape, but also the public presentation of self that is long associated with celebrity personas with regard to a distinctive split between the *I* (the verdical self) and the *Me* (the self as seen by others) with celebrity public life based upon the presentation of a self as 'a staged activity' (Rojek, 2001: 11). Thus, Crocker's 'Leave Britney Alone!' video produced a number of reactions that ranged from the 'superfan' utilizing social media, to a more calculated celebrity performance in its own right – but still highlighting the ways in which an anonymous individual could gain global visibility by millions of people across the world literally overnight.

PARA-SOCIAL INTERACTION AND FANS

In assessing the communal role that celebrity can play within contemporary cultures, Robert van Krieken refers back to Horton and Wohl's conception of para-social interaction, the relationship between social actors and celebrities through media consumption that nevertheless can produce a distinctive 'bond of intimacy' with media personalities. Surveying later work on the principle of para-social relations, researchers have explored the ways in which the activities of figures within media texts can provide guides for social actor's behaviour in their everyday lives and how they engage with media figures to the extent that they use them as a 'basis for communication and interaction within one's real-life relationships' (van Krieken, 2012: 84–5). A crucial factor here is that these modes of para-social interaction are avowedly communal and frequently linked with real-life relationships, be it TV shows or particular celebrity figures. Indeed, with reference to the latter, van Krieken argues that celebrity operates as a 'guide to life' and offer appropriate (or at least current) modes of social comportment and inspiration, from adopting the healthy and motivated lifestyle of a successful sports star, to publicly expressing devotion to a favoured celebrity in more extreme ways, for example the male Miley Cyrus 'superfan', Carl McCoid, who possesses over 20 tattoo designs and portraits of the singer.

The means with which to engage in this relationship with celebrities has developed in ways that have made the concept of a meaningful para-social relationship with a chosen celebrity more vibrant, and, potentially, less distant than that characterized by the traditional mass communication media. Initially, this development was established through the increasing use of Internet-based blogs attached to television programmes, especially in the science fiction and fantasy genre (*The X Files*, *Buffy The Vampire Slayer*, *Firefly*, *Doctor Who*, *Lost*, etc.). This development saw the space between fans and the producers of such texts become diminished through regular blogging sites through which production teams communicate with fans, usually in a way that is 'official' and thus preserves the sense of 'media hierarchy' that exists between producers and fans (Chin and Hills, 2011). Indeed, such developments have transformed, as Hills argues in relation to *Doctor Who* fan activities since the series' return in 2005 (last broadcast by the BBC in 1989), in that fans are no longer 'poachers' but have rather become 'collaborators' through convergent media networks either by becoming official producers (the writers of *Doctor Who* fiction, for example), or by being sought out to become 'part-time co-opted word-of-mouth marketers for the brand' (2010: 58).

Nevertheless, alongside communicative activity from producers, celebrity culture has similarly changed in terms of the space between it and its fans and consumers, most notably through the rise and proliferation of Internet-based social media and networking platforms, which have renewed interest in the ways in which social media have influenced and changed the nature of para-social relationships between fans and celebrities. To emphasize the ways in which social media are transforming the relationship between celebrities and their fans, Lucy Bennett (2013) cites the example of the eccentric but globally successful American female pop singer, Lady Gaga. With over 26 million followers on Twitter, more than 52 million 'Likes' on Facebook, and a substantial fan base on YouTube (with specific channel space such as LadyGagaVEVO), Lady Gaga is a prime example of how social media can be actively engaged with and used as a means by which to connect with fans. Nevertheless, as Bennett stresses, Gaga also uses social media to mobilize fan bases with regard to particular political debates and issues such as calling for the abolition of the 'Don't ask, don't tell' (DADT) official United States policy on gay people serving in the US military. In this regard, Gaga has established a relationship with fans in such a way that they can be positioned not merely as admirers and consumers of her music, but also as 'fellow partners' with regard to such political activism.

Bennett argues that such a perception of closeness is fostered by Gaga as she routinely communicates to fans via Twitter in ways that coalesce public and private elements of her personality, thus exacerbating the feeling within many fans that they are indeed her 'fellow partners' and that they are part of her creative world, even though, in reality, they are single individuals within a collective of millions of followers.

CELEBRITY FANDOM AND SOCIAL MEDIA

In examining the fan relationship with regard to popular music celebrity, Bennett cites the work of Nancy Baym and her analysis of the ways in which an increasing number of musicians are using social media not simply as a platform to release their music, but to directly communicate with fans online. For Baym, social media, with its emphasis on users as 'friends', represents a significant transformation that has occurred in the relationship between many musicians and how they interact and communicate with their audiences. This is explained as follows:

> Instead of engaging audiences only through broadcast media and live per-
> formance with tightly constricted social roles, performers are now likely to
> encounter them as individuals with whom they can have ongoing interactions
> online. (2012: 290)

Baym interviewed 36 musicians from North America and Europe and explored the ways in which they interacted with fans through social media, with a key result being that musicians increasingly heard first-hand (through private messages sent to them) examples of how their music is reacted to and emotionally utilized in terms of fans connecting with family members through concert attendance, or how particular songs helped listeners deal with personal issues such as grief. On a more professional level, some respondents simply appreciated the continuous interaction with fans, and the feedback to musical releases and live performances that can be achieved through social media. Alternatively, other musicians were more cautious about the increasing level of 'intimacy' between performers and fans, and the effect that this may have on the relationship between performer and their audience through social media. This is what one respondent stated:

> I think that artists should maintain a certain distance [. . .] We haven't really
> entered into this period. This is uncharted waters for artists, where everything is
> on display. And I'm old enough to grow up in a time when that's not – you don't
> expect that from your artists. You want there to be some mystique. You want the
> revelation at the end. You don't want the day-by-day minutiae. (2012: 304)

This quote again demonstrates and reinforces Rojek's point between the private *I* and the public *Me*, with the emphasis that the prevalence of famous individuals engaging in social media communication with their audience is reducing the tradi-tional space and privacy divide between celebrity figures and their fans. As another of Baym's respondents, Mark Kelly, the keyboardist with UK progressive rock band Marillion, stated: 'pop stars, rock stars used to just drop out of the sky didn't they? And now they're tweeting about what they had for breakfast or whatever' (2012: 292). But aside from potentially eroding the sense of mysteriousness that has tra-ditionally surrounded the private lives of celebrities, social media networks have re-galvanized discussions of the potency of the para-social relationship between fans and celebrities, which, through traditional modes of media, has always been marked by its unreciprocated nature with regard to the celebrity object of fandom, but, with a number of celebrities engaging in communicative practices through social network-ing sites, this long-established relationship is changing.

With reference to Twitter, Gayle Stever and Kevin Lawson's research, which monitored the tweeting behaviour of celebrities such as Kirstie Alley, Jeri Ryan, William Shatner, Katy Perry, Josh Groban, Tom Hanks, and Lady Gaga, argue that the social networking sites' unique characteristic from the perspective of celebrity users is that in response to fan messages a celebrity maintains control of the relationship and can reply to 'tweets', or, if they are unsuitable or offensive, ignore them and 'block' a particular fan from their site. Yet the sense of proximity between celebrity and fan is diminishing through such interaction. For instance, the American rap artist M.C. Hammer, a prominent user of Twitter, concluded that a direct effect of social media networks is that it 'effectively shortens the distance between the content that is created and produced for a brand and the consumer like no other medium. The same is true of with celebrities, artists, and entertainers like me who are now closer to fans than we've ever really been before' (Stever and Lawson, 2013: 339–40). Consequently, while the para-social relationship is one in which fans know celebrities well, but celebrities have no knowledge of the identities of individual fans, Twitter is arguably re-addressing this balance as it represents a medium that offers the potential for fans to be recognized by the particular celebrities that they follow on Twitter (and by extension alternative forums such as Facebook).

CELEBRITY TWEETING

While the tweets produced by celebrities are wide ranging (from marketing news of new product releases, to communication about political and social causes of interest to particular celebrities), Stever and Lawson did identify communicative practices that were directed towards what they dub the 'para-social realm'. For instance, with reference to the singer Josh Groban's tweets, it was evident that particular fan recognition was of great significance, and a relationship publicly admitted by Groban in which he has revealed that:

> He reads the fans' Tweets, and in several cases he illustrated the point by remarking that he knew and recognized someone's Twitter handle and/or post content. Such acknowledgements are also made within the context of Twitter itself and frequent posters were sometimes rewarded with a reply or ReTweet from Groban. (2013: 342)

Therefore, Twitter – which, due to its characteristic of generating 'followers', is founded 'on the idea of instant publicity' (Faina, 2012: 55) – can and does provide for fans a means with which to directly communicate expressions of fandom to celebrities and also connect with other fans within the social networking forum, and while this can also give more extreme and obsessive fans access, the celebrity has the ability to block and exclude such individuals. Hence, the development of social media has enriched and extended the para-social relation and enabled fans to communicate directly with celebrities, or at least produce the perception of access and recognition by them (Marwick and boyd, 2011). As an example of this development, One Direction's official website includes the standard components (news, events, photos, videos, merchandise, a newsletter, profiles of each band member) but also includes a tweet section in which the band address their fans with updates of their tours, media appearances, promotion of products, and asking fans to vote for their videos and fragrance line on website forums; but there are also more personalized messages, such as those thanking fans for concert attendance, and Harry Styles' messages wishing the fans luck in their school examinations and clearly indicating how the band are 'marketed to tweens and teens' (Redmond, 2014: 70).

Given the prevalence of online fan activity, some commentators have now called into question the traditional dichotomy of fandom that separates fans into either the obsessively pathological or the active and creative. For some commentators, (Cornel Sandvoss, for example), technologies such as the Internet and social media are now intimately interwoven into the fabric of daily life and cultural behaviour so that fan behaviour is not a rigorous 'artistic' or communal activity as it arguably was in the era of Jenkins' initial research, but a routine component of life. So, social media plat-forms have official pages for celebrities: fans can easily create one dedicated to their favourite celebrity; they can contribute to celebrity profiles on Wikipedia; they can follow celebrity lifestyles on mobile phones and tablets/I-Pads. In essence, fandom is arguably neither marginal nor a source of great cultural effort as it has been normalized and integrated into media consumption.

The perception of 'fans' as representing an irrational and obsessed social grouping, however, still remains within contemporary popular culture. To illustrate, Hills cites the example of fans of Stephanie Meyers' teenage vampire series, *Twilight*, and the film adaptations, starring Robert Pattison, Kristen Stewart, and Taylor Lautner. News media reporting of film releases habitually focused on (predominantly female) fans' 'hysterical' behaviour, particularly in relation to appearances of Pattison, who played the role of Edward Cullen. Even within fan culture, Twilight fans were similarly regarded in negative terms. For instance, at *Comic-Con* 2009, Hills notes the presence of pervasive displeasure at the screening of *New Moon*, the second in the series of film adaptations of the novel series, and the feelings expressed by general attendees of the convention that the female fans of Twilight 'ruined the convention' due to the 'invasion' of 'hordes of screaming fan-girls' (2012: 122). Such behaviour, argues Hills, represents a distinctive sub-division within fan culture whereby one section is engaged in the dis-tinctive pathologizing of another fanbase for displaying 'obsessed' behaviour of a type it itself has been routinely accused of (science fiction fans, for example).

The perennial issue of obsession in relation to fandom is one that is particularly attached to celebrity culture in ways that differ from that of fandom of particular texts and characters (from *Star Wars* to *Breaking Bad*). Although dismissed by Jenkins as perpetuating the stereotype of the obsessed fans, Vermorel and Vermorel's research into the feelings and fantasies that fans have for particular celebrity figures points to the ways in which fandom of texts and of particular individuals differs in terms of intensity. Indeed, for the Vermorels, the religious quality of fandom remains as celebrity is 'the religion of our consumer society. And fans are the mystical adepts of this religion who dramatize moods, fantasies and expectations we all share' (1985: 247). In this case, the creative and active aspects of fandom towards particular celeb-rities can take highly personal and fantasy-led directions into everyday life. For instance, from surveying fan diaries and letters and conducting interviews, Vermorel and Vermorel cite the example of 'Joanne', and her particular fantasy surrounding the American singer Barry Manilow, who stated that 'When I make love with my husband I imagine it's Barry Manilow. All the time. And after, when my husband and I have made love and I realize it's not him, I cry to myself . . . He helps me through my life' (1985: 11). To use One Direction again to contemporize this analysis, they are subject to intense reactions from teenage female fans. However, there is also a sizable middle-aged demographic grouping which routinely mobs the band when they appear at public events.

It is important to note that such an expression of fidelity to a pop singer is a fantasy and a means with which social actors utilize celebrities in their own lives, but it also demonstrates the depth of feeling that can exist, and an emotional connection that is not always satisfied through fantasy consumption or through the para-social relations. This is because there is a distinctive difference between fandom of texts and fandom of individuals, and although much of the consumption of celebrity is 'active' and uncontroversial, celebrity culture does produce distinctive fans that go beyond the para-social relation and proximity at a distance to contact the object of their fandom: stalkers.

EXTREME FANDOM: THE CELEBRITY STALKER

A key perception of the nature of celebrities, argues Rojek, is that they are regarded as inspiring a 'magnetic attraction' in relation to fans, but it is – in keeping with the parameters of the para-social relationship that they habitually have with their devotees – imaginary as they do not engage in direct interaction with fans. Moreover, there is a key distinction between their public persona and their private identities. However, argues Rojek, 'occasionally, the magnetic attraction of the public face erodes the distinction. In such cases celebrities may experience the mortification of the verdical self and fans may foster obsessional-compulsive neurosis' (2001: 65–6). Thus, some fans who develop deeper emotional connections with a celebrity can manifest a spectrum of behaviours that range from avidly collecting information on the celebrity, to locating addresses and loitering in their vicinity in the hope of initiating a meeting and establishing a reciprocal relationship, with stalking being the most intense expression of such fan behaviour. In this regard, stalking can 'be defined as the development of an obsessional-compulsive neurosis in respect of a celebrity, which results in intrusive shadowing and/or harassment' (2001: 66). In the view of David Giles (2000), stalkers differ from especially or overly devoted fans because of their unpredictable and distressing behaviour towards a celebrity, the threat of violence and communications that indicate the desire to meet, or evidence that they have been keeping the celebrity under surveillance in anticipation of a meeting. In some instances, a celebrity can be targeted by the stalker of a fellow celebrity, as was the case of Günter Parche who 'defended' the object of his devotion, the tennis player Steffi Graf, by stabbing Monica Seles in the back during at a Hamburg tournament in 1993 because she had defeated Graf on numerous occasions.

Within his analysis of the psychology of stalking, J. Reid Meloy, a clinical professor of psychiatry, states that stalking, from a legal perspective, typically involves three dimensions: the intrusion of one person into the life of another; tacit or overt threats;

and that the recipient of such behaviour experiences fear. Indeed, the word 'obsession' developed from the Latin word obsidere – 'to besiege' – and remains 'the most accurate word to be used to describe much of the object-related thinking of the stalker' (1998: 13). Such behaviour is frequently related to 'narcissistic linking fantasies' whereby individuals develop the belief that they have a sense of commonality with a celebrity that is built upon the fantasy that they are loved and admired by a celebrity, and that their lives are intertwined. It is important to note that stalking is not confined to the famous, but because of their visibility, and the fact that many celebrities appear regularly within the media, they are the primary group most at risk of stalking behaviour (Hoffman and Sheridan, 2008).

A key historical (and indeed now infamous) example of the narcissistic linking fantasy remains that of John Hinckley Jr., who stalked the American actress Jodie Foster, and who, in the wake of failed attempts to contact and 'court' her, decided that in assassinating the President of the United States, Ronald Reagan, he would attract her attention and ultimate love. And on 30 March 1981, Hinckley shot Reagan twice (the President survived the attempt) and was confined to a hospital on the grounds of being identified as having a narcissistic personality disorder, a factor reinforced by a note that he wrote just prior to the shooting which read: 'Jodie, I would abandon this idea of getting Reagan in a second if I could only win your heart and live out the rest of my life with you' (Reid Meloy, 1998: 20). In other instances, pathological narcissism can be exhibited in different ways, whereby the stalking of a celebrity is motivated not by a desire to be loved by them, but by the desire to acquire fame through them, as was the case with Mark David Chapman, who shot and killed John Lennon in 1980. Following the murder, Chapman confessed that:

> I've always known I'd be different and I've always known that I was destined for greatness ... I always knew the whole world would know who I was. I always felt different and felt special and felt odd and peculiar. (Reid Meloy, 2002: 115)

THE DARK SIDE OF THE PARA-SOCIAL RELATIONSHIP

While for the vast majority of fans the para-social relationship with celebrity culture is benign, stalking represents the 'dark side' of the para-social interaction whereby media consumption cultivates obsessional feelings for celebrities with the result that pathological degrees of 'celebrity worship' can develop (Spitzberg and Cupach, 2008). British researchers John Maltby and David Giles administered the Celebrity Attitude Scale to some 1,732 UK-based respondents and the results of the research articulated three degrees of celebrity worship. The first was the entertainment-social dimension, which consists of benign fan behaviour that is predicated upon a relationship with celebrities in terms of their entertainment provision and the ways in which this enables individuals to interact with like-minded fellow-fans. The core of this attitude is that of the 'active fan' and the pleasures of media consumption with no behaviour that seeks to minimize the proximity between them and the celebrity.

Conversely, the second expression of celebrity worship, the intense-personal dimension, revealed feelings of a compulsive nature towards celebrities that evoked the status of the 'obsessed fan', while the third form, the borderline-pathological dimension, revealed attitudes to celebrity figures that frequently were based upon regular fantasies and unmanageable behaviours. Thus, the second two modes of celebrity worship were those most associated with potential stalking behaviour as celebrities represented such intense components of such individuals' lives. Maltby and Giles state that those who register intense-personal levels 'may actually spend time worshipping celebrities at the expense of dealing with everyday events' (2008: 278), and for some this can lead to stalking, a form of behaviour that 'brutally underlines the power of celebrity to arouse deep, irrational emotions. In the psychology of the stalker, unconsummated desire is distorted into an overpowering wish to achieve consummation or recognition' (Rojek, 2001: 67).

So, while para-social interactions can be a healthy substitute for those who are, through no fault of their own, socially isolated, and stalking behaviour affects only a minority of fans, the number of fans who engage in stalking is still nevertheless significant, and, as such, there are numerous examples of celebrities who have become the target of stalking behaviour. For example, the actress Brooke Shields was stalked for over 15 years by Ronald Bailey, who sent numerous letters to her and then ultimately broke into her house (Cashmore, 2006). More recent examples include Robert Dewey Hoskins, who was ultimately imprisoned for stalking and threatening to kill the pop singer Madonna; Thomas Brodnicki, who stalked the former Disney actress and pop singer Selena Gomez; Jason R. Peyton's quest to marry the actress Jennifer Aniston; the Reverend David Ajemian, a priest who targeted the television talk-show host Conan O'Brien; Dawnette Knight, who stalked and threatened to kill the actress Catherine Zeta-Jones (due to professed feelings for her then-husband, the actor Michael Douglas); Mark Owen McLeod's harassment of the actress and pop singer Miley Cyrus; and Geneviève Sabourin's imprisonment for stalking the actor Alec Baldwin.

CELEBRITY STALKING AND SOCIAL MEDIA

Referring to the degree to which the proliferation of the Internet has enabled the rise of 'cyber-stalking' (whereby in addition to physical letters and face-to-face harassing behaviour from fans, stalkers can target figures of obsession through emails), Reid Meloy cites an email which flags the uneasy relationship that exists between celebrity and fans, which was received by the American actress Jennie Kwon and read: 'Everyone knows you haven't made it in show biz until you have your first obsessed fan' (1998: 10). This attitude has been exacerbated with the establishment of social media network sites such as Twitter and Facebook and the ways with which such media can change the stalking dynamic – a development that has become reflexively articulated by celebrities themselves. For example, the actress Kristen Stewart has stated that the rise of Facebook and Twitter have meant that it is more difficult for her to keep her locations secret from public knowledge. This is what she stated to news media of her status within a culture in which social media is widely interwoven:

Nowadays it's harder because everyone is on Facebook and everyone knows where you are all the time, and everyone's twittering . . . Like I'm going to die because somebody is going to say where I am and somebody is going to kill me. Someone's going to twitter my location and then it's going to be like, boom. (Thompson, 2012, MailOnline)

This highlights Spitzberg and Cupach's identification of the edgy relationship dynamic that exists between celebrities and their fans. In an immediate sense, fandom is what build and maintain a celebrity's public persona and indeed ensure that they have a celebrity career, but the alternative is that celebrities 'often suffer the consequences of living beneath the microscope of public attention' (2008: 308), a factor exacerbated by social media which have only intensified celebrity visibility. In the case of Kristen Stewart, her anxiety about the efficacy of Twitter to locate her was fuelled by hostile Robert Pattison fans who felt aggrieved at Stewart for having a relationship with Rupert Sanderson, the director of *Snow White and the Huntsman*, while still romantically attached to Pattison. In this instance, then, it was the fans of another celebrity who were regarded as the pathological threat, but Stewart's observation is apt in the age in which social media and sophisticated cameras installed within networked mobile telephones mean that celebrity sightings can be communicated and visually documented instantaneously. In this regard, contemporary media culture and its relationship with celebrity culture illustrates what the French philosopher of technology and social speed, Paul Virilio, calls 'the market of the visible' (Virilio, 2005: 61). Here celebrity images and activities – whether produced by the professional paparazzi or by citizens with i-Phones, and so on, and therefore with instant access to social media networks – dramatically demonstrate Virilio's views of a media world that is defined by the ever-increasing pace of media imagery and the dizzying pace of information communications. This conveys the general trajectory of Western media culture, but it neatly creates the situation that celebrity figures such as Stewart fear as it can potentially enable stalkers to gain ever greater avenues of access to the objects of their obsessional fandom with more rapidity than ever before. This sense of anxiety from impromptu public fan encounters is especially germane in light of the emergence of celebrity-based websites that have 'stalker' features which, in addition to monitoring celebrity movements via their own Tweets, enable 'fans to gather information about celebrity habits and whereabouts directly from other fans on the internet' (Ferris and Harris, 2011: 26).

Social media has rapidly established itself as a forum for fandom, from the active and celebratory, to that more pathological minority who seek to cross the para-social threshold, or to engage in negative behaviours. As Baym's qualitative research with musicians and social media discovered, while fans frequently and actively use such networks to reach out to the objects of their fandom, forums such as Facebook and Twitter were are also utilized by 'antifans' to communicate critical messages, provocative comments on musical output, or abuse (for example, One Direction's Zayn Malik has received numerous racist tweets). The use of Internet forums and social networking sites has become so prevalent that it has produced the 'troll' who engages in trolling, an online activity in which individuals deliberately provoke other group members with the intention of creating arguments (Bishop, 2012). As such, online behaviour is not necessarily always fannish or pathological, but instead 'active' in the sense that critics of celebrity culture and individual celebrities can utilize the likes of Facebook and Twitter to vent their ire. Indeed, such is the extent of negative comments directed against celebrities that US talk-show host, Jimmy Kimmel, has a periodic feature on his Jimmy Kimmel Live show entitled 'Celebrities Read Mean Tweets', that presents celebrities such as Selena Gomez, Dr Phil, Simon Cowell, Jessica Biel, Katy Perry, Larry King, Snooki, Kristen Stewart, Russell Brand, Jessica Simpson, Will Ferrell, and Justin Bieber reading out personally insulting tweets.

CONCLUDING POINTS

The ways in which insults can be expressed in social media platforms to the extent that celebrities can theoretically view them stresses the extent to which fan behaviour towards celebrities has been transformed in recent years in the wake of digital technologies. The category of active fandom has been invigorated through Internet and social media engagement, while negative elements such as stalking and pathological obsession with celebrity have also remained, and have been expended into the online world. But, regardless of the motivation of fan behaviour, the direct contact and visibility of celebrities that contemporary fans can – at least in principle – attain, and the rapidity of contact celebrities can have with their audiences, whether in terms of direct messages or general addresses of information, the degree to which the concept of the para-social relation has evolved since Horton and Wohl's analysis of the impact of television is extensive and unprecedented.

FURTHER READING

For a more extensive analysis of the sociological approach to fans and fandom, readers should consult:

- Hills, M. (2002) *Fan Cultures*. London and New York: Routledge.

- Hills, M. (2010) *Triumph of a Time Lord: Regenerating Doctor Who in the Twenty-first Century*. London: I.B. Taurus.

- Jenkins, H. (1992) *Textual Poachers: Television Fans and Participatory Culture*. New York: Routledge.

- Lewis, L.A. (ed.) (1992) *The Adoring Audience: Fan Culture and Popular Media*. London and New York: Routledge.

For detailed explanations of the concept of the para-social relation from a historical and contemporary perspective see:

- Horton, D.and Wohl, R.R. (1956) 'Mass communication and para-social interaction', *Psychiatry*, 19: 215–29.

- Stever, G.S. and Lawson, K. (2013) 'Twitter as a way for celebrities to communicate with fans: implications for the study of parasocial interaction' *North American Journal of Psychology* 15(2): 339–54.

6

REPORTING CELEBRITY

CHAPTER OVERVIEW

While the professional and personal activities of celebrities cover a wide spectrum of media discourses, our primary source of information still comes from the world of journalism and news production. From promoting products, appearances, and revealing relationships, marriages, and pregnancies – from Beyoncé, Kim Kardashian, and Kate Middleton, to being at the epicentre of scandals – Chris Brown, Tiger Woods, Paula Deen, Amanda Bynes, Lindsay Lohan, or Oscar Pistorius, celebrity and journalism has a long history and, according to many commentators, the connection between celebrity and journalism has never been closer, to the extent that the public demand for celebrity news is transforming the practice of journalism. However, the chapter will examine the modes by which social media have extended celebrity coverage in ways that complement, but increasingly go beyond the scope of, more traditional newspaper and magazine coverage. As such, the proliferation of *Twitter*, *Facebook*, *Instagram*, and so on, has resulted in coverage that is beyond the conventional parameters of celebrity control (PR and legal barriers) in which media audiences themselves play a role in transmitting news coverage through such platforms, and celebrities report upon themselves. Thus, inveterate tweeters and Facebook posters such as Stephen Fry, Kim Kardashian, Elizabeth Hurley, Ariana Grande, Katy Perry, and Lady Gaga now 'break' news stories about themselves that invalidate the traditional gossip column, as well as engage in public (but publicity-producing) celebrity-on-celebrity online arguments. To explore the relationship between celebrity culture and journalism, the chapter will cover:

- The development of celebrity reporting
- Celebrity culture as an inexpensive source of soft news
- Celebrity, defamation, and privacy laws
- Celebrity and journalistic practice
- The UK phone hacking scandal and the Leveson Inquiry
- Social media and celebrity reporting

To illustrate the relationship between changing news practices and celebrity, the chapter examines news coverage of Kate Middleton – from her relationship with Prince William, her marriage, and the birth of her son – in addition to discussions of Lily Allen, Tiger Woods, Sienna Miller, and Perez Hilton.

THE RISE OF CELEBRITY REPORTING

In the view of Ursula Smartt, 'it is our human craving for stories and gossip that helps keep the newspaper and magazine industries alive' (2011: 23), and as such, it is no surprise that the lives and activities of celebrities provide a pervasive focus for such public appetite and that one of the primary means by which contemporary celebrity culture is communicated is via journalism to the extent that, as Fred Inglis observes, celebrity:

> Is the staple of innumerable magazines on either side of the Atlantic, whether in the glossy and worshipful guise of *Hello!* and *Glamour* or the downright fairy-tale telling and mendacity of the *National Enquirer* and *Sunday Sport*; it fills a strip cartoon in . . . Private Eye and provides *all* the dailies, whether tabloid or broadsheet, with the contents of news, op-ed, gossip, and, not infrequently, contributed columns. (2010: 4)

However, a form of 'news culture' has existed for centuries, from the Forum verbal street communication of daily events in ancient Rome, block printed newsletters in sixth-century China, through to handwritten newsletters in Tudor England to (after the Gutenberg printing press) printed news pamphlets and the development, from the seventeenth century (in Europe and America), of newspapers, with them becoming established in the eighteenth century (Stephens, 2007). It was also, in Britain, the eighteenth century that saw the emergence of coffeehouse culture, trenchant political party debates, and the demand for the communication of public opinion – a demand furnished by a growing body of professional journalists, including 'star' writers such as the novelist Daniel Defoe (Marr, 2004). Regarding the development of the industry, it was in the nineteenth century that journalism became a commercial force and acquired definitive political and social authority (including, for example, the establishment of international news agencies such as Reuters in 1858). Because of these developments, it became known as the 'Fourth Estate' in so far as (somewhat idealistically) 'the press functions as a watchdog of the powerful in society and brings their misdemeanours to the attention of the public' (Conboy, 2010: 110).

Powerful 'press barons' such as Lords Northcliffe, Beaverbrook, and Rothermere generated considerable income thanks to advertising and increased sales of newspapers, due to the financial power that enormous newspaper sales and advertising income generated. This enabled newspapers to become independent of political funding although their financial might aroused anxieties that they might pose a potential threat to the idea of the Fourth Estate (so named by the eighteenth-century political philosopher, Edmund Burke in pre-revolutionary France alongside the aristocracy, the clergy, and the common people). The press did indeed institute a series of historical 'watchdog' functions against political forces, from William Randolph Hearst's newspaper efforts to bring about the Seventeenth Amendment to the US Constitution in 1912, to Bob Woodward and Carl Bernstein's exposure of the Watergate scandal connected with President Nixon in 1973, and the investigative and human rights activist journalism of figures such as John Pilger (Hampton, 2012: 3–6).

Later examples have included critical commentary on government military action in the post-9/11 'War on Terror' (Pilger, 2005) and Julian Assange's WikiLeak's website that has controversially disclosed government documents for public scrutiny (Fenster, 2012; McNair, 2012).

Alongside political reporting and lofty 'Fourth Estate' activity there has been a significant seam of stories about the lives and activities of the famous, and this is a feature of professional journalism that is longstanding. As Marshall (2005) argues, journalism and celebrity have been intertwined for some 200 years and emerged from business reporting and profiles of business figures, and opinions on political concerns. This focus was influenced by rapid processes of urban development and greater levels of visibility of influential individuals. As such, early twentieth-century American journalism began to increasingly include biographies of the famous, which, as public interest in the lives of such visible individuals grew, developed into 'hunt for news' journalism, revelation, exposure, and 'muck raking', and saw the establishment of gossip columns (Inglis, 2010), and for good commercial reason, as Marshall explains:

> American newspaper magnates of the late nineteenth century such as Joseph Pulitzer and William Randolph Hearst built their empires on a brand of news story that acknowledged a wider proportion of the population and attempted to cater to what was believed to be their interests and desires. Typically called yellow journalism, reporters developed stories that were both sensational and closer to the everyday lives of [a] new urban readership. Profiles of celebrity individuals emerged alongside the development of what were perceived to be more salacious stories and muckraking to discover scandal [and the] development of direct interviews with famous people in their private homes. (2005: 21)

At one level, this early rise in newspaper column space was a result of an emergent number of individuals who were 'stars', which was intensified as early Hollywood actors and actresses were increasingly recognized by members of the public and cinema audiences demanded to know more about these new 'idols' (Dyer, 1982). Thus, in addition to newspaper profiles, gossip columns, and scandals, this period also saw the establishment of celebrity/film star periodicals such as *Movie Stars*, *Photoplay*, *Hollywood Fan Magazine*, and *Confidential*, a journalistic tradition contemporaneously reflected in the glossy pages of *OK!* (with its subtitle 'First for Celebrity News') and *Hello!* Marshall places the growing demand for celebrity journalism within a wider social and cultural context.

THE CODES OF CELEBRITY JOURNALISM

For Marshall, a further key factor to explain the advent and development of celebrity journalism from the latter years of the nineteenth century and into the first decades of the twentieth century was that celebrity reporting marked a retreat from rigid class-based societies to venerate and celebrate individualism. As such, profiles of the famous within newspapers became central, and attractive to readers, because celebrities 'represented heightened examples of individual achievement and transformation and thereby challenged the rigidity of class-based societies by presenting the potential to transcend these categories' (2005: 21). In this regard, the structure of celebrity profiles that emerged in the first decades of the twentieth century remained surprisingly stable as the relationship between professional journalism and celebrity intensified, and broadly followed four major formats and settings:

1. The meeting of journalist and star in either a domestic setting or café.

2. The description of the casual dress and demeanour of the star.

3. The discussion of their current work – which is essentially the anchor for why the story is newsworthy.

4. The revelation of something that is against the grain of what is generally perceived to be the star's persona – something that is anecdotal but is revealing of the star's true nature. (2005: 25)

Ultimately, while celebrity reporting may have a crucial socially binding function (given that the news media are a significant component of the media-established para-social relationship that links celebrities with fans), Marshall stresses the extent to which the presence of celebrity within journalism constitutes an indication of the progressively central function of entertainment that has come to dominate news media.

CELEBRITY AS NEWS

As Graeme Turner argues within his book *Understanding Celebrity*, celebrity journalism is the dominant voice within the tabloid newspaper market, most significantly in the United Kingdom, and it is a focus that has developed in the wake of celebrity presence within glossy magazines. Referring to the work of women's magazine researchers such as Anna Gough-Yates and Joke Hermes, Turner argues that this process was initiated by the rise and subsequent popularity of weekly magazines that were heavily devoted to celebrity, which in turn led, in the 1990s, to the production of a definite 'genre of mass-market magazine, the celebrity gossip and news weekly' (2004: 73). Consequently, a number of celebrity magazines emerged, most notably *Hello!*, *OK!*, *Now*, *People*, *Closer*, *Grazia* (fusing fashion with celebrity) and, perhaps most prominently, *Heat* (launched in 1999 in the UK), which covers celebrities (from the A-list to the 'attributed' variety) and their lives, from Brad Pitt and Angelina Jolie, Victoria Beckham, Taylor Swift, Miley Cyrus, One Direction, Katy Perry, Kim Kardashian, and Kate Middleton, to its focus upon the members-of-the-public-turned-celebrity housemates of the Reality TV series, *Big Brother* and *The Only Way is Essex*, and key contestants that appear on the music television talent show, *The X Factor*. Furthermore, *Hello!* and *OK!* have strong relationships with the public relations industry and representatives of celebrities which is explained below:

These magazines deal with almost nothing but celebrity and thus they must be tightly articulated to the industry and its promotional needs if they want a reliable supply of pictures and stories. As a result, *Hello!* publishes uniformly appreciative features about celebrities' new marriages/houses/babies, recoveries from tragedy/divorce/career setbacks – clearly in collaboration with the celebrities concerned. (2004: 73–4)

However, Turner goes on to observe that a key aspect of this celebrity presence was a definitive sense of convergence between the editorial stance and position of celebrity-focused glossy magazines and weeklies and tabloid newspapers, the news form that is typically defined by its mixture of national and international news stories imbued with 'sensational, often salacious content' (McNair, 2009: 5). Given this editorial quality and focus, tabloid newspapers consistently devote column space and headlines to the activities of celebrities, and encourage readers to come forth for a fee (as was the case with the now defunct *News of the World*) with accounts of adulterous sexual scandals with famous individuals.

In Brian McNair's (2009) appraisal, the dominant presence of celebrity stories and images in tabloids has resulted in the charge that journalistic standards have steadily been 'dumbed down' and that 'hard news' (economic policy coverage, international coverage, party politics) is being replaced by more space devoted to 'soft news', such as celebrity lifestyles, achievements, scandals, and fashion choices. While the 'tabloidization' debate is longstanding (and much discussed) which potentially overlooks the complexity and diversity of journalistic output (that tabloids are not the only form of news product and have particular audiences who consume them precisely because of their soft news quality and scandal), it has proven to be durable, especially with regard to celebrity influence. A good example of this can be illustrated with regard to the journalistic coverage of the ex-President of France, Nicolas Sarkozy, who, within a matter of months after gaining office in 2007 divorced his wife, Cecilia, and shortly afterwards married the Italian model, singer, and actress, Carla Bruni. While the couple were reported on favourably by the British press, the French media were critical that the fusion of politics with the world of celebrity was a decisive example of the 'dumbed down' nature of his presidential style. But many news stories also covered the Sarkozy–Bruni relationship with acute reference to the role of women in twenty-first-century politics, and at one level, McNair concludes, 'The Nicolas and Carla show, whatever else it was, was a story about the changing nature of French culture and society' (2009: 73).

CELEBRITY AS INEXPENSIVE JOURNALISM

The focus on celebrity within journalism still raises acute concerns about the nature and trajectory of contemporary journalism, and also points to the power and influence that celebrity culture has as an ever-increasing source of news. At one level, the tabloidization debate taps into wider critiques of the nature of journalism which has been placed under ever-increasing commercial pressures and stresses which have in turn affected journalistic practice. As Robert W. McChesney argues in *The Problem of the Media*, commercialism has resulted in journalists increasingly pursuing specific reader demographics that are influenced by media owners and influential advertisers. Thus, political journalism has decreased while commercially viable story types have increased. Unlike (in an American context) the 'golden age' of professional journalism (from the 1950s to the 1970s), where journalists possessed considerable independence and financial resources to pursue stories, budget cuts and the need to feed 24-hour rolling news output and online bulletins has resulted in an increased demand for attention-grabbing news. Consequently, the 'great commercial success story of US journalism has been the Fox News Channel, which has cut costs to the bone by replacing expensive conventional journalism with celebrity pontificators' (2004: 79). Apart from costs, the pressure on journalists to provide entertainment over harder news is a factor that has resulted in the tabloidization debate continuing within critical media discourses and commentary upon professional journalistic practice. McNair's rebuttals against tabloidization are valid. Audiences who require news that is soft and threaded with celebrity stories turn to tabloids and know exactly what to expect from such newspapers (and their online equivalents), while broadsheets such as *The Guardian*, *Daily Telegraph*, or *The Independent* remain a bastion of hard news. Still, with McChesney's critique in mind, the lines between soft and hard news providers is arguably becoming more blurred as the drive to obtain larger readerships via engaging and entertaining stories becomes increaslingly dominant with the focus on celebrity as a driving force, as Conboy states:

> Tabloid tendencies to cross-reference celebrity and entertainment issues can be witnessed increasingly as part of the repertoire of the elite press and broadcast journalism in all its forms, and they are part of a strategy to reach new audiences in a crowded market and a changing cultural and technological environment. (Conboy, 2011: 123)

Yet, even within tabloids, recent years have seen their journalistic content diminish and be replaced with a distinctive 'storytelling' function. For instance, the former *Daily Star* journalist Richard Peppiatt cites Brian Cathcart's definition of journalism as a means with which to access how journalism is changing. For Cathcart, journalism is an endeavour that is 'demonstrably valuable to society. It tells us what is new, important and interesting in public life, it holds authority to account, it promotes informed debate, it entertains and enlightens' (in Peppiatt, 2012: 17). Nevertheless, while even tabloids were always guided by the imperative to be news- as well as entertainment-informed, the function of entertaining readers, Peppiatt argues, has progressively displaced and usurped the need to inform to the extent that editorial and journalistic commentary is impossible to tell apart from news and facts. In this regard, Peppiatt's first-hand British newsroom observations (which he calls 'the story factory') accords with McChesney's analysis of US journalism and its changing professional nature in the wake of commercial market forces. Here are Peppiatt's observations:

Journalism proper, driven by a truth-seeking impulse grounded in the real, is vastly more exhausting both financially and temporally than the type of agenda-rich storytelling that dominates the news market. The conditions of the modern newsroom, particularly, but not exclusively, tabloid ones, mean that journalists walk in the door and are forced by circumstance to behave as storytellers, abiding by the pre-defined narratives as part of an entertainment-seeking impulse. (2012: 23)

Furthermore, this process has accelerated apace given the increasing primacy of online newsrooms which, utilizing live blogs, can produce stories in time-cycles ranging from two hours to 30 minutes, which increasingly rely upon previously published sources, and which may affect verification processes (Thurman and Walters, 2013). In relation to celebrity stories, on the day after the wave of public protests in the Middle East in 2010, but largely emanating from Egypt and subsequently dubbed the 'Arab Spring', and which saw millions of people take to the streets in the name of freedom, Peppiatt ruefully points out that UK *Daily Star* newspaper's front-page headline read 'Jordan: The Movie'; however, this was not a reference to the political unrest in the Middle East, but instead referred to a proposed plan to produce a film about the life of model, Reality TV personality, and media entrepreneur, Katie Price, aka 'Jordan'. Thus, unprecedented civil unrest aimed at unseating national governments could not topple the centrality of celebrity as the dominant news of the day.

CELEBRITY REPORTING AND KATE MIDDLETON

The pantheon of celebrities who appear within news coverage is, as would be expected, varied, from actors, sports stars, and pop/rock figures, to socialites and Reality TV personalities, and celebrity is indeed a dominant force and presence in mainstream contemporary journalism. However, few individuals have dominated news media, from soft to hard news, tabloid to broadsheet to broadcast, in such a dramatic and global level as Catherine 'Kate' Middleton. Yet while Kate Middleton's celebrity status may indeed be that of Rojek's most 'disreputable' category of celebrity – the attributed celebrity, who has fame 'thrust upon them' without any discernible act of achievement, Kate Middleton is nevertheless one of the most famous women in the world as the result of her relationship, engagement, and marriage to Prince William, the Duke of Cambridge and the second in line to the British throne, and as the mother of their son, George.

The daughter of entrepreneurial parents who own a multimillion pound party supply and decoration company, Kate Middleton came to the attention of the world press when, as a fellow student at St Andrews University, she met Prince William in 2001 and they formed a relationship in 2002. Although they separated briefly in 2007, the couple were reconciled and announced their formal engagement in 2010, choosing to break with tradition to make the announcement on the social media platforms of Facebook and Twitter (Nicholl, 2011), and on the 29 April 2011, they were married at

Westminster Abbey and she became Duchess of Cambridge. From the outset of their relationship, Kate Middleton has become a persistent focus of journalistic interest and reportage, from news agencies as diverse as the *Sun* and the BBC breaking the story that she and William had split in 2007, to similar media coverage confirming their reconciliation in 2008. Her wedding constituted a major media spectacle which dominated newspaper front pages and television schedules and was watched by 2 billion people on television (with viewing figures of some 26 million in Britain). In terms of news coverage, stories likened Kate Middleton to William's mother and dubbed her 'The New Diana', while the *Daily Star* ran the wedding day headline: 'ONE BEAUTIFUL BRIDE . . . ONE GREAT DAY TO BE BRITISH'. Furthermore, when her pregnancy was announced through a press statement, but also via Twitter, the news:

> led to the couple's official website crashing. Within moments, there was a frenzy of excitement around the world, where twenty-four-hour news channels and newspapers dedicated their broadcasts to the conception of a new third-in-line to the throne. (Nicholl, 2013: 294)

Journalistic speculation ranged from the conception date to the identity of the godparents and the Lindo Wing of St Mary's Hospital, where the Duchess was due to give birth and was besieged by representatives of the global press, and this became known, in journalistic circles, as the 'Great Kate Wait'. When their child was born on Monday, July 22, 2012, it was announced on Twitter with the result that '487 million people tweeted messages of congratulations' (Nicholl, 2013: 301–4). Akin to the wedding coverage, the royal birth made headlines across the spectrum of newspapers, from souvenir editions of tabloids such the *Daily Mirror*, *The Sun*, and the *Daily Star*, to headline banners on broadsheets.

But it is not simply Kate Middleton's role as a royal girlfriend, then wife, that lies at the heart of reporting; she has demonstrably emerged as a major celebrity figure in her own right (eclipsing William as a journalistic subject of interest) as her image, fashion, and hair styles have become consistent features in news reporting and celebrity magazine covers and articles. Geordie Greig, the editor of *Tatler*, regarding Middleton's relationship with the media has stated: 'Kate has not put a foot wrong. She appears modest and beautiful, and is liked by the press' (in Cywinski, 2011: 129). As such, Middleton has appeared on the cover of *Hello!* magazine numerous times in connection with royalty, but she has also featured in lifestyle gossip features (one cover depicting Middleton and her mother shopping for cots), and in articles about her fashion choices. Indeed, Middleton has been dubbed a 'style princess' and *Grazia* magazine has called attention to the positive influence Middleton has had on the British economy due to what has been dubbed the 'duchess effect' that has seen Middleton's fashion choices emulated by consumers. The impact of this 'Kateonomics', based upon Middleton wearing fashion brands such as L.K. Bennett, Jimmy Choo shoes, and Reiss clothing, has been the generation of over £1 billion as the result of her fashion choices causing 'an army of copycat fans to empty shops and online retailers to recreate her signature style' (Vince, 2012: www.graziadaily.co.uk).

The royal wedding also afforded a moment in which a second Middleton ascended to the level of global celebrity, Philippa 'Pippa' Middleton. Although the subject of minor journalistic interest during her sister's engagement, it was her role as Kate's bridesmaid that catapulted her to fame, or rather, it was the media coverage of her from behind and her body in a Sarah Burton dress as she carried her sister's train. Consequently, Pippa Middleton caused 'quite a sensation in her figure-hugging bridesmaid gown. Unbeknownst to her, she was now a global superstar – her name was trending on Twitter, and by the end of the day, Facebook groups dedicated to her derrière had thousands of followers. People wanted to know all about Kate's younger sister . . .' (Nicholl, 2013: 249). Subsequently, Pippa Middleton similarly adorned numerous covers of *Hello!*, *OK!*, *Grazia*, *US*, and has become a persistent journalism subject, from her relationships to fashion choices, while her professional status has included editorial contributions to the *Tatler*. Indeed, such is her celebrity that the American magazine *Time* included Pippa (with Kate) in its list of the world's 100 most influential people of 2012 due to their status as 'avatars of inspiration' and a source of female style and bodily emulation (Mayer, 2012), with the latter point underscored by reports of a palpable rise in cosmetic surgery requests to obtain the posterior shape that led to her celebrity status. As such, Kate's – and to a lesser, but still significant extent – Pippa Middleton's lives are news and a staple of 'tabloid' journalism.

Kate Middleton's rise to fame and becoming Duchess of Cambridge has seen her represent a 'fairytale' life, rising from obscurity to a global position of fame, and her firm association with fashion and status as a fashion influence ensure that media coverage runs across the entire spectrum of journalistic coverage, from broadsheets and tabloids to fashion and celebrity magazines. And, because her lifestyle and daily activities are deemed newsworthy, coverage inevitably spreads across media platforms. In accordance with Garry Whannel's (2002) position, journalists and media agencies are compelled to report on her because of the 'vortextual' quality of news story that she generates. What Whannel means by this concept is that there are a number of social and cultural events that frequently have no intrinsic significance beyond the media's interest in them. Thus, vortextuality is the process whereby 'major news stories have the power to dominate the news media to such an extent that all attention appears, temporarily, to be directed towards them. Editorials, cartoons, columns, features, phone-ins are all focused on the same issue' (2010: 66). This creates, to reinforce the 'vortex' analogy, a distinctive media 'whirlpool' or 'whirlwind' effect in which news agencies and coverage become 'sucked' into an intense period of focus on a news event, and celebrities are an endemic focus of such news vortexes. To illustrate this process, Whannel cites examples such as the wedding of David Beckham and Victoria Adams in 1999, the reportage of Michael Jackson's 2005 trial on charges of sexual abuse of young people and the returned not-guilty verdict, and that which surrounded his subsequent death in 2009. With regard to Kate Middleton, her wedding to Prince William epitomizes the principle of vortexuality as it dominated global news and was impossible not to report, such was its significance. Soon after the wedding, while holidaying in the apparent privacy of Lord Linley's chateau in the South of France, Middleton was photographed by paparazzi while sunbathing topless and the photographs were subsequently published in the French edition of *Closer*, but although British newspapers collectively agreed not to publish them, they did, in a vortextual fashion, inevitably extensively run coverage because the 'story in itself was a front-page story broadcast around the world' (Nicholl, 2013: 289). Similarly, the interest and 'debate' concerning Pippa Middleton's rear created something of a media vortex-within-a-vortex in the royal wedding and became, regardless of its standing in terms of significance, a major news item communicated and debated across a platform of news and communicative forms.

CELEBRITY AND JOURNALISTIC PRACTICE

It is important to note that Peppiatt does not castigate the centrality of celebrity within this journalistic storytelling culture, arguing that news stories that focus upon celebrity activities and gossip have a legitimate place within the media system, but conversely, alternative commentators have stressed the degree to which journalistic standards and practices are being eroded in the search for celebrity stories. A particularly potent example of this process is documented by Chris Atkins (2012) and was presented within his 2009 documentary *Starsuckers*, which detailed the ways in which leading news media and tabloid newspapers acquire their celebrity stories.

Atkins and his team set out to see how prominent newspapers reacted to public stories about celebrities and fed a series of untrue stories to see if they would be printed without any form of verification taking place. The results were that celebrity stories *were* indeed published. The only basis in reality that the stories had was that they confirmed the location where a celebrity had been present, but the subject-matter of the stories was entirely fabricated and the newspapers were contacted via telephone lines dedicated to celebrity stories from the general public with a fee rewarded to those which were published. For instance, Atkins phoned in a story that concerned the Canadian pop star Avril Lavigne, that detailed the fact that she had fallen asleep at a London nightclub and had begun to snore loudly. The story was accepted by the *Mirror* and printed without any attempts by journalists to establish the accuracy of the story. Following this 'success', Atkins provided similar fictional celebrity stories to the *Daily Star*, the *Mirror* (again), *The Sun*, and the *Daily Express*. Their stories included the singer Amy Winehouse's distinctive beehive hairstyle catching fire because of an electrical fault during an improvised musical performance at a party held at her house; the film director Guy Ritchie sustaining injuries as a result of juggling with cutlery in a restaurant; Pixie Geldof confessing that she routinely padded her bra out with confectionary; and that Sarah Harding, a member of the British all-girl pop band, Girls Aloud, was a clandestine fan of quantum physics. Significantly, the Sarah Harding story was published in *The Sun*'s 'Bizarre' celebrity gossip column, but subsequently picked up and reported by a number of news sites across the world. Thus, not only celebrity news, but also the recent trajectory of journalistic culture has seen a demonstrable increase in personality and entertainment industry reporting, galvanized by the drive 'to connect with audiences by all available means' (Rowe, 2012: 359), and as Atkins' project demonstrated, the facts do not need to get in the way of a good celebrity story, or even be considered.

Alongside such issues, a far more serious concern regarding British journalistic practice, tabloids, and celebrity was expressed by what has become known as 'Hackgate' in relation to the Rupert Murdoch/News Corporation-owned newspaper the *News of the World* which saw the British government initiate the Leveson Inquiry 'into the culture, practice and ethics of the press in Britain' (Brock, 2012: 519) and addressing the need for more stringent regulation of the newspaper industry. Such was the severity of the hacking scandal that it ultimately resulted in Murdoch closing the newspaper down (Wring, 2012). In terms of detail, the scandal broke on 4 July 2011 when *Guardian* reporter Nick Davies (with fellow journalist Amelia Hill), who had been investigating hacking stories in relation to the *News for the World* for some time, wrote:

> Murdoch's tabloid *News of the World* had hacked the cell phone messages of Milly Dowler, a 13-year-old missing girl whose disappearance was a media sensation in 2002 . . . *The Guardian* reported that a [News of the World] employee had apparently hacked into Dowler's voice-message system, deleted messages, which gave her family and police hope that she was still alive, and used hacked material to write stories about this missing girl. Dowler was found murdered, and the revelation that [the News of the World] had hacked the murdered girl's phone and interfered with the police investigation created a British and global media spectacle in summer 2011. (Kellner, 2012: 1170)

The scale of the hacking scandal went far beyond the Milly Dowler case, as Brian Cathcart (2012), a leading Professor of Journalism and member of the campaigning group Hacked Off (which called for a full public enquiry into the newspaper phone hacking) outlines. In the period between 2000 and 2006, various *News of the World* journalists worked with a private investigator named Glenn Mulcaire in order to gain access to and listen to private mobile phone voicemail messages of a number of different people of interest. The targets of phone hacking were police officers, victims of crime, the royal family, cabinet ministers, other journalists, and, most commonly, celebrities. While numerous public and celebrity figures ultimately offered testimony to Lord Leveson (such as Steve Coogan, J.K. Rowling, Ed Miliband, Hugh Grant, and the singer Charlotte Church), it was the British actress Sienna Miller who was the particular focus of intensive phone hacking between 2005 and 2006. As Cathcart states, the extent of hacking directed against Miller was such that it was not merely her mobiles that were accessed, but also those of her close friends, family, and professional acquaintances. Upon investigation, police found within Glenn Mulcaire's notebooks PIN numbers and passwords for Miller's various mobile telephones, the telephone number of Miller's mother, and the mobile phone numbers of Miller's ex-partner, the actor Jude Law. The result of this hacking activity helped the

> *News of the World* to publish regular stories about Miller and in particular about her relationship with Law . . . While this went on, Miller also found that whenever she went even to places where she assumed she would have privacy, journalists and photographers would usually be waiting for her. (Cathcart, 2012: 16)

CELEBRITIES FIGHT BACK: MEDIA LAW

One of the key outcomes of the Leveson Inquiry was to establish a more rigorous regulatory system that, while supporting the integrity and freedom of the press and its independence from government, also firmly demanded the highest ethical and professional standards by journalists, news agencies, and media owners (Lord Justice Leveson, 2012). The issue of privacy and 'invasions of privacy' by journalists and public figures is a longstanding and much-debated facet of historical and contemporary media law, with celebrities figuring perennially in the arguments concerning press freedom and the right to privacy and confidentiality.

As Robin Barnes argues in his book *Outrageous Invasions*, citizens in the United States of America and the European Union have long been warranted constitutionally protected rights to privacy and freedom of self-expression. Nevertheless, these rights have come into conflict with regard to journalism in relation to the nebulous principle of the 'public's right to know'. In some instances, institutions such as the European Court of Human Rights have developed a set of boundaries to clarify what journalists can and cannot report. This is what happened in the United States:

> As the United States intensified its efforts to promote democracy world-wide, the quality of its own democratic institutions has come under closer scrutiny. Most significantly, freedom of the press as a core value has undergone significant change since the American Revolution. The changes wrought by the Civil Rights and Global Peace Movements included a series of cases starting in the mid-1960s, that granted the press consistently greater freedom. These developments enabled tabloid publishers to expand their cottage industry of disseminating the intimate details of the lives of the rich and famous. In the new millennium, there is disturbing evidence that the extension of protection to the tabloids led to a significant distortion of the public debate. (2010: xvii)

As such, Barnes illustrates the nature of this relationship with the view that, while the Fourteenth Amendment of the US Constitution protects citizens from harassment, it frequently fails in relation to tabloid-press intrusion into the private lives of celebrities. As such, celebrity tabloids such as the *National Enquirer* routinely attract lawsuits from celebrities due to the salacious and frequently outrageous stories it has published, from Cameron Diaz, Brooke Shields, and Tom Cruise, to Martha Stewart and Bill Cosby. And historically, there has been apathy in imposing restrictions on American freedom of the press.

To a large extent, argues Barnes, there has traditionally been a lower degree of legal protection of privacy of the famous compared to that of private citizens due to the particular classification of 'celebrity citizens' who are considered as a form of 'public property', and the often frenzied media attention, journalistic harassment, and inaccurate reporting they experience is frequently considered to be acceptable because public property which, in a wider context includes parks, public recreational areas, and so on, is for 'public use and pleasure', and Barnes suggests that celebrities are placed in a similar position. This process was keenly highlighted with regard to the scandal that involved the golfer Tiger Woods. In the wake of a minor car crash outside his Florida home, media speculation as to the cause of the accident (the vehicle had been travelling at a low speed) turned to reports of extramarital affairs which were rapidly picked up and disseminated by publications such as the *National Enquirer*. (These were then picked up by various other tabloids which sought out women who claimed to have had relationships with the sports star and who shared his text messages and voice mails with journalists.) Woods' response was to withdraw from public life and appeal for privacy on ethical grounds (Sánchez Abril, 2011b). Conversely, with regard to European legal frameworks and attitudes, 'the balancing of every person's right to privacy with free expression (as part of the fundamental commitment to fostering democratic society) is guaranteed in the Convention on Human Rights' (Barnes, 2010: 156). This was appropriated very quickly by a host of celebrities to combat journalistic coverage and image publication (Rozenberg, 2004).

DEFAMATION AND PRIVACY

Within a British context, the issue of defamation is a key element with regard to legal reactions to news stories and the 'threat of a libel action is the single most inhibiting factor to media freedom in the UK' (Carey and Verow, 1998: 109). Defamation is a key example of a tort, which is 'a civil wrong for which monetary damages may be awarded by a court' (Banks and Hanna, 2009: 303). The laws relating to defamation exist to defend individuals against untrue statements which could potentially damage their reputation, lead to them being avoided by others, lower their personal reputation, or lead to the individual being viewed publicly as a figure of ridicule (Quinn, 2013).

Ursula Smartt, whose work has focused upon law in relation to journalistic practice, defines the law of defamation in the following way:

> Defamation is the collective term for libel and slander, and occurs when a person communicates material to a third party in words or any other form, containing an untrue imputation against the reputation of a claimant. Material is libellous where it is communicated in a permanent form or broadcast, or forms part of a theatrical performance. If the material is spoken or takes some other transient form, then it is classed as slander. Whether material is defamatory is a matter for the courts to determine. (2011: 87)

Charges of libel against newspapers and news agencies have greatly increased in recent years in the United Kingdom, and they have involved major celebrity figures such as Nicole Kidman, Kate Hudson, Sir Elton John, Lily Allen, Kate Winslet, and David Beckham. As Frances Quinn (2013) states, many defamation cases do not go to court, but are settled between the parties with the payment of sufficient damages, and such settlements involving potentially libellous journalism stories have involved celebrity figures including Victoria Beckham (accepting damages from the celebrity magazine *Star* following its story that a television crew had made disparaging remarks concerning her character and behaviour); the heavy metal vocalist Ozzy Osbourne (who was awarded damages by the *Daily Star* for reports concerning an alleged health issue); and the footballer Cristiano Ronaldo (who received a large damages award from the *Daily Mirror* due to a story that the newspaper ran alleging that he had been drinking to an excessive degree in a Hollywood nightclub). The key issue within such cases is the balance between privacy and public interest and the often complex relationship between Article 8 of the European Convention on Human Rights: 'The Right to Privacy', and Article 10: 'Freedom of Expression'. With regard to Article 8, it states: 'Everyone has the right to respect for his private and family life, his home and his correspondence' (Smartt, 2006: 69). In this regard, the issue of personal privacy has seen the principle of press freedom challenged on the grounds of breaching confidentially and privacy. In this regard, it is celebrity culture that has provided landmark cases in pushing back against the 'freedom' of journalists. As Smartt explains, a key example to illustrate the degree to which Article 8 and Article 10 can come into conflict is the incident involving the actors Michael Douglas and Catherine Zeta-Jones against *Hello!* magazine in what became *Douglas v. Hello! Ltd* [2001].

The case surrounded the issue of exclusivity and privacy in relation to the publication of their wedding photographs in *OK!*, *Hello!*'s rival celebrity magazine. The issue was that Rupert Thorpe, a paparazzo photographer, had managed to covertly gain access to the Douglas's wedding at the Plaza Hotel in New York, taken photographs, and subsequently sold a number of them to *Hello!* The issue was *Hello!* had previously made an unsuccessful bid for the exclusive rights to publish the wedding photographs, but they had made a deal with *OK!* for £1 million. The result was an application by the Douglases and *OK!* for an injunction to be enacted to prevent publication by *Hello!* which was rejected by the Court of Appeal, with the outcome that both magazines published wedding editions. In response, the Douglases sought damages from *Hello!* for what they regarded as a direct breach of privacy and *OK!* were successful in the High Court and in the Court of Appeal. On the other hand, a more substantial victory was the freedom of expression complaint by the *Daily Mirror*, involving the supermodel Naomi Campbell, which was ultimately heard by European Court of Human Rights following articles the newspaper had published in February 2001 which revealed details about her drug addiction therapy. The newspaper contested the National Courts' finding that it had breached the privacy of the model with the outcome that the Court ruled in Campbell's favour and she won the privacy case.

CELEBRITY AND SUPERINJUNCTIONS

Further instances of injunctions being applied for to stop journalistic coverage have become more prevalent in the relationship between celebrity culture and the press since these two examples. Indeed, a recent development has been the increased use of 'superinjunctions'. As Smartt explains, there have been numerous cases in which celebrities have sought privacy injunctions but have been granted 'superinjunctions' by the courts. Superinjunctions serve to restrain the disclosure of the fact that a privacy injunction has been obtained (which is why they have been called 'double gagging orders' by the media) and they are used to block the reporting of stories that could bring public discomfiture. In this regard, they constitute a prime example of celebrity power as they have been used predominantly by sports stars, such as the footballer John Terry (in the wake of media reports that the England star had been in an extramarital relationship with the ex-girlfriend of one of his fellow England team-mates), as they possess the financial resources to employ highly expensive lawyers (unlike 'ordinary' members of the public). Thus:

> Superinjunctions are interim court orders which prevent news organizations from revealing the identities of those involved in legal disputes, or even reporting the existence of the injunction at all . . . In their simplest form, superinjunctions prevent the media from reporting what happens in court, usually on the basis that doing so could prejudice a trial or someone's right to privacy. (Smartt, 2011: 74)

If successful, then, superinjunctions are a legal recourse that can prohibit journalists even reporting the fact that they have been 'silenced' by courts, and that, in accordance with the Human Rights Act of 1998 and its specific clause pertaining to the protection of personal and family privacy, the journalists must recognize this, even if the subjects are celebrities. Nevertheless, not all appeals for superinjunctions are successful if stories are judged to be of sufficient interest to the public and contravene press freedom (the British footballer John Terry's injunction to stop press coverage of an extramarital affair was overturned, for example). Therefore, the relationship between privacy and press freedom is one in which celebrity culture can exert its power, but in which that power can still be curbed and stories can run. Furthermore, media technologies are affecting such issues, too, as many are publicly revealed on social networking sites such as Twitter and Facebook, 'making the double gagging orders effectively worthless' (Smartt, 2011: 74).

SOCIAL MEDIA AND CELEBRITY JOURNALISM

The issue of social media, while playing a role in circumnavigating legal blocks to press coverage, is also changing the nature of celebrity media coverage, and the agents who produce such coverage and news. As Gary Whannel states, the impact of digital communication technologies has resulted in a media landscape in which, via the extensive use of mobile telephones with cameras, video recording capabilities, and instant and rapid Internet access, 'images of anyone, caught in an indiscreet moment, can be circulated globally and instantaneously' (2010: 72) and is related to the co-existence of 'citizen journalists' producing footage and commentary in parallel with professional news agencies and journalists. Although a contested concept, the impact of digital and broadcast technologies has resulted in on-the-spot reports of events being broadcast via the web by 'citizens', while the development of the blogosphere has enabled individuals to produce news sites and assume the role of citizen journalist or 'citizen witness', albeit of a non-professional 'amateur' variety (Allan, 2006, 2013; Tremayne 2006; Anden, 2013).

Commentators on blogs in an everyday, 'non-journalistic' sense have drawn attention to the ways in which the technology has effectively represented the emergence of a 'generation of compulsive self-chroniclers' for whom 'confession' and intimate self-revelation is now endemic within a network society in which 'exposure may be painful at times, but it is all part of the process of "putting it out there", risking judgment and letting people in' (Nussbaum, 2005: 350–2). A major contributor to this process has been the development of social networking sites such as Facebook, Twitter, LinkedIn, and Jaiku, but perhaps more significantly, Twitter, with regard to self-revelation. While Twitter has become central to the citizen journalist debate, the use of the micro-blogging site is becoming more pervasive due to its ability to produce 'minute-by-minute' blogs, and newspapers have established official Twitter accounts; in 2009 the UK-based news broadcaster, Sky News appointed a Twitter correspondent to 'scour' Twitter for stories and to feed them back into Sky news stories (Hermida, 2010). This latter point is of particular interest in that the use of sites such as Twitter have resulted in transformations in the production and fan reception of celebrity information, as well as changes in the sources of such information: the celebrities themselves. Marwick and boyd argue that:

> Networked media is changing celebrity culture, the ways that people relate to celebrity images, how celebrities are produced, and how celebrity is practiced. Gossip websites, fan sites, and blogs provide a plethora of new locations for the circulation and creation of celebrity, moving between user-generated content and the mainstream media. The fragmented media landscape has created a shift in traditional understanding of 'celebrity management' from a highly controlled and regulated institutional model to one in which performers and personalities actively address and interact with fans. (2011: 139–40)

TWITTER

Launched in 2006 and based upon the enabling of individuals to microblog rapid 140-character updates ('tweets') to a personal network of followers, users can communicate a variety of forms of information, from statements of at-that-moment activities to philosophical musings, to posting photographs and postings to other users. However, Twitter has also attracted a number of celebrities, including Oprah Winfrey, Tom Hanks, Leonardo DiCaprio, Stephen Fry, Simon Cowell, Shah Rukh Khan, Lady Gaga, Charlie Sheen, Justin Bieber, Katy Perry, Miley Cyrus, Rihanna, and the Kardashian sisters. Indeed, there will be few major celebrity figures which do not possess an active Twitter account (although they may be managed by representatives). A key issue concerning celebrity use of Twitter is that it 'allows celebrity practitioners to create a sense of closeness and familiarity between themselves and their followers. Highly followed accounts vary in performed intimacy; while some mostly broadcast information about an upcoming tour or book, others write about personal subjects, post exclusive content, or chat about their daily lives' (Marwick and boyd, 2011: 147). The issue here is that celebrities are using Twitter to contribute to reports about themselves, and at one degree taking over aspects of traditional 'gossip' journalistic functions. As Marwick and boyd note, celebrities let intimate details sometimes slip into tweets, and often post private domestic images – for example, Rihanna and Kim Kardashian are notable exemplars of this practice, often in the form of 'selfies' which are images taken by a person themselves (holding the camera or mobile phone at arm's length) with the express purpose of uploading it to Twitter, Facebook, or Instagram, which enables users to filter photographs and digital footage into various social networking sites. At one degree, this sense of 'closeness and familiarity' may be highly performative – in that it is a controlled sense of access to the 'backstage' areas. Here Marwick and boyd employ Goffman's classic ideas as expressed within *The Presentation of Self in Everyday Life* (1959) and his 'dramaturgical' concept of the division between 'front stage' professional life and 'backstage' private life. With regard to celebrity culture, access to private space is tightly controlled (as we have seen with regard to legal actions against news stories), although social networking sites serve to erode this traditional barrier. But while the kinds of information and images released may be innocuous and controlled, nevertheless, it adds to celebrity news discourse, and in some instances creates news. For instance, celebrities frequently address rumours on Twitter, while in other instances they can engage in feuds with other celebrity figures.

CELEBRITY TWITTER WARS

For instance, while still attached to Disney and her teen show *Hannah Montana*, Miley Cyrus initiated a feud with fellow female Disney singers/performers Demi Lovato and Selena Gomez 'after posting a mocking parody of the girls' home-made video series on YouTube' (Marwick and boyd, 2011: 151), while in 2013 Cyrus engaged in a Twitter 'war' with the singer Sinead O'Connor in relation to O'Connor's views of Cyrus' risqué VMA performance (2013). More acidly, the Twitter exchange between the UK singer Lily Allen and female American rapper Azealia Banks constituted an ongoing feud played out publicly which saw Banks tweeting responses to Allen's charge that she was a 'one-hit wonder', to which Banks retorted with insults to Allen's children and the tweet: 'One hit, but am certainly NOT a wonder. Just played for 70k at glasto, critics STILL eagerly anticipating my debut. Suck on that hoe!' (NME.com, 2013). Banks has also engaged in public arguments via Twitter with the Australian rap artist, Iggy Azalea. Other instances of feuds include the actress Amanda Bynes and Rihanna, the celebrity blogger Perez Hilton and Will.i.am, and Robert Kardashian and the UK pop singer Rita Ora. The issue is that these stories crossed over into mainstream celebrity reporting, but they were stories created by celebrity figures.

As such, whether for anodyne promotional statements or publicly-broadcast arguments, social networking sites such as Twitter are adding a further dimension to the reporting of celebrity culture, and it is one that is created from within that culture itself. As such, while the paparazzi still take and sell images and newspapers and glossy magazines increasingly devote space to the lifestyles and activities of celebrities, an increasingly significant source of images and commentary is the product of celebrity culture itself, from within that culture. As such, while the relationship between journalism and celebrity was historically forged through the newspaper gossip column, given the degree of discourse produced by celebrity, the gossip column in the traditional sense may soon be a feature of the past. Indeed, this transformation is perfected with reference to the rise to prominence of the online celebrity gossip blogger Perez Hilton, who rose from being an amateur to attracting corporate sponsorship for his website, Perezhilton.com, and who 'figures himself as a journalist despite a lack of training or any institutional affiliation' but who is also a prime example of a celebrity who conforms to the sobriquet 'famous for being famous' (Salvato, 2012: 77). Beginning as the PageSixSixSix blog in 2004, Hilton's establishment of Perezhilton.com has seen him develop from an avowedly celebrity-obsessed blogger into an acerbic critic/celebrator of celebrity with the goal of, as Elizabeth Podneiks (2009) observes, bursting the bubble of celebrity culture. Certainly this has offended some celebrities (the pop singer Ke$ha, for example, as revealed within her MTV Reality series, *Ke$ha: My Crazy Beautiful Life*), but others have actively collaborated with Hilton, secure in the knowledge that their images will be uploaded to his site and extensively circulated.

CONCLUDING POINTS

Gossip and public celebrity interest remains at the heart of reporting the lifestyles of the famous, but, in the era of bloggers and social media, professional journalists are no longer the only producers of such discourse as it is celebrities themselves who engage in this process, from promoting products and appearances, to, as in the case of Vin Diesel in 2013, happily broadcasting footage of himself singing and dancing (badly, it must be noted) to Katy Perry and Beyoncé songs in his bedroom, pushing the boundaries of the 'carefully managed' social media persona P. David Marshall commented upon in 2010. Therefore, the media remain central to celebrity news, and professional news outlets still play a major role in this communication, but the agents of reporting are now more numerous and often more direct – from within celebrity culture itself.

FURTHER READING

To further explore the relationship between journalism and celebrity culture see:

- Inglis, F. (2010) *A Short History of Celebrity*. Princeton, NJ: Princeton University Press.
- Turner, G. (2014) *Understanding Celebrity* (2nd edn). London: SAGE.

Media law is a complex set of legislative measures that will be different within a global context. However, for accounts which provide clear and detailed explanations of the often tense legal relationship that exists between celebrities and journalists and which contain a number of incisive examples of privacy cases and defamation cases, see:

- Barnes, R.D. (2010) *Outrageous Invasions: Celebrities' Private Lives, Media, and the Law*. Oxford: Oxford University Press.

- Sánchez Abril, P. (2011a) 'A simple, human measure of privacy': public disclosure of private facts in the World of Tiger Woods', *Connecticut Public Interest Law Journal*, 10(2): 385–98.

- Smartt, U. (2011) *Media and Entertainment Law*. London and New York: Routledge.

7
GLOBAL CELEBRITY

CHAPTER OVERVIEW

This chapter counters the perception that celebrity culture is predominantly a Western global force that is consumed across the world. While Western figures such as Brad Pitt, Lady Gaga, Jennifer Lawrence, or Katy Perry do appeal to global audiences, and Western companies do use Western celebrities to visually front advertising campaigns across the globe, there are substantial alternative celebrity cultures that are either locally-consumed, appeal to globally dispersed diasporic audiences, or actively resist Western celebrity performances and their cultural presence (Indonesia's protests against Lady Gaga). As such, the chapter will cover subjects such as:

- Global media culture
- Non-Western media culture
- Bollywood and Indian celebrity
- Southeast Asian and Islamic celebrity cultures
- The popularity of K-pop

To demonstrate the global diversity of non-Western celebrity figures and culture, the chapter will consider examples such as Shah Rukh Khan and Jay Chou; Islamic, Japanese and South Korean pop; Nazril 'Ariel' Irham; and the South Korean pop star PSY, who achieved widespread fame in the Western world through social networking media.

GLOBAL MEDIA CULTURE AND WESTERN CELEBRITY

Globalization is a complex (and contested) concept which has numerous dimensions that encompass economics, markets, media, religion, and sport, to name but a few factors (Lechner, 2009). But, for Malcolm Waters, a definition of globalization that helps to clarify the multi-faceted term is that it is a 'social process in which the constraints of geography on social and cultural arrangements recede and in which people become increasingly aware that they are receding' (1995: 3). In terms of core characteristics, globalization involves:

- References to space as a distinctive 'space of flows'
- Compression of time and space horizons across the world
- The notion of a connected world
- The acceleration of information and image communication and reception on a global scale

Although explored predominantly from the perspective of economics and politics, media culture has also played a role in globalization debates, and frequently with a critical edge – for example, the now-classic critical argument that such transnational media output has been, as Jeremy Tunstall (1977) has argued, mainly American, with the result that the world's population has been habitually consuming Hollywood film products and Western television programmes and news broadcasts. Indeed, from representing merely a homogenized form of entertainment in the pursuit of profit, media imperialism formed a part of the American 'military industrial complex' goal of subjugating the world, but through culture rather than military might. It is not merely media products or news forms that constitute such 'imperialism', but the individuals who appear within media forms. With reference to the Hollywood star system that emerged from the 1920s onwards, Schiller argues that film stars constituted a major aspect of Westernizing images across the globe. Speaking of the power of early Hollywood celebrity and its worldwide power, Schiller cites the example of the film actors Douglas Fairbanks and Mary Pickford's 1920 visit to Europe. The result was that:

> The crowds were so thick outside their suite at the Ritz-Carlton in New York before they sailed that they couldn't leave the hotel. Word was called ahead to England, France, Holland, Switzerland and Italy that Doug and Mary were coming. (1977: 51)

Indeed, in the view of Anthony Giddens, celebrity is a product of the same technological drive that has produced globalization, in that 'celebrity itself is largely a product of new communications technology' (1999: 12). Furthermore, as Cohen states of film actors and celebrities in relation to global culture, 'media stars are recognized far beyond their national borders' (Cohen, 2005: 437), and so are also a central factor within globalization: the dominant and most visible global culture is that of the West. Thus, from Douglas Fairbanks and Mary Pickford through Charlie Chaplin, Marilyn Monroe, John Wayne, Arnold Schwarzenegger, Oprah Winfrey, Tom Cruise, Madonna, Angelina Jolie, Michael Jackson, Brad Pitt; from David Beckham to Lady Gaga, Jennifer Lawrence, Justin Bieber, or Miley Cyrus, Western celebrities have had and continue to possess a global status and a seemingly 'universal' level of fame, through either their cultural output, fronting campaigns for branded products, or their lifestyles and sometimes controversial lives garnering news coverage. Indeed, on the global stage, the issue of 'imperialism' and celebrity have been forces that have been linked.

One example of this is that Angelina Jolie and her celebrity partner, Brad Pitt, decamped to Namibia in 2006 for the birth of their daughter, Shiloh. Such was the impact of this major Hollywood celebrity power couple that the Namibian government was said to have acted in an undemocratic fashion through police reportedly banning overhead flights, and in conjunction with 'Brangelina's' own security force who carried out door-to-door searches in order to locate local and overseas media. Indeed, photographers from France and South Africa were expelled from the country (Carroll, 2006). Such was the influence of the stars that one journalist would dub the incident, with a distinctive imperialist nod to Joseph Conrad, 'Apocalypse Brangelina', with Jolie taking on the guise of 'Ms Kurtz' (Hyde, 2006). Thus, Western celebrities are not merely globally famous, but they are also globally powerful.

NON-WESTERN MEDIA CULTURE

Yet, other critics argue that the impact of the global media position is overstated and partial. As Ien Ang (1996) has argued, the idea of the whole world united through long-distance communication technologies gained renewed popularity as a result of a number of heavily televised historic events, such as Live Aid, the fall of the Berlin Wall, the Tiananmen Square Massacre, and the Gulf Wars (and extended to subsequent globally mediated events including the funeral of Princess Diana, the 9/11 terrorist attacks, the Live 8 concerts, the wedding of Prince William and Kate Middleton, and the funeral of Nelson Mandela). Still, this view needs to be complemented with the ways in which viewers receive such broadcasts and to question the perception that there exists a united 'global village'. What Ang means is that Western media can be interpreted according to specific cultural values and localized perceptions. Consequently, argues Ang, the concept of cultural imperialism is imperfect as an explanation of global culture. This is because cultural imperialism has presented the image of an all-powerful force that instils cultural homogenization and dominates indigenous cultures in its imposition of Western culture. As Mike Featherstone (1995) argues, it has long been far more desirable to discuss globalization in terms of much more complex and multilayered processes of global integration rather than in terms of the dichotomy of 'global' and 'local' and that the products of Western media are often modified and appropriated in local terms. Furthermore, within *The Myth of Media Globalization*, Kai Hafez (2007) continues this critical vein, but goes so far as to suggest that the perception of a globally-embracing media culture is not only limited, but is actually a 'myth'.

Referring to the staples of the globalization debate, US media imperialism, the global village, and the network society, and the idea that national sovereignty and nation-states have been rendered obsolete by Western media, Internet culture, and media broadcasts, Hafez points to numerous ways in which these processes have been overstated. For instance, in terms of 'user reach', proponents of global media culture fail to discriminate between technological reach and user reach. What

Hafez means here is that just because non-Western nations can receive Western media, it does not mean that they consume it. As such, the 'Internet may be a misjudged medium that is contributing far more to intensifying local connections (e-commerce, business) than to creating cross-border networks' (2007: 11). And where cultural products such as American-made films *do* have significant global reach, this has far more to do with the financial and economic marketing power of Hollywood than it does with the transmission of any pro-Western ideology. Yet while American films do have a powerful global presence (due in large measure, argues Hafez, to their general lack of cultural specificity), Hollywood films have not undermined Chinese, Indian, or Arab film cultures where locally-produced media productions dominate.

With reference to India, it is has a film industry that produces as many films as Hollywood and has become dubbed 'Bollywood', based upon the fusion of 'Bombay' (now Mumbai) and 'Hollywood', and produces films that keenly reflect Indian culture, social mores, history, and its legends. As such, Hafez states: 'Bollywood is a cultural bulwark for the South Asian sub-continent with its population of well over a billion. Its displacement by a foreign competitor is unimaginable' (2007: 92). Given the scale, economic power, and popularity of Bollywood, it has also created its own specifically Indian celebrity culture. However, the term 'Bollywood' has long attracted controversy due to its word play on Hollywood that implies that it is a mere imitative copy of the dominant US film industrial centre; but the label (regardless of directors' objections to it) became popularized within Indian film journalism and has consequently secured its perception as an international global brand in that Bollywood has become recognized as 'shorthand for India' (Chopra, 2007: 10).

BOLLYWOOD AND INDIAN CELEBRITY

In emphasizing the power and allure of Indian cinema and the men and women who appear in its films, Vijay Mishra states that they have been dubbed '"The temples of modern India". They are designed to seduce: monumental spaces gleam with light and color, vestibules are plastered with posters of gods and goddesses ... Devotees come in huge numbers to worship' (2002: 1). From *Raja Harischandra*, the first feature film produced in India and released in 1913, Bollywood has become a major global cinematic industry, making approximately 1,000 films per year (Nelson and Devanathan, 2006) that are frequently 'extravaganzas of song and dance, in which romance, melodrama, comedy, tragedy, and action are blended' (Chopra, 2007: 5). Thus, millions of Indians regularly go to the cinema and consume film magazines that are 'filled with tales of the stars' (Sansom, 2010: 7). These 'stars' of Indian cinema have been revered since the film industry grew apace in the early 1930s, but especially the leading actors from the 1950s onwards such as Dilip Kumar, Dev Anand, and Raj Kapoor (whose family were the founders of Indian cinema). From this powerful and charismatic trio, further stars emerged within the 1960s and 1970s such as Shammi Kapoor, Raaj Kumar, and, most famously, Amitabh Bachchan, famed for heroic action roles and dubbed 'the superstar extraordinaire of Bombay Cinema' (2002: xv), whose career and status as a

Bollywood icon is marked by film appearances that range from *Raaste Kaa Patthar* (1972), *Zanjeer* (1973), *Khoon Pasina* (1977), *Shaan* (1980), *Aaj Ka Arjun* (1990), to *Mohabbatein* (2000) and Baz Luhrmann's *The Great Gatsby* (2013).

Following Bachchan's impact within Indian cinema, a further host of stars emerged from the 1970s into the 2000s such as Anil Kapoor, Aamire Khan, Salman Khan, Shah Rukh Khan, Sunny Deol, Sanjay Duff, Hrithrik Roshan, Ranbir Kapoor, and Emraan Hashmi. And although initially less evident than their male counterparts, Mishra points to the emergence of female Bollywood stars who have also risen to considerable celebrity status within India, from the early industry actresses Devika Rani, Noor Jehan, and Meena Kumani, to later stars such as Rekha, Karishma Kapoor, and Aishwarya Rai (now Aishwarya Rai Bachchan), in addition to contemporary actresses like Kareena Kapoor Khan, Vaani Kapoor, Sonam Kapoor, and Deepika Padukone. This overview (and of course there are many more examples that could be cited), illustrates the centrality of an indigenous celebrity culture in India that matches, indeed easily surpasses, that of Hollywood in terms of local fandom and consumption. This, then, points to the degree, raised by critics such as Hafez, that Hollywood is not all-powerful, and that while many Western celebrities are clearly universally recognized, there are alternative celebrity cultures in the world that operate beyond the West.

CELEBRITY AND DIASPORAS

With regard to the scope, scale, and economic and cultural power of the Indian film industry, in the view of Rini Mehta, Bollywood reflects the dynamic and far-reaching economic and social transformations that have occurred in India since the 1990s and mark its global status as a dynamic emergent superpower, or the 'democratic . . . alternative to red China' (2010: 2), as India has assumed a powerful role in global relations. It was during this period that India shifted from its historic socialist-inspired mixed economy to embrace a Western-style neoliberal economy and culture, all of which was reflected in Bollywood. Indeed, Bollywood, in this regard, represents a contemporary example of the 'reverse flow' argument – that national cultures and products have influenced Western culture to the extent that:

> The post-global influx (and travel) of multinational capital and cultural apparatuses has had visible effects on Bollywood . . . [the] India International Film Festival in London, the current or planned drama schools owned by Bollywood personalities, the availability of Bollywood fare in Europe and the USA via satellite channels, and the renewed prevalence of Bollywood in the popular cultural imaginary of the Indian diaspora continue to sustain the most successful industry that ever existed in India. (2010: 13)

The issue of diaspora is a vital one with reference to the consumption of the Bollywood celebrity system. A key point that Gerrie Lim (2005) makes with regard to global cinema and international film stars, particularly those of South East Asia, is that although there have been highly successful examples of Asian films achieving success in Western markets, such as the action cinema of Hong Kong's John Woo, Zhong Yimou's *Hero, Crouching Tiger, Hidden Dragon, House of Flying Daggers*, and Japanese and Korean horror films such as *The Grudge* and *Ringu* (both remade in Hollywood for Western audiences), there have been, traditionally, few Asian stars breaking into Hollywood in a major way. Although there are key examples such as Jackie Chan, Chow Yun-Fat, Michelle Yeoh, and Zhang Ziyi, they have been more successful within Asian markets. Although, there are strong examples of non-Western crossover stars who have achieved substantial levels of global success, such as the pop singers Rihanna (from Barbados) and Shakira (from Colombia). However, there are there other ways in which non-Western films have significant presence and reception within Western nations, and that is in relation to diaspora populations.

In defining the concept of the diaspora, the anthropologist James Clifford refers to them as 'homes away from home' (1994: 302). Diasporas are communities that have moved away from an original homeland sometimes against their will, but who, crucially, preserve the memory or myths of that original homeland. They live in one place, and acutely remember and desire another place. This sensitivity remains and can be embraced through technological and cultural means. This is what Clifford states:

> And dispersed peoples, once separated from homelands by vast oceans and political barriers, increasingly find themselves in border relations with the old country thanks to a to-and-fro made possible by modern technologies of transport, communication, and labour migration. Airplanes, telephones, tape cassettes, camcorders, and mobile job markets reduce distances and facilitate two-way traffic, legal and illegal, between the world's places. (1994: 304)

Since Clifford's analysis, such global connectivity between diasporas and homelands has been intensified through the rise of the Internet, email, Skype, and social media, but also through popular culture and celebrities. Hindi cinema has played a central role in the life of the Indian diaspora across the world, the result of a migration process that began in 1830s (Parekh et al., 2003), and Bollywood has long acted as potent force in culturally unifying Indians dispersed around the globe. This process was established from the mid-1990s through specialized satellite channels such as B4U (Bollywood-for-You) and numerous websites dedicated to Indian cinema.

Consequently, Bollywood came 'to possess tremendous cultural and emotional value for expatriate Indians who grew up watching these films' (Punathambekar, 2005: 155). In this regard, Rajinder Kumar Dudrah examined the example of the Indian/South Asian diaspora in England (focusing specifically on the Birmingham-based community) and their identification with their homeland via Bollywood film productions. The consumption of Hindi films was initially stipulated in the 1970s through Asian-run cinemas that showed Hindi films, but they declined as the home video market expanded from the late 1970s and into the 1980s prompting the emergence of British Asian video shops where Hindi films could be rented (although the rise of satellite channels broadcasting South Asian films then sounded the death knell for such outlets). In the 1990s and into the 2000s, the spirit of the Asian-run cinemas returned as multiplex cinemas increasingly screened Bollywood films.

In terms of meaning and reception, Kumar Dudrah's qualitative research revealed that the films constituted more than a source of entertainment. One of his respondents, Gazella, stated: 'It means being an Asian. Being brought up in Britain I find being surrounded by people from various different backgrounds Bollywood gives me an opportunity to seek and delve into my heritage' (2002: 30). Consequently, as Kumar Dudrah observes, Bollywood represents a specific cultural conduit to a homeland that reinforces cultural identity, but also, in response to the perception of Western-dominated media global culture, Bollywood 'is able to serve alternative cultural and social representations away from dominant white and ethnocentric audio-visual possibilities' (2002: 23), and it is an alternative that also has its own non-Western celebrities with which diasporic communities connect.

BOLLYWOOD SUPERSTAR: SHAH RUKH KHAN

To emphasize the extent to which Indian cinema has established its own celebrities with legions of fans, this section will focus on the Bollywood actor and 'icon', Shah Rukh Khan (Shahrukh Khan or simply 'SRK'), whose defiant and India-focused Miltonesque mantra has long been, according to Lim, 'Better to rule in India than serve in Hollywood' (2005: 135). Born on 2 November 1965 in New Delhi, but with family roots in Peshawar, Pakistan, Shah Rukh Khan, whose career has lasted more than 20 years, first came to prominence through the changes that occurred in India's television industry and Doordarshan's move away from programming that reflected government interests and purely educational content, to entertainment in the form of comedy and soap operas. For Kahn, his path to fame came with a role in the series *Fauji*, followed by *Umeed*, *Wagle Ki Duniya*, *Circus*, and the mini-series *Idiot*, and then film comedies such as *Deewana* (1992). Anupama Chopra argues that Khan's move from television to film is a comparatively rare phenomenon in India. Furthermore, Khan is singular in that he is one of the few now-classic actors not to belong to one of the major Bollywood families, such as the Kapoors, who have now produced multiple generations of actors and actresses. On breaking into films, Khan would ascend to stardom through successful productions such as *Anjaam* (1994), but especially his role as Raj Malhotra in *Dilwale Dulhania Le Jayenge* (1995). The theme of *Dilwale Dulhania Le Jayenge*, with Khan's character a young man born in India but raised in Britain, gave him, argues Chopra, the position as a potent representative of the dynamic economic and cultural changes, or 'churning', that occurred within India in the 1990s and India's increasing presence on the global stage and embrace of consumerism, whereby 'Shah Ruhk as Raj was the best of the East and the West . . . Raj negotiated between tradition and modernity' (2007: 142). Further films such as *Dil To Pagal Hai* (1997), *Dil Se* (1998), *Ashoka the Great* (2001), *Devdas* (2002), *Don* (2006), *Don 2* (2011), and *Chennai Express* (2013) established Khan not merely as a successful actor capable of adeptly working across divergent genres (Denison, 2010), but as an Indian cinematic superstar.

Cementing such success, Khan has emerged as one of India's major brand endorsers (including Pepsi and TagHeuer), thus fulfilling a key aspect of celebrity power, but, argues Chopra, Kahn's celebrity plays a potent role in connecting people to Indian culture due to his worldwide fame and potent appeal to the globally dispersed Indian diaspora. And Kahn reflexively recognizes this, as he has stated of his massive international fan base:

> I feel very loved. I mean, I especially feel very, very loved. People keep saying that I make movies for the diaspora – the English or people living in England, America. But I think that I have just happened to have films which came at a time when people like you, or maybe even your family, parents or younger people. They kind of felt attachment to the country, and an attachment to the films so I was very fortunate . . . And so we stand for what India is – I'm not saying this is what India is, but somewhere when you've been staying to second, third generation away, it kind of connects you back to the country. (Dhaliwal and Rowe, 2013, TheGuardian.com)

The example of Shah Rukh Khan not only points to the power and influence of non-Western film and cultural industries, but also illustrates that Western celebrity culture is not the only producer of famous people whose lives fascinate and inspire devotion. In this regard, there are regions across the world that have no need of Western celebrities, and non-Western celebrity figures do not need to 'crack' US markets to attain global levels of fame. Certainly, Khan is one of Indian cinema's richest stars as a result of film success, extensive brand endorsement, his ownership of the production company Red Chillies Entertainment, and investment in enterprises such as the Kolkata Knight Riders cricket club (2010). Thus, as Chopra states of the levels of godlike 'worship' that have been bestowed on Khan by 'Indians and the varied non-Indian lovers of popular Hindi cinema, Shah Rukh is bigger than Tom Cruise and Brad Pitt combined' (2007: 11), and his prolific cinematic output demonstrates that his superstardom continues, within India and the Indian diaspora, to outshine his Western celebrity counterparts. This, then, points to the ways in which celebrity figures can connect in intimate ways with globally dispersed audiences, and keenly represent national connections back to homelands. Referring to Paul Gilroy's work on race and culture, Littler notes in her analysis of transnational celebrity, his example of the Reggae star, Bob Marley, in that Marley and his music 'symbolised the partial reconnection with African origins that permeates disaspora yearning' that increasingly became 'more planetary in nature, connecting to hybridised diasporic cultures' (2011a: 1).

SOUTHEAST ASIA: ALTERNATIVE GLOBAL CELEBRITY

As large as Bollywood and its pantheon of film stars is, India is not the only indigenous culture that has produced its own celebrity culture that reflects specific cultural values, and, in some instances, definitive political ideologies. For example, in his analysis of the Taiwan-born pop singer, Jay Chou, Anthony Fung points to the ways in which celebrity performance can be utilized to reinforce specific political positions. Although Jay Chou has made some inroads regarding a presence within Western media culture, most notably his role as Kato in Michel Gondry's film version of *The Green Hornet* (a 1966 television series based on the Green Hornet character starring the martial arts icon Bruce Lee in the Kato role), and his music has yielded hits in Taiwan and Hong Kong, his most substantial market has been within the People's Republic of China (PRC). A key issue regarding popular culture within China has traditionally been the state's role in reinforcing and transmitting key aspects of state policy, and as such popular music has frequently been subject to state scrutiny to ensure that it does not undermine Chinese political culture. For example, the Guns 'N' Roses' album 'Chinese Democracy' was banned due to its avowedly critical lyrical stance towards the Chinese state and its communist system, because it 'turns its spear point on China' and was avowedly pro-Western (Moore, 2008).

Alternatively, Jay Chou's marketing tactics have typically taken the form of appealing to the 'cool youth' market who are ardent consumers of cultural artefacts and premier brand names that simultaneously (and somewhat paradoxically) project a quality of individuality that does not compromise sanction from society and parental trust, while still carving out personal space from such authorities. As such, argues Fung, Jay Chou's image and lyrics encompass this attitude of humility combined with elements of non-compliance with regard to personal identity. However, the more significant component of Chou's success stems from the modes by which his musical output and style has fitted in with China's political programme. Here is Fung's explanation:

> His success lies in his capacity to sublimate himself into an icon of Chineseness while maintaining his popular and commercial façade, i.e., his cool image. Paradoxically, his most popular songs trigger the audience's emotions in a celebration of Chinese tradition and values, including conscientiousness, tolerance, and reservedness. (2008: 73)

This is routinely achieved, argues Fung, through the modes by which Jay Chou fuses Western musical styles (R&B, for example) with traditional Chinese melodies and traditional instruments such as the pipa and his donning of cool pop fashions with Chinese styles. Thus, Jay Chou has effectively brought 'western musical forms to the Chinese audience, but also evokes the national culture of the PRC' (2008: 74).

ISLAMIC CELEBRITY CULTURE AND RESISTANCE TO THE WEST

However, it is not merely political values that can be expressed by non-Western celebrity cultures, but also cultural and religious ones. For example, there are several artists in Malaysian popular music culture who closely connect Islamic religious beliefs and values within a pop music idiom and to considerable commercial success. As Bart Barendregt notes, a number of highly successful Islamic pop groups have emerged which have attained local and global levels of success. This emerged primarily from the practice of Nasyid, a musical form of recitation of the Koran which became a popularized and commercial form in the 1980s to the extent that pop groups which specialized in Nasyid rose to considerable prominence and fame, such as the group Raihan (which translates as 'Fragrance of Heaven'). As Barendregt argues, Raihan (consisting originally of Nazrey Johani, Che Amran Idris, Abu Bakar Md Yatim, Amran Ibrahim, and Azhari Ahmad), was the first avowed Muslim pop group not merely to attain national success, but whose first album Puji-Pujian (released in 1996) was the fastest selling album in Malaysia. Additionally, the band also acquired a distinctive level of transnational celebrity through musical collaborations with British Islamic Hip-Hop bands such as Mecca2Medina to produce a fusion of 'political activism and commercialism and religion and popular culture' (2011: 241). Similarly, the Malaysian female pop singer, Siti Nurhaliza – who has achieved considerable musical success, releasing some 15 albums, and combines her Muslim identity with Western fashions and looks – demonstrated the extent of her national celebrity when she became the first Malaysian pop performer to have had her wedding ceremony broadcast live on television (Taib, 2009). In other regards, Islamic values have formed a buffer against Western celebrity influence, for example the protests in Indonesia against the American pop star Lady Gaga. Having sold 52,000 tickets for a planned concert in Jakarta on 3 June 2012 as part of her *Born This Way* world tour, the flamboyant, but often controversial, performer faced conservative calls for the concert to be cancelled which resulted in street protests, primarily by the Islamic Defenders Front who denounced the singer as being 'dangerous and the producer of "Satanic lyrics"' which could constitute a clear moral threat (Springer, 2012). Ultimately, threats by the Islamic Defenders Front to mobilize 30,000 of its members to physically prevent Gaga from entering Jakarta resulted in the cancellation of the concert and she was unable to perform in Indonesia (Gardner, 2013).

CELEBRITY SCANDAL: ALTERNATIVE SOCIAL REACTIONS

The issue of morality within Indonesian culture also illustrates the stark differences that exist between Western celebrity culture and globally-diffused counterparts with regard to sexual scandal and the recent prominence of celebrity-featured 'sex tapes' leaked onto the Internet or appropriated for commercial release. As Daniel Harris argues, sex scandals involving film stars have long been part of Hollywood and later celebrity culture, from Fatty Arbuckle, a silent comedy star of the Keystone Cops cinematic troupe who was arrested for the rape and murder of the young actress Virginia Rappe, allegations via gossip magazines against performers in the 1950s and 1960s such as Desi Arnaz Jr. and Liberace, through to the public sexual exploits of film actors such as Hugh Grant. However, the increasing presence of celebrity sex

resented a curious relationship with acts that once would have ended one's
s Harris states with regard to celebrity attitudes' apparent embrace of a
phic candour', many 'celebrities have abandoned their traditional reticence
court controversy, leaking their own sex tapes in an apparent act of professional suicide that, much as they wring their hands and lament that the tape was
"stolen" in another unconscionable violation of their privacy, often breathes new life
into their careers' (2010: 146). While there have been a number of high-profile examples,
such as those of Rob Lowe, Pamela Anderson, and Dustin 'Screech' Diamond, star
of the 1980s teen show *Saved by the Bell*, the most prominent was that of Paris
Hilton, whose sex tape, made with Rick Salomon, was then titled *One Night in Paris*,
and was released in 2003 one week before the first broadcast of Hilton's Reality TV
series, *The Simple Life*. As Cashmore notes, the apparent controversy surrounding
the release of the tape, and the widespread media coverage that accompanied it, did
not tarnish the show, but rather played an encouraging role in its attainment of 13
million viewers for the debut episode. Furthermore, 'far from damaging her reputation,
it actually made it. Hilton went from rich kid socialite to the "must-have" celebrity
of the season' (2006: 144).

Interestingly, in 2007 Kim Kardashian, a friend of Paris Hilton, herself came
more centrally to media notoriety following the leak of a sex tape that featured her
with her then-boyfriend, Ray J. Paralleling the attention garnered by Hilton, a year
on from the leaked tape saw Kardashian and her family contracted to star in their
own Reality TV series, *Keeping Up With The Kardashians*. The issue of significance
is that sexual scandals no longer necessarily signal the end of stardom and celebrity,
but in some instances, its genesis. However, this is not a pattern that is always
mirrored in non-Western media cultures.

A prime example of a sex tape leak signalling not merely social condemnation and
scandal, but serious legal proceedings, was the case in Indonesia in 2010 involving
the prominent pop star Nazril 'Ariel' Irham, of the highly successful band Peterpan,
and the actress, Luna Maya. Like Paris Hilton and Kim Kardashian, Irham was the
subject of a graphic privately-made sex tape that was leaked onto the Internet in
the wake of a laptop theft, which then prompted the release of a second video showing Irham with another Indonesian television presenter. The outcome in the wake
of these video releases was prosecution under the country's anti-pornography laws
and Irham was the subject of widespread public criticism by Muslim groups. Yet,
unlike Hilton and Kardashian, the publicity generated through formal media coverage of the scandal resulted not in a form of publicity that boosted his celebrity, but
alternatively a three-year prison sentence imposed on 31 January 2011, having been
found guilty of 'giving an opportunity for others to spread, produce and prepare a
pornographic video'. Indeed, Irham's celebrity status was a factor in the verdict, as
the judge, Singgih Budi Prakoso, stated: 'As a public figure, the defendant should be
aware that fans might imitate his behaviour' (BBC, Asia Pacific, 2011). Aside from
the severe legal repercussions meted out to Irham that demonstrate that the activities of celebrity culture are not uniform throughout the world, the major communicative force within the Irham case was that the sex tapes were downloaded onto social
media platforms, most commonly Facebook and YouTube, but also communicated via

mobile phones, actions which prompted the Indonesian police to raid high schools to confiscate the videos (Karmini, 2010).

K-POP

The prevalence and use of social media in Southeast Asia (embracing the likes of Facebook, YouTube, and Twitter, but also indigenous platforms, such as China's Renren and 51.com) has inspired differing appraisals of the ways in which communicative technologies inspire global connections. Referring to the idea of an electronically connected global village (inspired by the work of Marshall McLuhan), Sun Jung (2011) points to the ways in which these processes are occurring at micro, or 'grassroots', levels via platforms such as Twitter. The key significance of Jung's analysis is that it points to global cultures crossing national boundaries, but within Southeast Asian cultures, and not necessarily those of the West. Focusing on Indonesian fandom of international pop music, Jung argues that throughout the 2000s, Korean popular culture has become increasingly adopted throughout Asia, especially South Korean popular music, or 'K-pop', with Indonesia establishing itself as one of the most significant consumers of K-pop and expressing fandom of its stars, such as Bi Rain, Super Junior, SHINee, TVXQ, and the Wonder Girls. The major elements of K-pop are 'pop tunes with simple, earworm-inducing melody, usually on the hegemonic pop music theme of love' (Jung, 2011). The primary reason, argues Jung, as to why Korean music has gained such a following among Indonesian youth is a result of the increasing liberalization of the country following the end of President Suharto's political regime, an authoritarian leadership that lasted from 1967 to 1998. Post-Suharto, young people were increasingly exposed to international cultural forms, including rock and punk music from North America and Europe, but also Japanese, Taiwanese, and Korean music and cinema.

Citing this as a key example of globalization, Jung also states that the sociocultural transformations that have rapidly occurred in post-Suharto Indonesia are also due to the fact that Asian nations such as Japan, Korea, and Taiwan have emerged as potent challengers to a Western-dominated global capitalism. As a consequence of this:

K-pop's popularity in Indonesia refers to the intricate intersection between capitalist desires of the Korean entertainment business sector, the globalized desires of the Indonesian media industry, and the local audiences' desire for cool, modern pop cultures. (2011: 7)

THE GLOBAL SUCCESS OF PSY

The economic processes that have become established in Southeast Asia have been complemented by the fast-growing acceptance and use of social media networks which has transformed how users search out and consume transnational cultural products though platforms such as Twitter and YouTube. In the case of Jung's qualitative research into the consumption of K-pop in Indonesia, he found that such technologies have produced, in the tradition of Jenkins' active fans, participatory cultures among fans that range from assimilating K-pop music, fashions, and dance styles into their lives and leisure behaviours, to creating homage and parody videos based upon key artists and posting them for wider viewing on platforms such as YouTube. In essence, although the 'reverse flow' model in relation to cuisine and world music is a long-established counter to the 'media are American' thesis (Barker, 1999), the impact of social networking has accelerated this process, as indicated by the acceptance of K-pop, and is best typified by the global success (indeed, phenomenon) of Korean pop singer PSY's hit song, 'Gangnam Style'.

Although a performer from 2001 with an extensive discography and considerable national fame in South Korea, it was in 2012 that PSY (real name Jae-Sang Park) released 'Gangnam Style', a track that would not only reach the number one position across the globe, but whose success was initially achieved though YouTube user sharing to the extent that the song and video became a 'viral' and the first video to pass the 1 billion view hit in YouTube's history (Gruger, 2012). This was partly due to the catchy nature of the song, but more significantly because the video featured PSY's (easily emulated and parodied) dance that simulated riding an invisible horse. In Andrew Lam's analysis of the crossover appeal and achievement of PSY and 'Gangnam Style', it is:

> The speed with which a cultural event can transmit these days; PSY burst like a supernova from regional to world stage within a few weeks' time. And he didn't even need to leave Seoul. The second thing to take note of is equally important, if not more so: His video, performed in Korean, is downloaded largely by people who don't understand one word of the language. (2013: 4)

K-POP AND ITS NATIONAL DIVERSIFICATION

The significance of PSY's success (which was followed by 'Gentleman', a track and video that, while not matching that of 'Gangnam Style', still garnered millions of YouTube hits), argues is that of 'reiterating the idea that globalization is no longer a one-way love affair' (Lam, 2013: 4). And indeed, K-pop is not alone in its crossover appeal, as evidenced by the global impact of alternative Asian musical forms, such as J-pop. Hailing from Japan, J-pop groups such as Morning Musume, ALiBi, and the solo artists Kyary Pamyu, Ayumi 'Ayu' Hamasaki, Shina Ringo, and Misia not only have extensive fan bases within Japan and throughout Asia, but also in the West, and have become key figures within Western club scenes (Toth, 2008; McCarthy, 2012). Yet there are immensely potent indigenous Asian celebrity cultures that are nationally-rooted and of significant influence. As Galbraith and Karlin observe, there is the Japanese 'national idol' (kokumin-teki aidoru) tradition, which consists of individuals and groups created by media industry professionals and agencies but which operate across multiple media platforms (pop music, modelling, television presenting) and are a significant source of cultural consumption.

Developing in the 1970s and reaching maturity as a cultural form in the 1980s, national idols have attained a pervasive presence within Japanese culture, but possession of talent is not paramount (pop group members are frequently changed as new idols are discovered) and they are typically related to Boorstin's 'person well known for their well-knownness' definition of fame. But, the talent issue does not diminish the celebrity influence and visibility of idols, as Galbraith and Karlin illustrate with reference to the pop groups AKB48 and Arashi:

> On a morning 'wide show', a news report discusses Arashi's recent concert. Billboards in train stations feature the members of AKB48 in advertisements for everything from computers to coffee. The magazine racks of convenience stores and kiosks are crowded with magazines featuring members of these groups on their covers. On the subway, a hanging advertisement for a tabloid magazine features gossip about the groups' members. On television, they star in dramas, host variety shows, and appear in commercials . . . In the daily routine of life in contemporary Japan, one might have more contact with a particular idol or celebrity than with one's own family. (2012: 8–9)

While there is no denying that Western celebrity culture is a globally visible force, and that Western cultural industries are consumed on a global scale, thus ensuring that celebrity is consumable throughout the world in the form of products (films, TV series, music, product endorsements, etc.), in addition to celebrity lifestyles being transmitted via news agencies, Western celebrity culture is not the only celebrity culture that has power within the world. Indeed, one does not have to look only to Asia for non-English-speaking pop music celebrities, but to Russia. Performers such as Timati, Valeria, Dima Bilan, Niusha, Oleg Gazmanov, Sergey Lazarev, and Kristina Orbakajte have all achieved considerable success and fame and constitute major celebrity figures within contemporary Russian culture, with no need to appeal to American markets.

CONCLUDING POINTS

As this chapter has examined, there are powerful indigenous celebrity cultures that have no need to connect with Western audiences, and when they do cross Western borders, it is to resonate with diaspora communities. Thus, Indian cinema-goers have little need for George Clooney, Matt Damon, Bradley Cooper, or Christian Bale, when they have Shah Rukh Khan (and not forgetting Arjun Rampal, Aamir Khan, or Hrithik Roshan); and when potent crossovers from Asia do occur, as in the case of PSY, K-pop, or Japanese idols, there are no concessions to conform to Western audiences, or, indeed, the English language. As such, while the discourse has long been dominated by a West-to-the-rest bias, this is another indication that celebrity culture in the twenty-first century needs to be reformulated and re-appraised in a global context.

FURTHER READING

To explore the classic examinations of 'media imperialism' and the concept of the global village,see:

- McLuhan, M. (1994) *Understanding Media: The Extensions of Man.* Cambridge, MA: MIT Press.

- Schiller, H. (1969) *Mass Communication and the American Empire.* New York: Augustus M. Kelly.

- Tunstall, J. (1977) *The Media are American: Anglo-American Media in the World.* London: Constable.

With regard to critical overviews of the concept of globalization and its relation to popular culture and media cultures, see:

- Bisley, N. (2007) *Rethinking Globalization.* Basingstoke: Palgrave Macmillan.

- Galbraith, P.W. and Karlin, J.G. (2012) *Idols and Celebrity in Japanese Media Culture.* Basingstoke: Palgrave Macmillan.

- Lechner, F.J. (2009) *Globalization: The Making of World Society.* Oxford: Wiley-Blackwell.

- Rojek, C. (2013) *Event Power: How Global Events Manage and Manipulate.* Los Angeles, CA and London: SAGE.

- Stiglitz, J. (2013) *Globalization and Its Discontents.* London: Penguin.

For a detailed account of the historical roots and development of K-pop, see:

- Lie, J. (2012) 'What is the K in K-pop? South Korean popular music, the culture industry, and national identity', *Korea Observer*, 43(3): 339–63.

8

REALITY TV AND CELEBRITY

CHAPTER OVERVIEW

According to Su Holmes, one of the significant factors to emerge from the growth of Reality TV is that it 'has made it impossible to escape the fact that we have seen an appreciable rise in the number of "ordinary" people appearing on television' (2004: 111). As such, the routes into celebrity culture have become more flexible as *Big Brother* contestants have become celebrity figures due to the media exposure they received while on television, as have affluent women who have taken part in the various *The Real Housewives*, in addition to tattoo artists, ice road truck drivers, dance moms, child beauty pageant hopefuls, and multi-millionaire duck call manufacturers. To explore the differing modes by which ordinary people are propelled into the celebrity world the chapter will investigate the following topics:

- The development of Reality TV
- The 'demotic' nature of Reality TV
- The transformation of 'ordinary' people into celebrity figures
- Celebrity-based Reality TV
- Screening 'ordinary' people who have uncommon lives

To illustrate the cultural points concerning the relationship between Reality TV and celebrity, the chapter will focus upon examples such as *Big Brother*, *The Real Housewives* series, Britney Spears, *Here Comes Honey Boo Boo*, and *Duck Dynasty*.

THE RISE OF REALITY TELEVISION

While clearly explaining the nature of celebrity in a wider context (appearances in cinema, popular music, television, etc.) the issue of visibility constitutes a primary force in the creation of celebrity. Certainly, this trend is manifest in relation to the inexorable rise throughout the 2000s of the television 'genre' widely known as 'Reality TV', particularly the reality gameshow formats such as *Big Brother*. The cultural responses to Reality TV initially bore a distinctly Frankfurt School-flavoured pessimism and critical cynicism. Contrary to any social experimental 'mission statements', Reality television, for many commentators, was argued to offer no social/psychological insights at all but instead merely represented 'a mixture of banality and emotional pornography' (Barnfield, in Cummings et al., 2002: 47). For others, it was an emergent genre explicitly predicated upon turning its 'characters' vices into virtues' (Cashmore, 2006: 189), and in its predictability and set format it is arguably a mode of television texts which limits and pre-establishes 'the attitudinal pattern of the spectator' (Adorno, 2001: 169), based as it is on mass audience participation. Such negative approaches were corroborated in the case of the reactions to *Loft Story*, the French version of *Big Brother*. While a significant ratings success, *Loft Story* was also subjected to various demonstrations by the protest group 'Activists Against Trash TV', which called for the programme to be removed from the air, and whose actions included demonstrators brandishing placards reading 'With trash TV the people turn into idiots' (Hill, 2005: 4), outside the television studio.

Conversely, alternative commentators perceived the development of Reality TV as an unprecedented advance within television, perceiving it as a medium by which the audience is actually *empowered* and rendered 'active'. In this analysis, Reality television has represented a dynamic development whereby the 'mass' was actually granted the ability to actively direct the narrative rather than simply receive transmissions in a docile, passive manner (Andrejevic, 2002; Tincknell and Raghuram, 2002). Furthermore, in relation to the example of *Big Brother* and its transmission in Denmark, some politically-minded critics viewed it as an incisive and instructive social experiment because of the ways in which the format was fundamentally based upon 'human relations, intimacy and security' (Biltereyst, 2004: 100).

Although considered a new cultural form, the roots of Reality TV arguably stretch back to at least the 1960s in the form of 'people shows' such as *Candid Camera* and through the 1970s, 1980s, and 1990s with docu-dramas and docu-soaps including *The Family*, *An American Family*, and *Airline*. Other notable examples include the 'DIY' webcam (Turner, 2004) experiments in the 1990s ('Jennicam', for example, which was self-broadcast to millions of web viewers). Further examples include distinctive Reality TV subgenres such as those which can be classified as 'Makeover' shows, in which participants undergo physical, attitudinal, or sartorial changes to achieve a prize, but also achieving media exposure and potential celebrity status. Prime examples of this now extensive expression of Reality TV includes *I Want a Famous Face*, *The Swan*, *Queer Eye for the Straight Guy*, *American Princess*, *Extreme Makeover*, and *America's Next Top Model* (Weber and Spigel, 2009). However, Reality TV's prime exemplar, in terms of influence, significance, and popularity, is undoubtedly *Big Brother*.

Big Brother was originally developed by Endemol Entertainment in the Netherlands in 1999 and would subsequently be syndicated in numerous countries including France, Germany, Italy, Poland, South Africa, Australia, and America.

Combining television and Internet surveillance (Griffin-Foley, 2004), *Big Brother* was launched in the United Kingdom on Channel 4 in the summer of 2000, becoming 'the definitive example of a whole range of programmes which have deployed combinations of the syntactical elements of forced confinement, competitive individualism and emotional conflict as entertainment' (Tincknell and Raghuram, 2004: 255). A Reality TV game show that combined with audience interactivity, the setting for *Big Brother* consisted (and still consists) of a specially constructed *Big Brother* House which is fitted extensively with cameras which serve to monitor the 'housemates' 24 hours a day until each housemate is voted out by the public, leaving a final winning contestant.

Yet for many commentators, the intrinsic appeal and distinctiveness of *Big Brother*, which is argued to represent a mixture of 'artificial entertainment and human reality' (Couldry, 2003: 106), is that it specifically involves 'real people', individuals who have been 'plucked from obscurity and turned into stars, not because of any special talent, but just because they seem personable' (Cummings et al., 2002: xii). Thus, Reality TV is a televisual experience which is 'located in border territories, between information and entertainment, documentary and drama' (Hill, 2005: 2). As Barnfield states: 'Our collective willingness to watch such material indicates an erosion of the distinction between public and private, an end to intimacy' (in Cummings et al., 2002: 63), and the *Big Brother* house represents an environment in which the contestants freely make 'themselves into a spectacle' (Scannell, 2002: 276) and as such many have become, to lesser and greater degrees, celebrity figures.

REALITY TV AND 'ORDINARY' CELEBRITIES

In the view of Su Holmes, the development of Reality TV, and *Big Brother* in particular, has resulted in a palpable rise in the number of 'ordinary' people who now are able to appear on television and who, by appearing on the programme, are inevitably granted the status of 'celebrity in process' (2004: 119). Yet it is a very novel form of celebrity because: 'celebrity in *Big Brother* is lacking some of the fundamental discourses of the success myth, largely the emphasis on work and traditional conceptions of talent' (Holmes, 2004: 119), although it may be argued to accord to some extent with the 'discovery narrative' (Turner, 2004) in which an anonymous individual suddenly finds fame and media attention. However, within *Big Brother*, there is frequently little sense of 'achieved celebrity'. It is rather an 'attributed celebrity' (Rojek, 2001) status because for those who participate, celebrity is ostensibly achieved via leisure, by frequently doing 'nothing'. Ultimately, *Big Brother* deliberately places 'ordinary people in an extraordinary situation . . . a world in which anyone can feel the glow of celebrity' (Holmes, 2004: 131–2).

This process rapidly became evident following the success of the first UK broadcast in 2000 and has become a clearly visible trend with regard to reflexive constants fully aware of the merits that can be obtained as a result of participating. In essence, since 2000, *Big Brother* has retreated from 'reality' or 'real people' being 'themselves' in favour of a parade of larger-than-life 'characters' steadfastly engaged in the maintenance of an entertaining persona. As Holmes states, in the wake of the potential rewards that were bestowed upon some housemates following their appearances on *Big Brother*, such as careers as television and radio presenters, in the second and third series of *Big Brother*, the contestants began to exhibit a self-conscious awareness of the conventions of the format. As *Big Brother 3* winner Kate Lawler stated: 'It's amazing to think the whole nation is watching *us*' (Holmes, 2004: 118). On leaving the *Big Brother* house, numerous contestants have forged careers within the media industry such as modelling (Orlaith McAllister), radio DJ-ing (Richard Newman), television presenting (Brian Dowling), glamour model-ling (Sophie Reade), and celebrity journalism (Josie Gibson). Regardless of duration, the equation is invariably *Big Brother* equals a celebrity status of some sort and accords with what Andrejevic (2002) has dubbed the 'democratization of celebrity'. Furthermore, the role that *Big Brother* could play in fostering this enhanced route to fame was reflectively recognized at the start of the phenomenon by its producers. The official Channel 4-produced narrative that was published in the wake of the first UK series concluded that the various contestants went into the *Big Brother* house 'unknown and came out with the kind of fame and celebrity it takes showbiz hopefuls years to achieve' (Ritchie, 2000: 247).

Alternatively, rather than lionize the wealth of 'democratic' routes to celebrity inaugurated by Reality TV, John Gray cynically observes that *Big Brother* is simply a device with which to perpetuate the 'illusion that celebrity is a universal entitle-ment that everyone can enjoy if they are lucky enough to be selected by everyone else' (2004: 207–8). Yet in the view of Anita Biressi and Heather Nunn, Reality TV did alter the landscape of media culture in its ability to provide a distinctive platform for 'ordinary people' to become media stars and attain fame 'without overtly draw-ing on education, entrepreneurial skills or even any obvious talent' (2005: 144–5). Biressi and Nunn note critical responses to the rise and proliferation of Reality TV and have held it up as further evidence of the 'tabloidization' of media culture, and that the Reithian vision of broadcasting as an educative apparatus has been eroded through game show formats and, in the wake of Reality TV, to focus upon 'confes-sional' formats whose function is 'not to take viewers outside of their own experience but to present them with a fully recognizable and familiar realm of the ordinary and the everyday' (2005: 146). Thus, the key moments within the genre are when partici-pants' personas are stripped away and their true feelings and emotions are revealed, through conflict, the pressures of the artificial media environment, or romantic/sex-ual attraction that are part of the experience, and the instances in which 'stressed-out contestants disclose their true feelings' (King, 2011: 7). As such, the process of celebrity associated with these formats is predicated upon the ways in which 'ordi-nary' people are unexpectedly rendered 'remarkable'. Yet Biressi and Nunn flag a distinctive ideological aspect to many Reality TV formats with regard to the 'celebri-fication' of some of its contestants with regard to social mobility and achievement: that individuals, often from working-class backgrounds, can rise from obscurity and mundane jobs to national fame and wealth.

REALITY TV AND THE DEMOTIC TURN

In the view of Graeme Turner, Reality TV constitutes a means by which the media industries actively and regularly 'manufacture' celebrity. And the format has proven itself to be highly commercially successful. Although *Big Brother* is the major (and most globally syndicated) example of the genre, there are numerous other expressions which have created an entirely new kind of celebrity pantheon. This is what Turner states:

> There is a wealth of Reality TV formats that have attracted large audiences, both national and transnational, as well as creating their own stable of personalities and stars: *Survivor, Airport, Airline, Driving School, What Not To Wear, Jersey Shore, The Hills* and *Keeping Up With The Kardashians.* (2014: 58–9)

In terms of theorizing the ways in which Reality TV has produced distinctive celebrities drawn from the world of the 'everyday', Turner devised 'the demotic turn' (2004), a concept used to explain 'the increasing visibility of the "ordinary person" as they turn themselves into media content through celebrity culture, Reality TV, DIY websites, talk radio and the like' (Turner, 2006: 153). Of course, as Turner notes, 'ordinary people' have long been discovered and drawn into the world of celebrity, such as individuals 'discovered' by talent agencies, etc., and propelled into the worlds of the film and music industries; but this process has increased significantly since Reality TV established itself as a major cultural genre to the extent that, via the likes of *Big Brother*, 'the contemporary media consumer has become increasingly accustomed to witnessing what happens to the "ordinary" person who has been plucked from obscurity to enjoy a highly specified and circumscribed celebrity' (2006: 155). A key aspect of the effectiveness of Reality TV is, of course, its 'reality', its immediacy, even though, as Turner states, the 'reality' is of a constructed form (edited highlights that accentuate drama, conflict, or romantic/sexual possibilities and otherwise establish a 'narrative' that engages viewer attention). The ways in which Reality TV shows such as *Big Brother* embed themselves into the lives of viewers is a key aspect of their appeal as well as offering viewers the opportunity to engage with contestants that appear on it as they are constantly onscreen and can be viewed across media platforms (highlight programmes, 24-hour TV streaming, Internet viewing, etc.). Nevertheless, Turner is keen to stress that the 'demotic turn' does not translate into a notion of 'media democracy'. What he means here is that while it may appear that the era of Reality TV has opened up celebrity to all, that is not necessarily the case as the entertainment industry is hierarchical and exclusive. Therefore:

> No amount of public participation in game shows, Reality TV or DIY celebrity websites will alter the fact that, overall, the media industries still remain in control of the symbolic economy, and that they still attempt to operate this economy in the service of their own interests. (2006: 157)

Nonetheless, the nature of exclusiveness is masked by the nature of the audition process which, at face value, suggests that any member of the public can indeed gain access to media exposure and celebrity status, and the thousands of hopefuls who attend recruiting events held in major cities reinforce this. These events are of course *auditions*, and the selection process is not random. Although the contestants are 'ordinary' in that they are not media personalities, nor do they have to display some defined talent (as is the case within television talent shows such as *American Idol*, *The X Factor*, *Britain's Got Talent*, *The Voice*, etc.), successful candidates still must possess something that will engage viewers because Reality TV or not, it still must entertain for an intensive three-month (or more) period. As such, Reality TV's 'apparent tolerance of a lack of exceptional talents or achievements is available as long as the person concerned (paradoxically) can perform their ordinariness with some degree of specificity or individuality' (2006: 160).

CELEBRITY-BASED REALITY TV

While Reality TV has arisen as a platform to enable the public to become celebrities (however short-lived the status may be), a curious alternative has developed by which Reality TV has been embraced as a means to *re-energize* celebrity status and to some degree to 'normalize' or render 'ordinary' apparently 'extraordinary' celebrity figures. For instance, the *Big Brother* format has been adapted to include celebrities in the form of *Celebrity Big Brother*, which was first broadcast in the UK in 2001 and sent culturally 'known faces' into the *Big Brother* house to subject themselves to the viewers' gaze. Although the 'metanarrative' of the *Celebrity Big Brother* format is more or less the same as *Big Brother* (the running time is much shorter and is usually restricted to three weeks), the major difference is that within the world of *Celebrity Big Brother*, the viewer (ideally) 'knows' the contestants who enter the house. As Hill states, unlike the conventional *Big Brother*, which deals with 'real' people drawn from the general public, *Celebrity Big Brother* alternatively 'takes celebrities and turns them into 'ordinary people', before releasing them back into the world of the media' (2005: 38). Indeed, the nature of celebrity in relation to Reality TV is now so elastic and circular that *Celebrity Big Brother 11*, broadcast in the UK in January 2013, featured the married couple Heidi Montag and Spencer Pratt who collapsed into the 'power couple' persona dubbed 'Spiedi', who had actually attained their celebrity status by appearing in the US Reality TV series, *The Hills*.

A seemingly paradoxical aspect of the series is that for many contestants there is little difference between them and the 'ordinary' members of the public who take part in the conventional version of the series, as the 'celebrities' frequently range from veteran stars to unknown models or minor pop stars, and see the series as a platform to rekindle fame or actually attain a respectable level of celebrity. Alternatively, a selection of such celebrities annually elect to appear on the television series *I'm a Celebrity, Get Me Out of Here* in which they routinely submit themselves to various 'bush tucker trials' that invariably involve eating objects such as worms, wichetty grubs, kangaroo testicles, or fish eyes, or take part in activities that invariably involve them being covered by cockroaches, spiders, or snakes in enclosed spaces for the entertainment of the viewing public. With the advent of the Reality TV format, numerous celebrity figures have engaged in this revelatory process that it offers to viewers, and show the world previously private aspects of their lives. Consequently, the 2000s would see a vogue for such formats, from classic heavy metal/rock stars such as Ozzy Osbourne (*The Osbournes* 2002–2005) and KISS's Gene Simmons (*Gene Simmons: Family Jewels* 2006–2007), to wrestling icons such as Hulk Hogan (*Hogan Knows Best* 2005–2007) and more controversial figures such as Anna Nicole Smith (*The Anna Nicole Show* 2002–2004). Paris Hilton (with Nicole Ritchie) would embrace Reality TV to show the 'reality' behind her $360 million heiress status in *The Simple Life* (2003–2007). But the most notable and successful example of a personal and domestic form of the genre was Jessica Simpson within MTV's *Newlyweds: Nick and Jessica* (2003–2005), which charted their married life and their relationships. Although the couple would subsequently divorce, the series garnered each of the widespread publicity and raised their respective celebrity profiles. Subsequent celebrity-focused shows have included *Kathy Griffin: My Life on the D-List*, Paris Hilton's *My New BFF*, *Giuliana and Bill*, *Married to Jonas*, as well as the quasi-parody Reality TV show starring Joan Rivers, *Joan and Melissa: Joan Knows Best*, *Ke$ha: My Crazy Beautiful Life*, and Lindsay Lohan's *Lindsay*.

The motivation in engaging with celebrity is that it is a medium worth exploiting due to its popularity as a television genre, and the potentially profile-raising attributes it can bestow if successful, 'even if it can cast them in less-than-flattering lights that can work in opposition to their cultivated media images' (Lai, 2006: 225). With regard to *The Osbournes*, the series not only cast the heavy metal vocalist Ozzy in a charmingly befuddled light, but it propelled son and daughter Jack and Kelly to various levels of media fame: daredevil adventure and ghost hunting TV shows for Jack and pop music and TV presenting for Kelly, and a high-profile role within *The X Factor* for wife Sharon. However, not all celebrity TV forays worked, as Britney Spears discovered.

BRITNEY SPEARS AND THE PERILS OF CELEBRITY REALITY TV

With regard to public perception, Douglas Kellner argues that celebrities 'have their handlers and image managers, who make sure that their clients continue to be seen and positively perceived' (2003: 4). However, in 2005 the pop singer Britney Spears actively took over her own image management and in the process, arguably, began to dissolve her public brand image via the production of her Reality TV series *Britney and Kevin: Chaotic*. Behind the scenes pop exposés are not unprecedented, as Madonna demonstrated within *Truth or Dare/In Bed with Madonna,* in which the singer 'allowed cameras access to areas of her private life . . . Even talking bitchily behind the scenes of her "Blonde Ambition" tour, she came over as an ordinary mortal. It is difficult to imagine any other performer inviting cameras to examine them close-up in this way' (Cashmore, 2006: 45). In this regard, Madonna's film reflected a precursor to Paul Virilio's assessment of Reality TV as a 'confessional' form of television programming (2005: 90). Yet, as Reality TV established itself, Britney Spears echoed Madonna's candid filming of the hitherto private aspects of her life within her Reality TV series.

In terms of structure and content, *Britney and Kevin: Chaotic* represented a televisual form of autobiography and frequently was a confessional narrative. Although the title features both Spears and Federline, Federline was frequently background presence and only a sketchy (and rather sanitized and selective) biography was provided for him. It was Britney Spears who was at the centre of the show and it was Spears who engaged most consistently in the process of protracted self-revelation. Although on one level the acceptance of Reality TV was part of an effort to cast her 'brand' image in a firmly mature direction, the confessional aspect was central because this would be the intrinsic nature of Spears' programme, serving as the means for her to persistently confess her thoughts, feelings, and growing sexual attraction to Kevin Federline, all direct-to-camera.

Regarding its apparent 'metanarrative', *Britney and Kevin: Chaotic* was ostensibly an autobiographical 'visual love story'. As a narrative resonating with key autobiographical aspects, such as being filled with 'personal expressions' peppered with a consistent motif of 'self-advertisement' (Sayre, 1977), *Chaotic* charted the inception and growth of a relationship between Britney Spears and Federline that would ultimately result in marriage. *Chaotic* consisted of five half-hour episodes, and was direct and raw. Framed with studio-bound interview sequences and concert performance footage from the *Onyx Hotel* European tour, the majority of the *Chaotic* material consisted of hand-held digital camera 'home video' footage shot by Spears and Federline themselves. As such, the dominant visual tone was subsequently crude and unprofessional, but hence seemingly more intimate and candid. This is because the tone of the programme was upon capturing the reality of Spears' life, as she states at one point directly to the camera: 'Can you handle it? Can you handle my truth?' These assertive and provocative questions were further underscored by the taglines for the series which disclaimed: 'It's real. It's our lives.' Furthermore, in line with its confessional flavour, whereas sex and sexuality progressively became more manifest within her recordings and image, but still remained circumspect and playful, the references to sex were explicit and frank within *Chaotic*. Throughout the episodes, there are a series of stark ruptures with the 'public Britney'. Such collisions are heightened with interweaving of Spears' DIY 'guerrilla' footage and polished and professional concert footage – manifestly establishing two distinct worlds represented literally by front- and backstage spaces which foreground the 'differing' aspects of Britney Spears.

From a social psychological perspective, according to Erving Goffman in his classic text *The Presentation of Self in Everyday Life* (1959), human beings can be interpreted as manipulative performers always engaged in creating a 'front' in their relations with other social actors. In the process of social interaction, individuals are continuously communicating (giving and giving off) self-impressions in all they do, for everything they do displays their social character as persons in one way or

another. Goffman explains this through use of the metaphor of the theatrical performance to articulate self-presentation in daily life. On stage, an actor has the task of
presenting themselves to the audience as a particular character in a play, and they
must make manifest exactly what role is being played, an effort assisted through
the use of costume, props, scenery and movement, as well as dialogue. They are also
aided by other actors on the stage and those behind the scenes. From the perspective
of Goffman's analysis, in many instances, the social actor in everyday situations can
be perceived as having exactly the same problem as the stage actor. For instance,
when an individual enters a setting or occasion, they are faced with the task of communicating to others who and what they are. The only way others can judge what
type or kind of person that individual is comes initially through their conduct and
through their appearance.

While social actors may not literally 'put on a performance', they can, argues
Goffman, be seen to be using the resources at their disposal to communicate an
impression to a given social 'audience', to put on a show 'for the benefit of other
people' (1971: 28). While this may suggest a facile and even manipulative aspect
to social presentation and personality interpretation, it is manifestly recognizable
when applied *back* to the world of dramatic performance and the example of Britney
Spears. In *Chaotic*, the public Britney Spears performs precisely within the dramaturgical milieu Goffman draws upon. As a pop star, Spears is a professional role
player whose performances are meticulously stage-managed, and thus she *does*
project a dramaturgical self. As part of this process, Spears projects a 'front' which
includes the Goffman inventory of clothing, posture, speech patterns, facial expressions, bodily gestures, and insignia of office or rank. With regard to everyday performances, Goffman argues that akin to the theatre production, social settings can be
divided into 'front' and 'back' regions. The front region refers to the place where the
performance is given, while conventionally the backstage area is cut off from public
view, often physically so that the 'audience' is unable to witness what is occurring.
The backstage area is the space in which only professional participants are allowed
to participate. This is because if backstage areas were witnessed, then the 'reality' of
a social scenario may result in a state of profound disillusionment. Goffman used
the background processes within a court as an illustration, but it is also evident
within *Chaotic* as Spears persistently lifts the dramaturgical curtain. Indeed, that
is the central point of the series as, within the various backstage moments, Spears
is often determinedly unglamorous and, unlike the 'public Britney', she is shown frequently smoking, swearing, and drinking alcohol, sometimes to excess, and undercuts
an image that was previously centred on being 'respectable, fun and responsible'
(Gauntlett, 2004: 163) Britney Spears.

In this respect, the 'real' Britney Spears functions as a dissonant image with regard
to the Britney which adorned album covers or performed in pop videos. In essence,
Spears deliberately visualizes herself as an autonomous adult and *not* the 'innocent'
teen of her earlier career. *Chaotic* is thus a reflective exercise in the 'demystification'
of her public image. The very choice of title of the programme was designed to lay
an emphatic emphasis upon undermining the polished image that Spears had been
perennially associated with.

CELEBRITY-BASED REALITY TV AS A DAMAGING FORCE

Reality television, therefore, is a genre that actively seeks to break down the front-backstage divides and reveals them to televisual scrutiny in which the private becomes public, the central theme of examples such as *Big Brother*. Of course, there is choice, but within *Chaotic*, Britney Spears chose to show boundary dissolution and engage in onscreen confessions. Unfortunately for Spears, the critical response to her confrontational 'Can you handle my truth?' challenge, was a resounding no. If iconic status in pop music is achieved by the combination of many elements, primarily musical talent but also image, presence, and personality (Hoare, 1999: 5), then in producing and starring in *Chaotic*, Spears systematically diminished her iconic brand. She deconstructed the nature of her celebrity and her status as a 'fantastic icon'. Returning to Spears' show, Reality TV is viewed as a genre whose principal quality is that it turns its 'characters' vices into virtues' (Cashmore, 2006: 189). However, with regard to Britney Spears, this was not the outcome. Instead, her vices did not become virtues, but overwhelmed her established 'public Britney' role. This is what one reviewer acerbically stated in an evaluation that was based centrally upon the nature of the 'truth' *Chaotic* revealed and the image it portrayed of Spears:

> One does not expect a generally accepted sex kitten or pop princess to have bad skin, frazzled hair, or the manners of a goat, but from one unnaturally long hour with Ms. Spears, one can only take away the notion that in her private time, without the lights and glamour of the stage, she is even worse than we ever suspected. (*Ruthless Reviews*, 2005)

Yet for all of the caustic irreverence of the latter review, the problematic aspect that it draws attention to is exactly the consequence of leaving the comfort zone of a carefully contrived and managed world of media spectacle to reveal what lies behind the carefully-crafted pop performer visage, and highlights the risk of revealing the mechanics of what occurs in the backstage zone. By way of comparison, remembering their attitude to the 'classic' film stars and celebrities of the 1940s and 1950s, one respondent within Jackie Stacey's research stated that, above all, they considered them to be 'very special people, glamorous, handsome and way above . . . ordinary mortals' (Stacey, 1994: 142). One of the processes which helped to achieve this audience perception was the distance at which such 'stars' were kept from the gaze of their audiences, underpinning Rojek's conception of the veridical 'I' and the 'Me' as seen by others. Spears' recording career was similarly constructed to represent her as an 'icon', an image to adorn products and to be consumed and predicated upon a public presentation of self as a 'staged activity' (2001: 11). But in embracing Reality TV, a medium which is based upon the blurring of this public and private sense of self (Holmes, 2004), in providing a raw insight into her 'reality', Spears deconstructed the glamour and celebrity mystique to reveal instead her 'ordinariness', which, in that period her life, was typical of what Moya Luckett stated was 'Spears's customary habit of disclosi innermost angst on TV' (2010: 40).

Post *Chaotic*, Spears' professional and personal lives collided in a spiral of seemingly inescapable turmoil, and she entered into what Smit described as a period of popular cultural 'exile' (2013: 92). Her marriage and subsequent divorce from Federline, incessant partying, and the infamous public hair-shaving incident in 2007 caused Spears' public/private roles to implode in a whirlpool of conflicting images and perceptions, evoking Jean Baudrillard's warning of the risk of living a life of 'obscene' visibility. According to Baudrillard, 'If all enigmas are resolved, the stars go out' (1990: 55). Subsequently, Spears has never returned to Reality TV and instead rebuilt her pop brand and public self through successful album releases, collaborations with the likes of Will.i.am, and a two-year residence in Las Vegas (2014–2015), decisively closing off public access to her private world and demonstrating that, while Reality TV can open up private spaces and resurrect ailing celebrity status, it can also reveal too much.

THE NEW WAVE OF REALITY TV: 'EXTRAORDINARY' ORDINARY PEOPLE

Although Britney Spears' attempt to visually erode the line between her private and public selves was regarded as a failure, it would become a central factor in later examples of Reality TV, especially those which returned the focus back to the 'demotic' potential of the genre. Indeed, whereas Spears' candid and open approach tarnished her celebrity, it became the primary cause of success for the Kardashian family. However, the Kardashians were something of a hybrid as they represented an interesting family subject for Reality TV, but were also on the margins of celebrity culture – the factor that motivated mother Kris Jenner to pitch a show that chronicled the 'crazy' domestic world of her family to Ryan Seacrest at the E! television channel.

As explored in Chapter 3, Jenner's entrepreneurial seal was initially built upon revitalizing an Olympic medallist's public persona, and extending daughter Kim's initial media notice based upon her status as Paris Hilton's friend, marketing their life as a Reality TV series, *Keeping Up With The Kardashians*, which was predicated upon exposing all facets of their lives and exposing the public/private zones of their mediated lives. Since its first showing in 2007, the level of fame accrued by the Kardashians has expanded, especially with regard to Kim Kardashian. The dominant ethos of *Keeping Up With The Kardashians* has been to show every aspect of the family's life regardless of how frenetic and out of the ordinary it may be. Kris Jenner, who also serves as an executive producer, stating her intention for the series said: 'I think the only way to make this show successful is to really be real about it, and if stuff happens . . . we have to be able to roll with it and let them tape it and show it, no matter what' (2011: 263–4). Whether or not, as Turner (2014) states, the media attention bestowed upon Kim Kardshian is 'disproportionate' to her talents, the series, which to date has resulted in nine seasons, has shown the trappings of the family's celebrity lives and the wealth, glamour, and luxury which comes with it, but also family disputes, relationship breakdowns, and divorce, health crises, pregnancies, and births. Given that the Kardashians are essentially famous for being themselves, they *must* continually reveal themselves in order to garner media attention.

Yet the Kardashians were clearly not 'ordinary', even before their Reality TV fame and subsequent brand extensions, and they are part of a more recent addition to the Reality TV genre that focuses on 'people of interest', but with a similar level of celebrity effect. For example, there are a number of series that feature domestic and career lifestyles, relationships, conspicuous consumption, and interpersonal conflicts of affluent, fashionable, and attractive individuals, such as *The Hills*, *Jersey Shore*, and its spinoff *Snooki & JWOWW*, *The Real Housewives of Orange County*, *The Real Housewives of New York City*, *The Real Housewives of Beverly Hills*, and the latter's spinoff *Vanderpump Rules*, and UK examples such as *The Only Way is Essex*, *Made in Chelsea*, and *Geordie Shore*. As such, participants in these shows, from Lauren Conrad, the Situation, Snooki, Bethenny Frankel, and Lisa Vanderpump, to Joey Essex, Amy Childs, Mark Wright, Spencer Matthews, and Vicky Pattison, have attained considerable media attention and celebrity status. Referring to *The Real Housewives* series, Nicole Cox and Jennifer Proffitt (2012) point to the audience interest in the shows being predicated upon the insights that they provide into the 'real lives' of the women who live in a variety of affluent American gated communities. The huge success of the series and its spinoffs demonstrates the key aspect of Reality TV's proliferation in which high viewing figures equal high profits due to advertising revenue. Hence Cox and Proffitt also identify the ways in which the allure of the series, with its consistent displays of conspicuous consumption, does raise political issues regarding gendered audiences (a large proportion of the viewer base is female) and valorizes consumerism, including cosmetic surgery and body enhancements. Accordingly, *The Real Housewives* offers an aspirational lifestyle of luxury brand consumerism coupled with celebrity lifestyles. As Cox and Proffitt state: 'The housewives are shown in cahoots with celebrity hair/makeup stylists, chefs, designers, fitness instructors, and plastic surgeons. They purchase goods and services from the same people and places as the "stars", as if to suggest that their spending has granted (or earned) them entrance into the same social stratum as bona fide celebrities' (2012: 302). But of course, due to the demotic nature of Reality TV, the real housewives *are* celebrities.

Alongside the 'glamorous lifestyle' format, alternative recent adaptations within the Reality TV genre have included individuals with novel lives, such as *Breaking Amish*, and out-of-the-ordinary professions. Of the latter variety, recent years have seen the production of shows based upon a variety of individuals with 'interesting jobs' such as bounty hunters (*Dog The Bounty Hunter*), tattoo artists (*Miami Ink*, *LA Ink*, and *New York Ink*), pawnbrokers (*Pawn Stars*, *Hardcore Pawn*, and *Cajun Pawn Stars*), storage bin bidders (*Storage Hunters*, *Storage Wars*), deep-sea fishermen (*Deadliest Catch*, *Lobstermen*), haulage (*Ice Road Truckers*, *Shipping Wars*), repossession agents (*Lizard Lick Towing*), and child beauty pageant and dance contestants (*Toddlers and Tiaras*, *Dance Moms*). Reality TV is clearly a genre of trends, and one significant trajectory in recent years has been that of family-based shows rooted in distinctive regional areas, such as the American rural South, a trend best exemplified by *Here Comes Honey Boo Boo*, which was first broadcast in 2012.

TALES FROM THE AMERICAN SOUTH

A spinoff from the reality show *Toddlers and Tiaras* and produced by The Learning Channel (TLC), the premise of the Georgia-set *Here Comes Honey Boo Boo* series is based upon the everyday activities and working-class family life of seven-year-old pageant contestant Alana 'Honey Boo Boo' Thompson, her mother June (also known as 'Mama'), June's partner, Mike 'Sugar Bear' Thompson, and sisters Anna 'Chickadee' Shannon, Lauren 'Pumpkin' Shannon, and Jessica 'Chubbs' Shannon. Critical and viewer reactions to *Here Comes Honey Boo Boo* have vacillated between viewing the 'redneck' antics of its cast as charming, endearing, and unsophisticated humor, and charges that the series is highly exploitative in its focus on class, educational levels, unhealthy diet, and the bodily size of the family (June weighs some 303 pounds and the family are routinely shown eating junk food and rejecting healthy options). This is what A.J. Maréchal states (with a heavy hint of an Adorno-style critical attitude) of the latter position, not simply of the series, but also of wider cultural critiques of Reality TV – those it bestows fame upon, but also the voyeuristic aspect of filming 'reality':

> You know this show is exploitation. TLC knows it. Maybe even Mama and HBB know it, deep down in their rotund bodies. *Here Comes Honey Boo Boo* is a car crash, and everybody rubber-necks at a car crash, right? It's human nature. Yes, except that if you play that card, you also have to realize that human nature comes with the capacity to draw a line, to hold fast against the dehumanization and incremental tearing down of the social fabric, even if this never-ending onslaught of reality television suggests that's a losing effort. You can say no to visual exploitation. You can say no to TLC. And you can say no to Honey Boo Boo Child. Somebody has to. (2012: 25)

Nevertheless, the vogue for setting Reality TV shows in America's rural South has also resulted in very different representations of families than that of *Here Comes Honey Boo Boo*, including *Swamp People* and *Moonshiners*. However, the most prominent recent example is A&E channel's series *Duck Dynasty*, which was first broadcast in 2012. As with *Here Comes Honey Boo Boo*, the Robertson family who are the feature of *Duck Dynasty* are similarly avowedly Southern 'rednecks', with the major difference that they helm a multimillion dollar company, Duck Commander. In essence, therefore, having made their fortune through the invention and manufacture of handmade duck callers for the hunting market, the Robertsons represent Louisiana 'backwoods millionaires' and a further instance of entrepreneurial celebrity figures, but with a distinctive twist.

The principle dynamic of *Duck Dynasty* are the ways in which the families' 'hybrid' identity is negotiated. The central theme is the differences between the family patriarch, Phil Robertson, who invented the distinctive duck callers and founded the company in 1973, and son Willie, the current CEO of Duck Commander, and the driving force that has seen the enterprise become a major financial and business success. In essence, then, the series explores the differences between Phil's traditional, Christian, and conservative values and Willie's modern ethos (extending the brand of the company and introducing mechanized production techniques into a craft-based manufacturing approach), supported by his brothers Jep and Jase and their respective wives and children. The series lays a heavy emphasis on family, with each episode ending with a family meal and a non-diegetic voiceover provided by Willie that communicates a homily based upon the particular episode, but the family also represents, as Phil states, a space 'where the swamp meets corporate America'. As such, the family combines capitalistic business acumen with a commitment to 'fishing, hunting, shooting, and killing animals', visually communicated by the wearing of heavy beards, camouflage gear, the brandishing of guns, and patriotic bandanas.

Nonetheless Phil Robertson's 'Old Testament' qualities, the key to his screen persona, have resulted in controversy for the series and the network that produces it. A notable example was the furore that arose in response to comments made by Robertson in relation to Biblical attitudes towards homosexuality in an interview for *GQ* magazine. As a result of complaints made by groups such as the Human Rights Campaign and the gay rights group GLAAD, he was suspended by the series' producing company, A&E. The issue saw further public condemnations by celebrity figures such as Martina Navratilova and Piers Morgan, but support from Sarah Palin and the broadcaster Sean Hannity in relation to freedom of speech. Further expressions of support came from the series' extensive fanbase, with online petitions and Facebook groups demanding Robertson's re-instatement to the series, which did occur.

CONCLUDING POINTS

Although it has a comparatively recent history as a mainstream genre, Reality TV has changed perceptions of the kinds of individuals who appear on television and who can potentially be a 'celebrity'. Thus, a series such as *Duck Dynasty*, which in 2013 achieved the highest viewing figures for a non-fiction series in A&E's broadcast history (Boyle, 2013), demonstrates not only that the demotic potential of Reality TV continues apace long after its inception through the likes of *Big Brother*, but that 'ordinary' people have the ability to become part of much wider media debates when they enter into celebrity culture and become the epicentre of controversies. Consequently, whether competing for a cash prize under 24/7 surveillance, resurrecting faded celebrity careers, or combining business with duck hunting, Reality television remains a significant route into celebrity culture due to the longevity of the genre and the public appeal and interest that it continues to garner. And as such, beauty pageant trainers, hoarders, ice truckers, pawnbrokers, and affluent housewives rank alongside film stars, models, and pop stars in celebrity culture, a factor that would be of great interest to commentators such as Daniel Boorstin.

FURTHER READING

For more detail concerning the development of Reality TV as a distinctive and increasingly influential and multi-faceted television genre, see:

- Hill, A. (2005) *Reality TV: Audiences and Popular Factual Television.* London and New York: Routledge.

- Taddeo, J.A. and Dvorak, K. (2010) *The Tube Has Spoken: Reality TV and History.* Lexington, KY: The University Press of Kentucky.

In terms of directly linking Reality TV with celebrity, readers will find the following useful sources:

- Cox, N.B. and Proffitt, J.M. (2012) 'The housewives' guide to better living: promoting consumption on Bravo's "The Real Housewives"', *Communication, Culture & Critique,* 5: 295–312.

- Holmes, S. (2009) '"Jade's back, and this time she's famous": narratives of celebrity in the *Celebrity Big Brother* "race" row', *Entertainment and Sports Law,* 7(1): http://www2.warwick.ac.uk/fac/soc/law/elj/eslj/issues/volume7/number1/holmes (accessed 5 January 2014).

- Holmes, S. and Jermyn, J. (2004) *Understanding Reality Television.* London and New York: Routledge.

CELEBRITY INFLUENCE

CHAPTER OVERVIEW

The glossy celebrity magazine industry's products are dominated by articles promising readers the exact steps by which they too can 'get Rihanna's body', possess the flawless complexion of Cara Delevingne, or how women can regain their pre-pregnancy body just like Kate Middleton, Jennifer Lopez, or Kim Kardashian (and even look glamorous while giving birth); while for males, they can glean from the pages of periodicals such as *Men's Health* how to imitate Zac Efron's abdominal muscles, sculpt the *Wolverine* physique of Hugh Jackman, or build Chris Hemsworth's Thor-style biceps. This chapter, then, looks at the ways in which celebrity culture can be perceived to exert direct influences upon wider society, from copying their fashion choices to attempting to shape our bodies to mirror theirs. However, this aspect of celebrity culture raises a number of issues that, on the one hand present celebrities as arbiters of fashion and the promoters of trends, while on the other, there are fears concerning the deleterious effects such influence can have. This is especially acute with regard to unrealistic attempts to copy celebrity body shapes, which themselves may be 'illusory' due to the centrality of digital manipulation or 'airbrushing' of celebrity images within media forms.

To examine the various ways in which it is argued that celebrity culture can and does exert influence on wider society, the chapter will examine the following topics:

- Celebrity fashion
- Celebrity body role models
- Celebrity self-help and fitness texts
- Body dissatisfaction and celebrity culture
- Airbrushing and the digital manipulation of celebrity images
- The positive celebrity influence regarding attitudes to health and as a source of empowerment with regard to homosexual identity

To illustrate the substantive cultural issues and ideas underpinning the debates surrounding celebrity influence, the chapter will cite celebrity examples that include Georgiana, Duchess of Devonshire, Cher, Cameron Diaz, and Angelina Jolie.

CELEBRITY INFLUENCE AND FASHION INSPIRATION

Considering the issue of the rise and efficacy of celebrity product and service endorsements, Cooper Lawrence notes that the primary rationale for companies to pay substantial sums to celebrities is to tap into the levels of public worship they attract. Consequently, the equation is that if 'we worship celebrities and aspire to their lifestyle, who better to influence our decisions; who better to tell us what to buy, who we need to be' (2009: 108). There is of course a need to be cautious here as marketing research routinely stresses that consumers do not slavishly purchase products just because a notable celebrity endorses them; connection to the brand is also paramount. However, the idea of celebrities serving as figures of influence is potent and it predates the advertising and endorsement expansion that has arisen in recent years and can be traced back to the era of early Hollywood.

As Dana Thomas states within *Deluxe*, the influx of top designers to dress film stars inspired considerable public interest. For example, the designer Adrian's gowns for Greta Garbo resulted in the actress receiving copious numbers of letters from fans imploring her to be able to buy them from her. Similarly, when Adrian produced a gown worn by Joan Crawford for her role in the 1932 film *Letty Lynton*, 'Macy's sold half a million copies', while 'Grace Kelly's wedding dress, designed by MGM's Helen Rose for Kelly's 1956 wedding to Prince Rainer III of Monaco, was one of the most copied ever' (2008: 104).

Exploring fan reactions to early Hollywood, Jackie Stacey's (1994) ethnographic research identified a range of audience–star identification practices and her interviews uncovered remembered responses from a number of women about their memories of Hollywood fandom and the influence that classic film stars had upon them. For instance, some responses recalled a strong desire to be just like actresses such as Bette Davis as they represented potent role models, but role models who stood as ideals of feminine attractiveness. As such, film stars frequently provided 'blueprints' for a particular archetype of femininity for adolescent women. Other respondents recalled the games of make-believe they would play pretending to be favourite film stars and of consciously imitating the behaviours of film stars, especially the imitation of body movements which were incorporated into the respondents' own deportment in their everyday lives. Significantly, this process of imitation centred upon the relationship of copying film stars and achieving this through acts of consumption. Therefore, respondents recalled actively copying the hairstyles of famous stars in a bid to produce a new self-image established through the pleasure derived from fandom of a particular star image.

Stacey's research points to the influence that celebrity culture arguable exerts in relation to gender norms and bodily representations, and, as Ellis Cashmore concurs with regard to the impact that Hollywood had on the public in the 1930s, it did not merely establish a potent economic creative industry, but also, in establishing a celebrity class, established 'benchmarks' for bodily representation. As Cashmore argues, with the rise of Hollywood there also 'came a new standard of beauty, one that drew near-unanimous agreement, defining a kind of gold standard of beauty' (2006: 109), and one which set in train a source of cultural imitation, whether through acts of product consumption or more radical routes such as cosmetic surgery. But how and why does celebrity culture have such an effect, to the extent that it can define modes of gender and bodily image? To begin to explore this question, it is usual to illustrate the extent to which this is not an entirely new development and has antecedents, most notably that of Georgiana Spencer.

EIGHTEENTH-CENTURY CELEBRITY INFLUENCE: GEORGIANA, DUCHESS OF DEVONSHIRE

While the idea of celebrities representing key contemporary arbiters of style is now a common presence within media discourses, it is not a new phenomenon, as evidenced by the fashion impact exerted by Georgiana Spencer, Duchess of Devonshire. Born in 1757 and the eldest child of the Earl and Countess Spencer, Georgiana grew up to be a source of social and cultural interest in relation to her command of fashion and her public status, traits continued by her later family member, Diana Spencer, Princess of Wales. As Amanda Foreman states, Georgiana grew up surrounded by a 'celebrity-filled' environment due to the frequency with which famous visitors called at her London house, such as the actor David Garrick, and the novelist Laurence Sterne. However, her rise in social standing was secured by her marriage to the Duke of Devonshire in 1774, and she thus became Duchess of Devonshire. Yet, although the marriage was ostensibly established in order for the Duke to have heirs (and for Georgiana to fulfil her various official duties), she rapidly acquired celebrity. For instance, Georgiana's presence was much prized by society figures due to the prestige that it bestowed upon them, but it was her understanding of fashion, and the value of making bold and frequently outrageous fashion statements, that cemented Georgiana's fame and sartorial influence.

At one level, this was established through her display of modish London fashions at rural English social events, but it was underpinned by her conscious knowledge of how to stand out (demonstrating a potent example of Georg Simmel's sociological discussion of the way in which people established individuality in crowded and impersonal metropolises through the adoption of outré fashion choices). To achieve this effect, Georgiana created 'signature' styles, most famously the drooping ostrich feather which she positioned so that it hung in an arch across the front of her hair, a look unique to her own style. Yet Georgiana's striking style was not merely noteworthy, but routinely caused a social 'sensation' when she made appearances at public events and, more importantly, her look rapidly become hugely influential. Thus:

> Whatever she wore became instantly fashionable. Women's hair was already arranged high above the head, but Georgiana took the fashion a step further by creating the three-foot hair tower. She stuck pads of horse hair to her own hair using scented pomade. Sometimes she carried a ship in full sail, or an exotic arrangement of stuffed birds and waxed fruit, or even a pastoral tableau with little wooden trees and sheep. Even though the towers required the help of at least two hairdressers and took several hours to arrange, Georgiana's designs inspired others to imitate her. (Foreman, 1998: 37)

Given such influential power, Georgiana rapidly established herself as a major celebrity figure whose fame transcended that of her husband. Furthermore, her rise to fame was directly due to growing interest in both her and her newsworthy fashion statements, and reports of her activities fed into the increasing public interest surrounding lifestyles of the famous. Thus, as newspapers proliferated and circulations grew, reports centered on a range of famous individuals 'Georgiana among them, which the whole county read about, and discussed, and with whom they could feel some sort of connection' (1998: 38).

Hence, celebrity culture, from its true beginnings, has exercised social power, with fashion at its heart. Aside from the marriage parallels that have been drawn between Georgiana and Diana (like Prince Charles, the Duke of Devonshire had a mistress who was his 'true love' – a relationship conveyed in the film *The Duchess*, starring Keira Knightley as Georgiana), Georgiana and Diana were both striking in their roles as fashionable women with singular images, a baton now picked up (or established by media discourses) by the Duchess of Cambridge, whose fashion effect and influence, as discussed in Chapter 6, is similarly dramatic (if not as eccentric as her royal predecessor) and rabidly communicated throughout the media.

MODELS OF FEMININITY

Georgiana's creation of a public self through fashion choices accords with the view of the fashion researcher Jennifer Craik in her book *The Face of Fashion*, in which she argues that the function of fashion is that it serves as a 'mask' that individuals use to effectively disguise themselves. According to this view, the ways in which people use dress represents a series of 'technical devices' which go beyond simply adorning the body, but actually can and do express a precise relationship that exists between an individual's body and the society in which she or he lives. To explain this process, Craik draws upon the work of the sociologist Pierre Bourdieu, and specifically his concept of habitus (as articulated within his text, *Distinction*). What Bourdieu means by habitus is a set of very specialized techniques and knowledge that individuals acquire from their given culture which then enables them to move through their lives effectively. An essential feature of habitus is that these techniques appear to be unconscious or 'common sense' notions of appropriate 'techniques and modes of self-presentation' (1994: 4).

Although the concept of habitus is frequently connected to the concept and expression of social class, habitus has also been related to gendered practice to explain the ways in which gender is culturally replicated and communicated through fashion styles. The importance for celebrity culture here is that people look to particular cultural 'role models' to guide them and to prescribe the acceptable and 'unacceptable' modes of clothing the body. A key example of a fashion role model, argues Craik, is the fashion model, a figure that has proven to be intrinsic to changing ideas about gender representation and changing definitions of femininity, but a female figure that is fundamentally associated with the need for bodily discipline that underlines Western conceptions of beauty and the appropriate maintenance of the body.

This is because a central element of modelling is the requirement to meet exact bodily specifications, but these change over time, suggesting that models are difficult and problematic 'role models' to follow. Indeed, even within the industry itself changing conceptions of beauty rapidly established a drive towards cosmetic surgical procedures to fit particular demands. For example, the model Twiggy came to symbolize a specific 1960s concept of femininity. This was because:

> Twiggy was the perfect model for the time. She weighed six and a half stone and took size six in dresses. She was flat chested and stick legged, she was guaranteed to look good in a mini. She had a small, thin face capped with boyish haircut and large dark eyes underlined with penciled lashes. (1994: 84)

The problematic aspect with regard to Twiggy's image was that whereas her thinness was natural and not the product of physical effort, other models struggled to emulate her singular and iconic look with the result that dieting and eating disorders became prevalent within the industry, but of course each decade has seen differing idealizations of the fashionable body (from Jerry Hall in the 1970s, through to the era of the 'supermodel' typified by Cindy Crawford, and then the 1990s rise of the superstar model Kate Moss, whose mantle has been assumed by Cara Delevingne).

However, this changing pattern of preferred model bodies, the types of women selected by agencies and advertisers, have attracted considerable criticism. These ranged from the fears that trends such as the late 2000s 'size 0' look, which controversially presented models with thin bodies and 'dangerously' low Body Mass Indexes that were not representative of the majority of women (and thus potentially served as damaging role models for young women), to models selected for major fashion shows who were 'far too white [and] nearly exclusively Anglo-looking' (Mears, 2010: 22). Therefore, changing body images, the promotion of bodies that are dangerously unrealistic, and a lack of ethnic diversity raise concerns for a celebrity group that is extensively disseminated within fashion periodicals and advertising in relation to their possession of enviable and 'perfect' bodies.

CELEBRITY BODY ROLE MODELS

While the model has represented a key focus for the transmission of social and cultural conceptions of bodily habitus, models have also firmly assumed their place as major celebrity icons alongside, celebrities from the world of cinema who have served as a longstanding source of public aspiration. As Pamela Church Gibson states in her study of celebrity and fashion, the 'intense interest in Hollywood stars, which combines a wish to emulate their style and perhaps their perfect bodies . . . has lasted for a hundred years' (2012: 53). In the early decades of Hollywood, as explored in Chapter 6, new magazines dedicated to movie stars were increasingly filled with features that promoted fashionable star styles and offered them as sources of emulation to readers. This is a process that has continued within fashion, and celebrity-based magazines and stars have long been influential with regard to styles being adopted by the public: from

Jennifer Aniston's hairstyle in the early seasons of the hit TV show *Friends* (inspiring the 'Rachel' request in hair salons), Elizabeth Hurley's association with Versace, Sarah Jessica Parker's link (via her *Sex in the City* character, Carrie Bradshaw) with Manolo Blahnik, to Cheryl Cole's hand tattoo design. Yet celebrity influence extends beyond fashion because celebrities 'promote not only ways of dressing and making up, but also have been instrumental in creating the desirable body shapes of each decade' (2012: 73).

To demonstrate this process, Elizabeth Arveda Kissling examined the nature of the body image and femininity message that was actively promoted by celebrity figures in a series of glossy celebrity self-help books that were produced in the 1980s by Victoria Principal, Raquel Welch, Elizabeth Taylor, Brooke Shields, and Cher. Although produced by very different kinds of celebrities, a unifying theme within such texts was the clear association of female confidence and self-worth with enhanced levels of health, fitness, and beauty. Consequently, rather than serving as empowering manifestos, what these celebrity self-help books actually contained were conservative acceptances of idealized principles of female physical appearance which offered few challenges to the prevailing bodily ideology. For example, within the singer and actress Cher's book (a celebrity famed for numerous cosmetic procedures), she declared: 'Look, we're a visual society. I didn't make this society. I just live here. I adapted to it' (2006: 554).

Such acceptance reflects and upholds what numerous feminist critics argue is a dominant factor within the patriarchal oppression of women: that they are primarily valued on the basis of their appearance and thus must 'work' on their looks in order to succeed. This resonates with Naomi Wolf's now-classic work which proposed that women in the Western world are routinely subjected to a prevailing 'beauty myth' based upon a cultural perception that the 'quality called "beauty"objectively and universally exists. Women must want to embody it and men must want to possess women who embody it' (1990: 12). Wolf argues that the parameters of the beauty myth have been routinely transmitted via fashion magazines and advertising imagery, and that its desirability is reflected in the growth and power of the diet and cosmetic surgery industries, both of which have expanded significantly since the publication of Wolf's work.

Returning to celebrity within this process, in her assessment of celebrity self-help books Kissling found that their prevailing message was that of promoting exercise and diet as the guaranteed route to achieving beauty and health and they therefore sustained oppression through their appeal for women to objectify their own bodies. Consequently, these celebrity diet and fitness books do not acknowledge or criticize sexist culture but, alternatively, stress that the source of female unhappiness lies within and can therefore be combated and overcome through bodily recreation through exercise and beauty regimes.

CELEBRITY SELF-HELP: THE NEXT GENERATION

The trend for celebrity-produced diet and fitness self-help books has continued beyond the 1980s to become a distinctive sub-genre with figures such as Kirstie Alley, Tyra Banks,

Alicia Silverstone, Jessica Alba, and Gwyneth Paltrow producing successful texts (with style and fashion guide versions written by Victoria Beckham, Mary Kate Olsen, Whitney Port, and Lauren Conrad). Moreover, some celebrity books have been forthright, like the earlier examples, in their message concerning the value of physical attractiveness and the need for body maintenance. For example, in Joan Rivers and Valerie Frankel's *Men Are Stupid . . . And They Like Big Boobs* (2009), for all of its acerbic and irreverent tone as one would expect from the comedienne, the book is a detailed account of cosmetic surgery procedures (Botox, skin peels, face-lifts, liposuction, rhinoplasty, and tummy tucks) and their effectiveness for female confidence (indeed, she had undergone many of the procedures she discusses in the book). Here she states of the philosophy of the book:

> I've been the public (lifted) face of cosmetic enhancements since the Stone Age. My luck was to realize early on the degree to which looking good helped my life and career – and to start having work done early, too. My abiding life philosophy is plain: *In our appearance-centric society, beauty is a huge factor in everyone's professional and emotional success* . . . In our society, looks 'matter more than anyone would like to believe, and it's senseless to go through life angry about it when you can just embrace it. Looking good equals *feeling* good. (2009: 2)

However, a notable contemporary example that does not avowedly advocate such drastic measures is that of the Hollywood actress Cameron Diaz's *The Body Book*, which alternatively presents readers with extensive information concerning nutrition, fitness, and wellbeing. Diaz's book is addressed explicitly to women (the opening line is 'Hello, Lady!'), and she unhesitatingly offers herself as a role model to readers, stating that 'Everything in these pages is information that I use to live my life, information that makes me feel so excited and joyous that I just had to share it with you' (2014: 1–2). Throughout the book, Diaz emphasizes that nutrition, fitness, and the discipline required to attain and maintain a healthy lifestyle are sources of empowerment for women and that the body is a personal possession and:

> How well you care for it will determine how well you are able to live your life. So whether you wish you had longer legs or smaller hips, bigger boobs or less pointy ears, this book is for you. It's a guide to maximising your strength and endurance so that your body can take you everywhere you want to go in life: to all of your success, to the love of your life, to your passions and adventures. (2014: 3)

At one level, Diaz's book could be argued to reflect a similar sensibility to the earlier celebrity-based texts that Kissling examined, and indeed Diaz's image is presented throughout *The Body Book* and shows that she is the possessor of a 'perfect' celebrity body. Also, the route to success offered to readers is again an individualized proposition – it is a matter of acquiring mastery over the body with no acknowledgement of any external social or cultural barriers that may serve to block empowerment.

Diaz is keen to stress diet and fitness as life-enhancing rather than health-enriching, however, instead of a means by which idealized celebrity bodies can be emulated. As such, the book contains detailed discussions of nutrition, body chemistry, physiology, biology, and information on the major muscle groups in tandem with advice to reject sugar and fast food, and embrace growing old gracefully. Such information and advice is, of course, routinely transmitted by health groups, but the issue here is that Diaz personalizes the project of healthy living with her own identity and biography, and 'validates' the message given by her own healthy and athletic body. Indeed, to emphasize the degree to which Diaz is regarded as an influential figure, the promotional blurb on the back cover of the book states: 'Cameron Diaz has been a role model for millions of women all over the world throughout her career.'

CELEBRITY FITNESS

While self-help books continue to promote the celebrity as either the source of bodily inspiration or as a personal guide to a healthier life, a more prevalent development in the diffusion of celebrity body role models has been the rise of the celebrity fitness video and DVD market in which various celebrities have presented themselves as trainers to take viewers on step-by-step workouts designed to emulate their bodies. In her study of such products, Vanessa Russell (2007) argues that the trend emerged due to the increasing mass commercial availability and popularity of the VHS video recorder in the early 1980s. This permitted individuals who did not wish to exercise in public to avoid 'gym humiliation' due to unfit bodies and to exercise in their homes guided by aerobic video instructors. A prominent video to meet this consumer demand was the *Jane Fonda Workout*, performed by the Oscar-winning actress.

Selling over a million copies, the initial video was followed by numerous further workouts (including two in 2010 aimed at older viewers). The success of the video sparked an industry focused upon celebrity fitness videos predicated on the promise to viewers that by faithfully emulating the exercise techniques shown, their bodies could similarly be transformed to mirror that of the celebrity. In Fonda's case this was especially attractive given that the actress was in her early forties when she released her first video, and thus she stood as impressive proof that a body could be remodelled and honed into an athletic and aesthetically appealing shape. Therefore, by purchasing and performing the video workouts as demonstrated by the celebrity, viewers could transform their body to look just like a celebrity's.

While Jane Fonda's video range remains arguably the most iconic example of the trend, numerous other celebrities have released similar workout videos in recent years, such as Cher, Paula Abdul, Chuck Norris, Mel B, Geri Halliwell, Claudia Schiffer, Carmen Electra, Davina McCall, Mike 'The Situation' Sorrentino, Kim Kardashian, and *Geordie Shore*'s Vicky Pattison. Furthermore, professional trainers who have released videos, or worked with celebrities, such as Billy Blanks, Josh Salzmann, Harvey Walden, and Jillian Michaels, have themselves become celebrity figures.

But, the issue with such videos, argues Russell, is that their promise – to enable viewers to remould their bodies to mirror that of a celebrity – is problematic and, unsurprisingly, in most cases it is idealized and unrealistic. The major stumbling block for viewers is that the instructor is not in the same position as they are, but is rather at the end point, already in possession of a 'perfect' body. Furthermore, the video/DVD (many sequences can now be downloaded or viewed via YouTube) format is not live and so the constructed nature of the narrative is not apparent to viewers. For instance, the featured celebrity instructor is most commonly highly groomed and their onscreen image is produced through the assistance of physical trainers, makeup artists, dietitians, stylists, lighting technicians, and expert choreographers (all unseen) and the workouts are frequently segmented so that the celebrity is never depicted in a tired or physically unappealing manner (sweaty, hair and makeup in disarray, etc.). Furthermore, while the celebrity is positioned to act as a 'mirror' to the viewer's body and the aspirational role model, in many cases the workouts are actually *disempowering*. This is because few viewers can match the celebrity's level of fitness (the work has already been done and the ideal body acquired), therefore many viewers must start with the low-impact workouts while the celebrity can undertake what Russell calls the 'hardcore' expert level.

Thus, while the exercises are undoubtedly useful, it will be a long journey until the 'celebrity level' is reached and many viewers will feel distinctly inferior to the celebrity who performs the routines with aplomb and apparent mastery, and who, of course, looks good doing it. Ultimately, what such products visually offer, from their covers to their content, is, like the earlier self-help books, a reflection of a social and cultural idealization of the thin and muscled body, with celebrities as the major source of influence and constituting the ideal that social actors feel they should both admire and aspire towards.

CELEBRITY AND THE ENHANCED BODY

To explore the cultural context of such bodily motivation in relation to celebrity culture, I will now turn to the work of the feminist writer, Susie Orbach. Within her book *Bodies*, Orbach (who organized demonstrations against the fashion industry in relation to its use of size zero models) argues that the quest for bodily perfection has increasingly become individualized due to fundamental social and industrial transformations, such as the decline of manual labour (in the Western world, at least), which have altered bodily activity and galvanized the rise of the pursuit of the gym-sculpted body and both the growth of the diet industry and the increase in demand for cosmetic surgery. However, celebrity culture in partnership with the advertising industry has also played a decisive and influential role in inspiring body transformation, resulting in an increased surge of exercise in pursuit of specific aesthetic outcomes, but also of cosmetic alteration and modification. This is what Orbach states:

> Late capitalism has catapulted us out of centuries-old bodily practices which were centred on survival, procreation, the provision of shelter and the satisfaction of hunger. Now, birthing, illness and ageing, while part of the ordinary cycle of life, are also events that can be interrupted or altered by personal

endeavour in which one harnesses the medical advances and surgical restruc-turings on offer. Our body is judged as our individual production. (2010: 5)

According to this view, the body is now routinely viewed as a project to be actively worked upon, and celebrities are a significant source of role models who inspire this labour. This is a point that Hamish Pringle develops with explicit reference to celeb-rity culture and the position that celebrities hold as visual role models. Yet Pring-le's view, while acknowledging the impact in terms of fashion choices and workouts, points to more radical dimensions of celebrity influence in relation to the cosmetic surgery that is undertaken to emulate specific celebrity attributes in the form of demands for cosmetic operations such as breast implants, lip plumping, liposuction, Botox, and buttock implants (the latter popularized by the hip-hop star, Nicki Minaj). Hence, encapsulating the degree of influence that celebrity is argued to have, Pringle concludes that in addition to offering lifestyle and fashion advice:

> Increasingly, they are telling us how to modify our appearance, not just by means of cosmetics, clothing and other accessories, but by use of medical treatments and cosmetic surgeries. The fact that such a significant number of people are actually going through with this, often using celebrity features as a reference point for their surgeon is indicative of the powerful influence that stars can have. (2004: 46)

Although based upon an extensive study of the 'toy celebrity' Barbie, Mary F. Rogers emphasizes the degree to which cosmetic surgery demands are reflecting the cultural view of the human body as a 'plastic' instrument within a consumer market in which desires that are driven by fantasy role models can be realized via technologies that can transform human flesh (including numerous individuals who have surgically enhanced themselves with the express desire to be human Barbie dolls). Rogers argues that contemporary bodies are no longer constrained by natural factors, and as such they reflect what she calls a distinctive ethic of 'somatics'. This concept refers to a technological approach to the body that is motivated by the sentiment that 'bodies can be whatever we like if we devote enough money and attention to them. This development makes the body an aerobic instrument, a surgical object, a dietary experiment, a fleshy clay capable of endless remoulding' (1999: 113).

Returning to the view of Susan Bordo, celebrity culture has long promoted the idea of the malleable body, such as the extreme gym-sculptured body of Arnold Schwarzenegger whose championship body-building status was the foundation of his film action hero cinematic persona (from Conan to the Terminator), but is also applicable to many subsequent stars (Hugh Jackman, Chris Hemsworth, Vin Diesel, Dwayne 'The Rock' Johnson, etc.). However, in addition to worked-out bodies, celebrities have become intimately immersed within the world of cosmetic surgical culture to the point that it has defined their celebrity identities, for example, Cher and Michael Jackson. The danger, though, argues Bordo with direct reference to Cher, whose var-ious cosmetic surgeries have consistently enabled her to appear much younger than her actual age, is that she 'has not made the aging female body sexually more accept-able. [She has instead] established a new norm – achievable only through continual cosmetic surgery – in which the surface of the female body ceases to age physically as the body grows chronologically older' (1993: 26).

This culture is so prevalent, argues Bordo, that many female stars over the age of 25 are 'the plastic product of numerous cosmetic surgeries on face and body' (1993: 104). To underscore this assessment, there are a number of contemporary female celebrities whose cosmetic procedures have become well documented within the media, such as Tara Reid, Nicole Kidman, Meg Ryan, Janice Dickinson, Katie Price, Heidi Montag, and Jwoww, in addition to older performers whose surgeries have drawn particular (invariably critical) attention like Kim Novak, Liza Minnelli, and Joan Van Ark (not forgetting male stars such as Burt Reynolds or Mickey Rourke). However, rather than simply representing an expression of 'vanity' or routine somatic behaviour, the drive towards cosmetic surgery within celebrity culture itself is arguably a reaction to the pervasive culture of ageism that is prevalent in the entertainment industry and which valorizes youthful bodies over old ones (Holmlund, 2010; Jermyn, 2012).

THE RISKS OF CELEBRITY INFLUENCE

One of the most severe effects commonly attributed to the media's glamourization of celebrities is the degree to which they are routinely perceived to possess ideal body shapes and fêted within media discourses as bodily role models. As such, a link between negative self-perceptions of body image in relation to such media-communicated body ideals and the adoption of harmful eating behaviours such as anorexia nervosa has been extensively investigated (King et al., 2000; Blond, 2008; Rogers and Chabrol, 2009). Although a complex issue with regard to how and why many people develop anorexia and other eating disorders, Bordo nevertheless links them with the growing postwar cultural obsession with 'keeping our bodies slim, tight, and young' and 'meanings of contemporary beauty ideals' (1993: 140). However, to investigate the explicit role that celebrity culture may play within this configuration, John Maltby, with David C. Giles, Louise Barber, and Lynn E. McCutcheon, empirically explored the link between celebrity worship and body image, with a special focus upon female adolescents.

In their study, Maltby et al. examined the perceived relationship posited to exist between celebrity worship and perceptions of body image, and more specifically they addressed general social fears that media glamourization of slender celebrities may inspire young people to have unrealistic and ultimately unattainable aspirations, with the risk of developing eating disorders. The study, utilizing the Celebrity Worship Scale, focused upon adolescent para-social relationships that have the potential to lead to intense attachments to celebrities considered to be influential role models. With regard to the researchers' methodological approach, they selected three distinctive samples consisting of 229 school-aged adolescents aged between 14 and 16, 183 full-time university undergraduate students, and 289 adults aged between 22 and 60. The results of the study suggested that a 'relationship between celebrity worship for intense-personal reasons and attention to body shape occurs in female adolescents but not female students and adults sampled from a general population' (2005: 27). However, with regard to body image measures, female respondents were found to score significantly higher than males in relation to their attention to body shape, and to be more significantly preoccupied with body image.

In terms of the overall conclusions of the research, the findings suggested that although there is a palpable degree of comparison and idealization of celebrity bodies among adolescents, the link between celebrity worship and body image wanes as young people enter into adulthood. However, alternative studies have raised differing views. For example, Willinge et al. (2006) have also examined the criticism levelled at media representations of ideal bodies and their potential influence in instigating eating disorders. The issue within this study was to examine the ways in which research has questioned the media link to eating disorders on the basis that although wide audiences are exposed to the same idealized media messages relating to celebrity bodies, only a relative minority of individuals are adversely affected by them. This study was based upon samples of body-satisfied and body-dissatisfied female and male university students (who were shown images of Australian celebrities such as Kylie Minogue), and suggested that for individuals who class themselves as body-dissatisfied, mediated idealized images can play a role in contributing to the preliminary development of body dissatisfaction.

While many body-satisfied participants endorsed body sizes that were realistic and larger than the sizes of the celebrity images they were exposed to, thus rejecting media images of idealized slender bodies, a significant aspect of the research was that many male students, whether body satisfied or body dissatisfied, viewed thin celebrity body sizes as the ideal for females. This endorsement of thin ideal body sizes for females thus contributed to the social pressures that the young female respondents reported feeling from males in comparison with slim celebrity bodies.

CELEBRITIES AND POST-PREGNANCY BODIES

The suggestion that celebrity influence in terms of bodily ideals is a phenomenon largely restricted to younger people and that fades with adulthood is interesting, but is problematized by Hilary Cunningham's (2002) analysis of media coverage of celebrities and their post-childbirth bodies. In this study, adult women potentially face pressures regarding their bodies during and post-pregnancy. As a natural process within pregnancy, the body changes that occur are essential to ensure a healthy birth, and a key change is the development of a protective layer of abdomen fat that functions to ensure that the foetus is appropriately insulated. However, a prominent focus that has emerged within magazines, argues Cunningham, is the rise of celebrity-focused 'Getting-your-body-back' post-pregnancy features and 'Hollywood's hottest new moms' news stories that arose in the early 2000s.

To illustrate this apparent trend, Cunningham identified a number of stories based on celebrities who had rapidly returned to their pre-pregnant physical shapes, such as Demi Moore, Pamela Anderson, Madonna, Catherine Zeta-Jones, Cindy Crawford, and Victoria Beckham. But the issue of concern in terms of the reception of these articles and the images that accompany them, is that non-celebrity women who have given birth do not have the facilities to engage in workouts in the home (employing professional trainers and nutritionists) and that it is an activity that 'ordinary' women have to do in their own time in addition to childcare and/or employment. The key issue, therefore, is that media features emphasize not merely the fact that celebrities have regained their pre-pregnant bodies, but that they have achieved this in a matter of months, implying that the post-pregnant body is a condition that needs to be rectified as quickly as possible and body 'normality' re-established.

The features that Cunningham identifies in the early 2000s have proliferated, and numerous celebrity-based magazines (such as *Hello!*, *OK!*, and *Us Weekly*) habitually focus upon celebrities who have given birth, such as Jennifer Lopez, Bethenny Frankel, Padma Lakshmi, Penelope Cruz, Alicia Keys, Kate Middleton, and Kim Kardashian, with headlines disclaiming the likes of 'Jaw-Dropping Post Baby Bods', 'I Got My Body Back: How She Lost 40LBS in 40 Days', and 'My Best Body Ever: How I Did It'. Therefore, celebrity influence linked with media-transmitted unrealistic body images is not confined to adolescents, but also affects adult women adjusting to their post-pregnancy bodies consuming images of celebrities whose own pregnant bodies are regarded as negative states that must be banished as rapidly as possible, with the window for returning to 'normal' getting ever shorter, as illustrated by the widespread celebratory coverage that marked the supermodel Adriana Lima's return to the Victoria's Secrets catwalk eight weeks after giving birth to her second daughter in 2012.

CELEBRITY IMAGES AND DIGITAL MANIPULATION

A further issue that is problematic with regard to employing celebrities as bodily role models and as key sources of image influence is the degree to which the images of celebrity figures found within magazine culture and advertising/brand imagery actually reflect any sense of realism. For instance, in the view of Margo DeMello, many of the images of women within modern media discourses actually promote standards of beauty that are utterly unattainable for most women. However, this is because the celebrities or models which are the subject of such imagery are frequently subjected to photoshopping visual techniques that alter the images before they are communicated publicly. Hence, the 'perfect' bodies that saturate consumer culture are invariably the result of deliberate digital manipulation to the extent that waists are reduced, thighs thinned, and facial lines are smoothed away with the result that frequently 'the photoshopping is so overdone that the results no longer even look realistically human' (2014: 177).

In conceptualizing and theorizing Western attitudes to the female body, Susan Bordo's analysis of surgically enhanced bodies utilizes the work of the French postmodernist thinker, Jean Baudrillard, with particular regard to his influential concept of simulation, which she uses to emphasize the degree to which advertising images deliberately manipulate reality. In defining his concept, Baudrillard describes simulation as an action that is designed explicitly 'to feign to have what one doesn't have' (1994: 3), and this is the very essence of what DeMello attributes to advertising images, and what has been applied to many of the images of celebrities by critics who argue that what they purport to represent is actually unreal. For example, the idea of simulating reality lies at the heart of the practice of digital image manipulation within magazine culture, and especially in relation to celebrity representation.

This trend is extensively (and critically) examined by Jennifer Nelson, in her book *Airbrushed Nation*, and she argues that retouched images of celebrities and models are now the norm within glossy magazines to a degree that dramatically transcends their real-life attributes. However, the practice is defended by the industry on the basis that such magazines deal in fantasy, not reality, and that the digital manipulation of celebrity images in order to present visages to the public that appear 'perfect' is not a form of deception, but rather constitutes a form of 'art'. For example, referring to a digitally enhanced image of the American singer Kelly Clarkson, the editor of *Self* magazine stated, on the rationale for using the singer's image, that:

> Portraits like the one we take each month for the cover of *Self* are not supposed to be unedited or a true-to-life snapshot. This is art, creativity, and collaboration. It's not, as in a news photograph, journalism. It is, however, meant to inspire women to want to be their best. (2012: 125)

The problem with such images, counters Nelson, is that airbrushing/photoshopping establishes a standard of beauty that is in reality unattainable and thus difficult to justify as a source of inspiration. As Maggie Wykes and Barrie Gunter similarly argue in their book *The Media and Body Image*, such images act to normalize desirable bodies that are (in the manner of Baudrillard) intrinsically illusions because they represent bodies that are not possible in reality, but which may be reacted to by members of the public as if they are real. *GQ* magazine published a cover portrait of the British actress Kate Winslet that was digitally altered to render her slimmer than her natural build and she critically spoke out against it (but she has been the subject of further 'airbrushing', most notably her 2013 appearance on the cover of *Vogue*). But in the wake of the furore, an editor of GQ magazine stated that the normalized publishing industry approach to 'airbrushing' was that 'Practically every photo you see in a magazine will have been digitally altered in this way' (2005: 122). However, there are also critical voices from within celebrity culture, with a notable example being that of the teenage singer Lorde, who criticized images of her live performances that had digitally removed all traces of her acne scars, and she tweeted alternative images that revealed her 'flaws' to her fans.

With reference to the studies of celebrity worship, and the risks of health problems and eating disorders that can potentially arise from feelings of body dissatisfaction, the dilemma is that celebrity visual influence becomes even more problematic as the standards of beauty that are culturally communicated by celebrity images are (again to use an idea from Baudrillard) 'realer-than-real', and thus, utterly impossible to mimic because the subject of the image itself does not fully possess these attributes. Other commentators point to the degree to which the viewers of digitally enhanced images are fully aware of their 'fake' and exaggerated qualities of many fashion and celebrity images. The reason for this, argues Hany Farid, is that the altering of digital imagery 'is now ubiquitous. People have come to expect it in the fashion and entertainment world, where airbrushing blemishes and wrinkles away is routine' (2009: 44). This view raises the important perspective that we are not passive consumers of images displaying 'perfect' bodies and recognize them for what they are: exaggerations (few would take the Vogue Kate Winslet picture or the image of Mariah Carey on the cover of her *Me. I am Mariah* album as accurate reflections of their real bodies). Indeed, obviously airbrushed celebrity images are now routinely the subject of scepticism and ridicule in media discourses and Internet sites.

There have been serious political backlashes, however, against the practice of airbrushing celebrity images and the potentially harmful influence this may exercise. In some cases this has been expressed in calls for 'health warnings' to accompany images so that viewers are fully cognizant that they do not reflect reality and are thus not to be used as a personal guide to beauty or bodily form. More dramatically, the ethical nature of advertising campaigns that have utilized extensively altered images of celebrities to promote beauty products have been the subject of political protest.

For instance, in the United Kingdom a number of complaints were levelled against the cosmetics company *Lancôme* by the British Liberal Democrat MP Jo Swinson in response to a L'Oréal advertisement featuring Julia Roberts and Christy Turlington, on the grounds that they were excessively airbrushed. The complaints were upheld and the campaign was ultimately banned in the UK, with Sweney stating:

> Pictures of flawless skin and super-slim bodies are all around, but they don't reflect reality . . . Excessive airbrushing and digital manipulation techniques have become the norm, but both Christy Turlington and Julia Roberts are naturally beautiful women who don't need retouching to look great. This ban sends a powerful message to advertisers – let's get back to reality. (Sweney, 2011, TheGuardianBeta)

Compelling as the airbrushing debate is with regard to the establishment of unrealistic imagery and 'impossible role models', it must also be acknowledged that many celebrities themselves are frequently subjected to critical pressure regarding their body sizes. To illustrate this point, Deborah Lupton mentions in her book *Fat* that female celebrities are regularly ridiculed and criticized by magazines for gaining weight or displaying evidence of 'negative' body issues, such as bulging stomachs or cellulite.

As such, female celebrities whose weight is perceived to markedly fluctuate, such as Kim and Khloé Kardashian, Oprah Winfrey, Tyra Banks, Britney Spears, Kirstie Alley, and Kelly Osbourne, are routinely commented upon and subjected to bodily judgement, usually in the form of critical 'before and after' photographs that display their bodily changes in minute detail. Furthermore, on numerous websites devoted solely to chronicling the lives and statuses of celebrities who have gained weight, negative adjectives abound in relation to such images to the extent that, as Lupton observes, while 'many of the celebrities featured still look attractive and well-groomed in the "after" photographs, they are deemed "ugly" simply because they have gained weight' (2013: 53). Moreover, such issues have extended into the formal media, as evidenced by the film critic Rex Reed, who said that the actress Melissa McCarthy was 'tractor-sized' and a 'female hippo' in his review of her film *Identity Thief.*

THE CELEBRITY EFFECT

With regard to countering the emphasis on celebrities possessing 'super-slim' bodies, there are instances of celebrity figures which are celebrated for presenting alternative, but still highly fashionable, body shapes. So far this chapter has examined the influence of celebrity primarily from the perspective of celebrities serving as visual role models reflecting fashions and idealized bodies. As such, the linking of celebrities with body dissatisfaction tends towards the negative influence and effects of celebrity culture. However, Mary C. Beltrán, whose research is centrally concerned with representations of ethnicity, class, and gender in television, film, and celebrity cultures has championed the Puerto Rican actress and singer Jennifer Lopez of portraying a potent Latina image that does not conform to conventional standards of Hollywood body ideals. In this respect, Jennifer Lopez's ethnic identity becomes empowering and disruptive to body norms. This is how Lopez describes her body and cultural reactions to it:

I guess I'm a little hippy. Latinas and black women have a certain body type. We're curvy. It's in the history books. I didn't start a revolution. But I don't mind if the big-butted women in the world are a little happier because of a few cameramen's obsession with my behind. (2007: 283)

However, an alternative, and more serious, example of socially positive celebrity influence concerns health issues, with particular significance in relation to celebrities who have been diagnosed with cancer. For example, although the Lance Armstrong Foundation has been rebranded as the Livestrong Foundation (in response to Armstrong's performance-enhancing drug scandal), the foundation was established by Armstrong in the wake of his battles against cancer 'to inspire and empower' cancer survivors and has raised millions of dollars through sales of its 'Livestrong' wristbands. In other cases, celebrities who have shared their experiences of fighting cancer have directly inspired others who are living with the disease.

For instance, there was a substantial increase in Australian women booking mammography tests following the singer and actress Kylie Minogue's diagnosis and treatment for breast cancer. Similarly, the E! channel reporter and Reality TV personality Guliana Rancic publicly shared her decision to undergo a double mastectomy, as did the actress Angelina Jolie, when she discovered that she had inherited the BRCA1 gene that had caused her mother's fatal cancer at the age of 56. With regard to Jolie, the discovery of the gene meant that Jolie was estimated to have an 87 per cent risk of breast cancer and a 50 per cent risk of ovarian cancer, and as such she elected to have a preventative double mastectomy. To share her decision to have the surgery with the public, Jolie wrote a piece for the *New York Times* entitled 'My Medical Choice', in which she stated:

I wanted to write this to tell other women that the decision to have a mastectomy was not easy. But it is one I am very happy that I made. My chances of developing breast cancer have dropped from 87 percent to under 5 percent. I can tell my children that they don't need to fear they will lose me to breast cancer . . . For any woman reading this, I hope it helps you to know you have options. I want to encourage every woman, especially if you have a family history of breast or ovarian cancer, to seek out the information and medical experts who can help you through this aspect of your life, and to make your own informed choices. (Jolie, 2013)

Medical authorities have since reported a distinctive and significant 'Angelina Jolie effect' in the dramatically increased number of women who have sought testing for the BRCA1 gene and a rise in similar preventative double mastectomies, reinforcing the positive (if not life-saving for some women) influence of a major global celebrity. However, as a coda to the chapter that echoes earlier points, the 'Angelina Jolie effect' did, as some medical authorities have reported, lead to a number of women requesting mastectomies who, although diagnosed with cancer, did not have the BRCA1 gene and thus would potentially not benefit from such preventative measures. But, the motivation for the requests was through learning of Jolie's surgery, and as one doctor stated: 'These are patients who say, "can you do for me what Angelina Jolie had done?"' (Harris, 2013, medicaldaily.com). Hence, celebrity influence is palpable and potent.

CONCLUDING POINTS

Celebrity culture is an influential force in numerous ways, from communicating and inspiring fashion choices and epitomizing cultural body ideals, to inspiring people to follow their prescribed exercise regimes or make medical decisions in response to their own experiences and actions. The chapter has largely focused upon the fashion and body debates in relation to celebrity as these are the areas that tend to raise social concerns, primarily surrounding the risks of body dissatisfaction in relation to people who compare themselves unfavourably to an idealized celebrity. And this 'risk' is exacerbated when the reality of such inspirational images are open to question with regard to the levels of digital manipulation that is rife within media industries.

There is, however, a further degree of celebrity influence and inspiration. For instance, as part of Richard Dyer's analysis of Judy Garland in his book *Heavenly Bodies*, he explores the empowering influence that she had on the gay community in the 1950s (and beyond). Dyer argues that this appeal arose from her post-MGM film work as it was a period of her career that saw her develop as an open and emotionally available performer who spoke frankly on TV chat shows about her suicidal behaviour and marital troubles. What this openness offered to the gay community was the revelation that the Garland image that had been efficiently crafted by MGM's publicity machine as 'a story of difference' (2004: 154). Hence, her openness and difference resonated with many who were effectively 'invisible' and marginalized in terms of cultural and political representation, a factor corroborated by a gay man who stated of the significance of attending a Garland concert: 'It was as if the fact that we had gathered to see Garland gave us permission to be gay in public for once' (2004: 140).

Although not gay, Judy Garland demonstrates the effective influence celebrity can have upon sexual discourses, and there have been numerous other female celebrities who have also been subsequently positively celebrated by members of the gay community (including Liza Minnelli, Barbra Streisand, Cher, Madonna, Princess Diana, and Lady Gaga). Furthermore, celebrity figures who are openly gay are increasingly playing a role in countering social and cultural sexual prejudice nationally and across the world. As such, the examples of Elton John, K.D. Lang, Ellen DeGeneres, Sir Ian McKellen, Ricky Martin, Portia de Rossi, Zachary Quinto, Jim Parsons, Neil Patrick Harris, Adam Lambert, Tom Daley, and Ellen Page illustrate the ways in which celebrity culture can be seen to provide an effective public forum for gay representations, the articulation of gay identity, and political opposition against sexual intolerance and discrimination. Therefore, celebrity influence is multidimensional, often controversial, but a potent social and cultural force.

FURTHER READING

Readers wishing to further explore the concept of habitus and an example of the concept applied to celebrity culture should consult:

- Barron, L. (2007) 'The habitus of Elizabeth Hurley: celebrity, fashion, and identity branding', *Fashion Theory*, 11(4): 443–61.

- Bourdieu, P. (1984) *Distinction: A Social Critique of the Judgement of Taste*. London: Routledge & Kegan Paul.

- Craik, J. (1994) *The Face of Fashion: Cultural Studies in Fashion*. London and New York: Routledge.

Regarding the feminist approaches to the wider issue and pressures of body image and airbrushing, readers should consult:

- Bordo, S. (1993) *Unbearable Weight: Feminism, Western Culture and the Body*. Berkeley, CA: University of California Press.

- Nelson, J. (2012) *Airbrushed Nation: The Lure and Loathing of Women's Magazines*. Berkeley, CA: Seal Press.

Finally, for readers who wish to learn more about the thoughts of Jean Baudrillard and the application of his theory to media debates (including that of Daniel Boorstin's idea of the pseudo-event and Reality makeover TV), see:

- Baudrillard, J. (1994) *Simulacra and Simulation*. Ann Arbor, MI: The University of Michigan Press.

- Merrin, W. (2005) *Baudrillard and the Media: A Critical Introduction*. Cambridge: Polity.

- Toffoletti, K. (2014) 'Baudrillard, postfeminism, and the image makeover', *Cultural Politics*, 10(1): 105–19.

10
EXTREME CELEBRITY

CHAPTER OVERVIEW

This chapter examines extreme examples of celebrity culture with the focus upon the levels to which criminals can acquire fame and even adulation due to the degree to which the line between fame and notoriety has been blurred so that there is little to no difference between 'good' and' bad' fame. From the perspective of mainstream celebrity culture, this process is arguably evident in relation to the activities of young actresses such as Lindsay Lohan and Amanda Bynes, both once successful young performers who now more commonly gain media attention due to their issues with DUI offences and erratic public behaviour. However, such behaviour does keep them in the public eye and the subject of journalists and celebrity commentators (a factor that also now surrounds the pop singer Justin Bieber). However, the degree to which infamy has become a legitimate source of celebrity status has extended to criminal figures and their relationship with fame to the degree that individuals who have committed heinous criminal acts, such as serial killers, have acquired celebrity status and 'fan' followings. This chapter, therefore, examines the degree to which celebrity culture has few limits regarding those who can be publicly 'celebrated' with a focus upon the figure of the serial killer. Therefore, to investigate this development and set of arguments, the chapter will look at the following areas:

- Scandal and celebrity
- Crime and media
- The rise of the serial killer
- The serial killer as celebrity
- Murderabilia
- Killing for fame

To elucidate key points regarding instances of extreme celebrity and criminality as a source of 'celebration', the chapter will refer to examples such as Bonnie and Clyde, Jack the Ripper, H.H. Holmes, David Berkowitz, Dennis Rader, John Wayne Gacy, Ted Bundy, and Jeffery Dahmer.

BAD CELEBRITY

In the view of Ellis Cashmore, the relationship between celebrity and scandal has experienced a process of distinctive transformation in recent years. At one stage, he argues, scandals, from sexual revelations to engagements (or even the suspicion of involvement) in illegal acts, inevitably spelt the end of a media career, although it was not until the full establishment of the Hollywood system that the more problematic and personal aspects of the then still nascent celebrity culture began to become the staple of journalism. It was, as Richard deCordova argues, in the early 1920s that newspaper and magazines significantly turned their attention towards the marital problems of Hollywood film stars, especially divorces, infidelities, and more shocking scandals. Of the latter variety, the most significant Hollywood incident of the 1920s was that of the Keystone Cops comedian Roscoe (Fatty) Arbuckle, who, during one of his lavish 'gin jollification' parties, was accused of the sexual assault of the actress Virginia Rappe, whose bladder was ruptured (allegedly due to Arbuckle's weight), and the resulting peritonitis ultimately led to her death.

The repercussions of the Arbuckle case signalled the beginning of a change in the perception of Hollywood, and the stars who comprised it could no longer 'function as a guarantor of the cinema's morality' (2001: 128). In the early Hollywood years, the relationship between studios and cinema/star magazines had been formal, because, as Harris observes, the sexual transgressions were seldom reported on. This was because:

> Early twentieth-century gossip columnists were not rumor mongers but little more than flacks for an industry determined to overcome its image as a hotbed of sexual perversion . . . [because the] . . . major studios restricted the media's access to their famous assets through their own in-house PR departments. (2010: 151)

This seemingly harmonious relationship changed with the collapse of the studio system, and in a world in which now-independent stars represented themselves and attempted to determine press access and copy, 'journalists, previously content to parrot the press releases of studio propaganda machines, became private eyes hunting for scoops' (ibid.); and, argues deCordova, the Arbuckle scandal dramatically changed public perceptions of Hollywood 'debauchery', and the more intrusive and lurid celebrity reporting that followed was centrally defined by the search for celebrity disgrace. After being charged with manslaughter, Arbuckle was ultimately acquitted (subsequent reports alleged that Rappe's death was the result of complications caused by an illegal abortion said to have occurred shortly before her attendance at the 'jollification'), but the damage to his reputation and career was extensive: his films were withdrawn from cinemas and Paramount terminated his contract. Thus, from being one of Hollywood's highest paid stars, 'in the wake of the Rappe scandal film studios ignored him while creditors pursued him. He turned to drink and died destitute aged 46, in 1933' (Cashmore, 2006: 143). However, scandal has, in relation to contemporary celebrity culture, changed from such negative career outcomes.

Referring to Paris Hilton's ascent from famous-as-socialite-heiress to multi-portfolio celebrity figure in the wake of her *One Night In Paris* sex tape, scandals that capture the public's attention with a fusion of 'outrage and delight' work to great strategic advantage in that modern scandals habitually 'create rather than destroy their careers' (ibid.). A survey of scandals involving celebrities as diverse as Rob Lowe, Robert Downey Jr., Winona Ryder, George Michael, Hugh Grant, R. Kelly, Mel Gibson, and Tiger Woods has demonstrated that famous individuals who survive scandals flourish in most instances or at least experience temporary fluctuations in their celebrity status. There are of course notable exceptions, such as the racism scandal surrounding television chef Paula Deen which resulted in the loss of a range of endorsement deals and her television cookery programmes with the Food Network in 2013. The cycling champion Lance Armstrong's 'celebrity brand' was also irreparably tarnished by revelations of performance-enhancing drugs during his Tour de France victories.

Alternatively, there are celebrity figures who have engaged in illegal activities and, in many instances, experienced legal sanctions, for example Roman Polanski, who was arrested and charged in the United States with sexual offences against 13-year-old Samantha Gailey, in 1977. Facing likely imprisonment, Polanski fled to France and still faces arrest if he returns to the United States. Other celebrity figures who have faced legal action include Mike Tyson who was imprisoned for rape, Kobe Bryant who was charged with sexual assault, and Chris Brown who was charged with domestic violence against the pop singer Rihanna, not to mention Lindsay Lohan and Justin Bieber's DUI arrests, Phil Spector's imprisonment for the murder of Lana Clarkson, and the trials of Oscar Pistorius, Michael Jackson, and O.J. Simpson. With regard to Simpson – NFL footballer, sports commentator, and latterly actor – his 1995 trial for allegedly murdering his ex-wife Nicole Brown and her friend Ron Goldman became a media 'megaspectacle'. This was due, according to Douglas Kellner, not only to Simpson's extensive celebrity status and his reputation as an American sports hero, but also to his attempt to evade arrest in a white Bronco (with his friend, A.C. Cowlings), which was pursued by police and filmed by news helicopters and broadcast live on television. The subsequent trial resulted in deep divisions of public and professional attitudes along class, ethnic, and gender lines towards Simpson with regard to the pro and anti-Simpson positions that surrounded the murder trial (and the following civil trial), and accounts of Simpson's behaviour towards Nicole Brown (extra-marital affairs, domestic violence, stalking) were made public.

Consequently, the Simpson trial also, argues Kellner, represented a decisive transformation point 'of news into infotainment and the decline of journalism in a media culture' (2003: 96) as it was broadcast live each day on channels such as CNN and E! Television. As such, the 'affair was a *celebrity spectacle* as well, with the tabloids and mainstream media alike focused on every detail of Simpson's life and the coverage creating new celebrities [such as Simpson's friend and house guest, Kato Kaelin but also Judge Lance Ito] with every twist and turn of the investigation and trial' (2003: 99), and this extended to the reading of the verdict, itself a major media event as people 'gathered in their homes, in public places, in classrooms, and even the stock market stopped doing business and airline flights were delayed so that the TV nation and indeed the Global Village could watch the verdict' (2003: 107). The not-guilty verdict, reached in only four hours, created a media storm of debate, and a continued attitudinal divide that Ellis Cashmore argues was clearly dependent upon Simpson's ethnicity. Opinion polls were carried out during and after the trial and African American respondents believed he was not guilty whereas white Americans felt that he was. In this regard, Simpson was not able to regain his pre-trial media status or re-establish his then burgeoning acting career, and for Cashmore, the reason was related to the relationship between ethnicity and celebrity. As he explains: 'Scandals that once killed careers now boost them: unless the celebrity is black, in which case their status doesn't enhance perceptions of them in the same way as it does for whites' (2006: 159). However, while high levels of public interest can ensure that black celebrities can maintain their celebrity status in the wake of scandals, as Michael Jackson did, Simpson did not. Indeed, his life has been embroiled in further legal problems, such as tax issues in 1999, but most significantly, his arrest for his part in an armed robbery in Las Vegas to recover sports memorabilia he claimed had been stolen from him, for which he was imprisoned in 2008.

A further element of scandal that has emerged concerns individuals who have seemingly used their celebrity to coerce 'fans' to participate in criminal acts, or whose celebrity status has served as a 'mask' to conceal their true deviant identities. An example of the former is the case of Ian Watkins. Watkins was the lead singer of the successful Welsh hard rock band Lostprophets, and was sentenced to 35 years in prison for sexual crimes against the children of two female admirers of the band. The fanatical view of fandom quickly became a factor in the case (indeed, it was even the foundation of Watkins' barrister's defence, saying that her client was subjected to fans who would 'do anything' to keep his attention). The presiding judge, Mr Justice Royce, emphatically singled out the 'Svengali-like' power of celebrity as a key motivator for the crimes in his summing up, stating that:

> You, Watkins, achieved fame and success as the lead singer of Lostprophets. You had many fawning fans. That gave you power. You knew you could use that power to induce young female fans to help satisfy your insatiable lust and take part in the sexual abuse of their own children. (Morris, 2013, theguardianbeta)

The issue of the sexual abuse of children was also at the heart of the posthumous charges levelled against the formerly iconic British entertainer, Jimmy Savile, which formed the basis of an intense subsequent media scandal that affected the BBC. With a career that spanned decades with the BBC on radio and television, Savile, whose trademarked sartorial eccentricity consisted of tracksuits, gold chains, ostentatious rings, sunglasses, and ever-present cigars, was, argues Frank Furedi, at the time of his death in 2011 aged 84, regarded as 'a larger-than-life philanthropist and a national treasure' (2013: 13). This perception was to change radically in the light of revelations made in a television documentary, *Exposure: The Other Side of Jimmy Savile*, broadcast on 3 October, 2012. It effectively 'unmasked' Savile as a sexual predator of young girls whose criminal activities stretched back to the 1960s, taking advantage of his charity work that frequently involved visits to schools and hospitals. The resulting media scandal saw the 'rapid transformation of Savile from a celebrity-saint into the personification of evil' (2013: 13), and a number of well-known British veteran entertainers were subsequently arrested on similar charges.

BONNIE AND CLYDE: EARLY MEDIA 'SUPERSTARS'

The flipside of celebrities who have become involved in scandals and criminal acts (or at least subject to criminal charges), and whose celebrity status has been compromised and, in some instances, ended, are those individuals who have attained celebrity status through avowedly criminal acts and who have garnered widespread media coverage and public interest that has bordered on acclaim and support. While many convicted criminals receive media attention because of their crimes, some have reflexively become aware of their fame and sought to extend and enjoy it. Historically, there are numerous examples of individuals who have achieved a 'Robin Hood' status for their criminal acts – Jesse James, for example, but with regard to palpable celebrity status, the classic example remains that of Bonnie Parker and Clyde Barrow, known 'Bonnie and Clyde'. Embarking upon their short-lived criminal reign of robbery and eventual murder between 1932 and 1934 in Dallas, Texas, their exploits coincided with the Great Depression, which caused widespread unemployment throughout America and resultant poverty which led to a dramatic fall in newspaper consumption (newspapers were considered a luxury few struggling families could afford). In response, Texas newspaper proprietors increased stories about 'colourful criminals' and Bonnie and Clyde were perfect. They were young and daring and their two-year spate of bank robberies (with the wider Barrow Gang) across the state caught the public's attention.

As Jeff Guinn states, 'Clyde and Bonnie came to epitomise the edgy daydreams of the economically and socially downtrodden. Resentful of their own powerlessness and poverty, Barrow Gang fans liked the idea of colourful young rebels sticking it to bankers and cops' (2009: 4). Furthermore, Bonnie and Clyde were aware of this fame and of their status as 'criminal celebrities' and the need for self-publicity. Thus, photographs taken of them by members of their gang were found by the police, and the images were quickly transferred to cinema newsreels and transmitted to the American public.

> So the nation became familiar with nattily dressed Clyde brandishing a menacing Browning Automatic Rifle, and with Bonnie assuming unladylike postures on the bumpers of stolen cars . . . Thanks to the media, Clyde and Bonnie had quickly come to be considered the epitome of scandalous glamour. (Guinn, 2009: 3)

Achieving fame by scandal was (and remains) at the heart of the appeal of Bonnie and Clyde, who were effectively mythologized in their own time (although the Barrow Gang murders of the motorcycle police officers H.D. Murphy and E.B. Wheeler turned public opinion against them) and demonstrates the range of who can enter the realm of celebrity culture. At one level, the 'romance' of Bonnie and Clyde's out-law life reflected the times and served as a real-life Hollywood production, complete with a tragic and brutal ending before the guns of the retired Texas Ranger Frank Hamer's posse. The criminal figure, therefore, has acquired a sustained mystique (think of the allure of the gangster within film noir) and within contemporary culture there has emerged a significant (and profitable) sub-genre of 'true crime' consisting of the publication of memoirs by ex-criminal figures that have propelled them to liter-ary fame and attracted fervent followers. Yet there is another kind of real-life crim-inal figure who has also seemingly attained celebrity status. These are figures who lack the 'romance' of the 1930s gangster, and who are the perpetrators of the most heinous and brutal crimes that have ever been committed, namely the serial killers.

SERIAL KILLERS AND FAME

Debating the appeal of the 'lovable' television serial killer character Dexter Morgan, eponymous star of *Dexter* (2006–2013), Susan Amper concludes: 'Without doubt, serial killers, both real and fictional, fascinate us' (2010: 105). With regard to defi-nitions, serial murder is 'the killing of three or more people over a period of more than 30 days with a significant cooling-off period between the killings' (Holmes and Holmes, 1998: 8). Previously referred to as 'repeat killers', the term 'serial killer' was coined by the FBI detective Robert K. Ressler with the added elements that frequently the victims have no connection to the killer (which is why an earlier term for the crime was 'stranger killing') and that there is no apparent motive (Ressler and Schachtman, 1992; Stratton, 1996; Haggerty, 2009). Yet, while serial killers have become a staple of crime reporting and popular cultural representations, their presence within society is a longstanding one. As Amanda Howard (2010) argues, the first recorded serial killer was Liu Pengli, a member of the Han royal family, and who, as a result of being made Ling of Jidang in 144 BCE, embarked on a murderous reign of terror that resulted in the murder of up to 100 people. A similar body count was reached in ancient Rome by Locusta, a poisoner whose deadly arts inspired a school for poisoners. Later in history, the Renaissance witnessed a series of killers whose infamy has resonated throughout subsequent history, such as Gilles de Rais, who raped and murdered hundreds of children. In the fifteenth century, Vlad Tepes III personally impaled his conquered military enemies, while the sixteenth century produced Countess Elizabeth Bathory who was found guilty of the murder of over 600 women (and who, like Vlad Tepes, would inspire later literary and cinematic Gothic vampire lore).

Despite these historical mass murderers, the first significant acknowledged exam-ple of serial killing is historically related to the brutal murders of five women that occurred in the Whitechapel area of London in 1888, and which have been attributed to the figure known as 'Jack the Ripper'. The perpetrator was never captured, spawn-ing decades of speculation and conspiracies surrounding the killer's identity, and exac-erbated by the 'ritualistic' nature of the bodily mutilation of four of the victims. As

Schmid states, a key element of the Ripper case was the public appeal of the crimes which was rapidly capitalized upon in the form of waxworks, plays, and a tourist trade which began at the time of the murders (with one entrepreneur charging the public a penny to enter the yard that was the scene of one of the murders) and has continued ever since ('Jack's London'). Consequently, 'there was something about the Ripper (and the type of murderer he quickly came to represent) that appealed to thousands of otherwise ordinary people' (2005: 37). Furthermore, the issue of the 'fame' associated with extreme acts of murder was reflected at the same time as the Ripper murders in America by H.H. Holmes who committed a series of killings in his 'Murder Castle', a structure built by Holmes between 1888 and 1890 (Holmes confessed to 27 killings) in order to claim life-insurance policies. Unlike the Ripper, Holmes was apprehended and subsequently executed, but while awaiting execution, he quickly seized upon the economic benefits of the public's interest in him. For instance, he claimed to news reporters that he was taking on the physical charac- teristics of Satan, a bold attempt, argues David Schmid, to exaggerate his 'gothic monster' persona. Furthermore:

> Even after his arrest, Holmes remained attentive to the financial opportunities created by his notoriety, both publishing his own version of events to compete with the flurry of books that appeared about him and, even with the shadow of the gallows hanging over him, negotiating with a newspaper to provide it with an exclusive version of his confession for thousands of dollars. (2005: 55)

Despite Holmes being arguably America's first 'official' serial killer (although other commentators/historians have cited William 'Billy the Kid' Bonney as an earlier example) and was followed by later early twentieth-century individuals such as Carl Panzram and Albert Fish, the 1960s and 1970s constituted the 'Golden Age of Serial Killers' with the crimes of David Berkowitz, John Wayne Gacy, Ted Bundy, and Jeffrey Dahmer. Howard argues that this was the period in which such figures 'were revered as the epitome of psychopathy, both by criminal and psychological profes- sionals and by the general public' (2010: 62).

The issue that has characterized the status of serial killers has been related to the *nature* of their fame, and it is a specific type of recognition. As Schmid argues, the primary characterization of fame revolves around its intrinsically positive qualities – the preserve of singular individuals who have stood out from the general population through the possession of admirable traits, uncommon achievements, or compelling lifestyles. As such, individuals who have acquired fame through criminal acts, while accorded media and public attention, have traditionally been placed within suitably 'negative' categories of fame such as infamy and notoriety, and represent antiheroes rather than heroes. Yet the public prominence and cultural reaction to serial killers implies, according to Schmid, that, within contemporary American culture at least, this traditional dividing line has blurred, if not completely collapsed, and he asserts that there is now little to no difference between fame and notoriety. This is not to say that the notion of fame as a consequence of a meritorious achievement (within sport, politics, music, art, acting, etc.) is still not predominant within celebrity culture, but there has been a palpable decline in the position of merit as an essential dynamic in achieving fame to the extent that now to be 'famous and to be notorious are frequently the same thing (2005: 9).

With hints of Boorstin's approach to fame, the argument to explain this process is one in which fame was historically based upon the performance of a meritorious achievement. Technological developments in printing, and especially the media created since the Graphic Revolution (magazines, radio, cinema, and television), served to 'democratize' celebrity, lessen its elite status, and open it up to more people. Also, crucially, it has been a distinct form of fame progressively concentrated on public visibility rather than purely on the possession of talent. While there is always a risk of falling into the overly-pessimistic position of completely disregarding the role of merit as a means by which to attain fame, a decisive transformation has been the prominence of individuals who are famous because they have been able to attract the public's attention; indeed, comply with Boorstin's classic 'famous for being famous' definition of celebrity.

SERIAL KILLERS AS CELEBRITY FIGURES

While, as Neal Gabler (2001) states, Boorstin's concept does not cover the majority of celebrities who are famous and have attained fame through considerable achievement (from Marlon Brando and Michael Jordan, to Tom Hanks), the contemporary celebrity landscape certainly can provide Boorstinian examples such as Paris Hilton, Snooki, or Kim Kardashian, all expressions of what Gabler calls 'the "Zsa Zsa Factor" in honour of Zsa Zsa Gabor, who parlayed her marriage to actor George Sanders into a brief movie career and the movie career into a much more enduring celebrity' (2001: 2). But regardless of Boorstin's somewhat sweeping statement, a key element remains in the merit issue as a passport to fame to explain the ascent of serial killers to celebrity status, and this is the increasing primacy of contemporary fame being based upon visibility rather than achievement. The result of this, argues Schmid, is that there is little ground between good and bad forms of fame, and with the decline of merit as the *only* qualification for fame, public recognition and self-exposure are of equal weight and notoriety is no impediment to fame. At one level, this process is arguably discernible with regard to 'fallen' celebrities whose negative lifestyles have eclipsed their professional statuses but which keep them within the public gaze, for instance the actresses Lindsay Lohan and Amanda Bynes, both former child stars who have publicly-documented DUI arrests, and the pop singer Justin Bieber. But in a wider context, the erasing of the line between fame and notoriety, and the centrality of visibility within securing renown, mean that crime is not only not an obstacle to achieving fame, but is a virtual guarantor of celebrity status. As Schmid states:

> The iconic status of serial killers in contemporary American culture is compelling evidence of the collapse of the difference between fame and notoriety. In particular, the decline of merit as a defining factor in fame means that nowadays to be famous and to be notorious are frequently the same thing. (2005: 9)

A crucial factor here is that the media technologies which have enabled individuals to become famous are also little different in relation to creating celebrities from criminal figures. Therefore, just as early twentieth-century mass communication technologies such as newspapers, photography, and film established Hollywood film stars as a newly emergent celebrity class, the same technologies were simultaneously employed to bestow celebrity status upon criminals (as evidenced by the reporting of Bonnie and Clyde, for example), and as a result the exploits of criminals have been widely publicized. Indeed, sensationalized accounts of crime have long played a prominent role within journalism, especially the lurid accounts of criminals and their crimes within classic 'yellow journalism'. Regardless of earlier examples (Jack the Ripper, etc.), the serial killer, argues Schmid, was truly 'born' around 1985 within American news media as a result of changes in the news reporting of crime. This is linked to the apparent 'tabloidization' of news agencies and changing editorial practices in response to the success of the likes of *National Enquirer*. Consequently, dramatic (but uncommon) crimes such as serial murder attained more concentrated levels of news coverage and news primacy, but with a strong degree of over-reporting incidents of serial murder and exaggerating the extent of the phenomenon.

The result of such reporting, argues Schmid, is that the previously 'faceless' figure of the multiple murderer was personified as the serial killer, a tag that came with a roster of 'characters' such as Ted Bundy, John Wayne Gacy, and Jeffrey Dahmer to ensure that within this period, there was both a distinctive moral panic and a definitive 'folk devil', a social grouping held to be a source of fear and disruption (the concept of the folk devil is most closely associated with Cohen's (1980) classic book, *Folk Devils and Moral Panics*). As such, the sudden 'discovery' of the serial killer in American culture was similarly reported as a unique form of emergent crime, with an exceptional and terrifying different type of criminal figure that constituted a threat to both social norms and values, but also a represented a terrifying source of physical threat in the form of unimagined acts of violence and murder. Schmid argues that:

> The key element of this panic was that serial murder was a qualitatively new phenomenon, that it was growing rapidly, that there were a large number of serial murderers active at any given time, that serial murder was a distinctly American phenomenon, and that the crime had reached epidemic proportions, claiming four thousand victims a year – with different forms of media conjoining to disseminate the myth and to establish a few 'representative' serial killers as household names. (2005: 15)

Thus, the moral panic not only dominated crime reporting and fictional media forms (novels, cinema, and popular music), it also established serial killers as celebrities. Haggerty picks up this point with reference to the ways in which crime and celebrity stories have proliferated within the era of Internet news and multi-channel television, again emphasizing the ways in which committing a 'sensational' crime is one of the most direct ways in which an individual can gain media and public attention and, consequently, celebrity. Indeed, the celebrity status of serial killers is not lost on serial killers themselves. As Haggerty observes in relation to John Wayne Gacy's attitude to his 'fame', Gacy 'took pride in his sinister celebrity, bragging that he had been the subject of eleven hardback books, thirty-one paperbacks, two screenplays, one movie, one off-Broadway play, five songs, and over 5,000 articles' (2009: 174).

MURDERABILIA

A crucial point of significance is that Gacy's own sense of celebrity was matched by public interest and the existence of 'fans' of his grisly route to fame. As Fox and Levin argue, hero worship was conventionally and historically bestowed upon meritorious individuals, but the process has extended to the fandom of antiheroes who have 'distinguished themselves in the worst possible ways by reaching the pinnacle of "success" as murderers' (2005: 6). As evidence of such fandom, they cite the marketing of serial killer merchandise such as collector card ranges featuring Edward Gein, Jeffrey Dahmer, Theodore Bundy, and Charles Manson, while magazines such as *People* have featured serial killers such as Jeffrey Dahmer on their covers. Consequently, such developments have served to glorify serial killers and established a market for personal effects related to them, which ranges from serial killers' hair and toenail cuttings, to the artwork of Gacy which became highly collectable following his execution in 1994 for the murder of 33 young men (their bodies were found in the crawlspace beneath his house).

Further examples also include the controversial decision made by the rock band Guns 'N' Roses to record a song composed by Charles Manson for their 1993 album, *The Spaghetti Incident*. The marketing of items associated with serial killers and cultural products which feature them, dubbed 'murderabilia', constitutes what is now a considerable serial killer industry (films, television, T-shirts, collecting cards, books, websites, television), have granted serial killers maximum visibility and, given the primacy of visibility as a key element of contemporary fame, established some of them as 'stars'. The existence and profitability of murderabilia, argues Schmid, 'reminds us that celebrity culture and consumer culture intermingle just as complexly with serial killers as they do with film stars' (2005: 21). And, although serial killers are usually reserved for mention by brutal death metal music, Jeffrey Dahmer has been referenced in mainstream pop songs, most notably Ke$ha's 'Cannibal' and Katy Perry's 'Dark Horse'.

Of course, the psychological, neuropsychological, and sociocultural motivations that drive individuals to engage in serial murder are complex. As Lawrence Miller observes, serial killers are often found to have extensive past criminal histories and patterns of anti-social and criminal behaviour that are rooted in adolescence, and the killers are invariably motivated by violent fantasies that inexorably are built in tandem 'with a neuropsychodynamically driven hunger that only the orgiastic release of torturing and murdering another human being will provide' (2014a: 1). However, the issue of fame is, for many commentators, a significant one. Therefore, there are no ostensible obstacles the serial killer being part of celebrity culture. Indeed, the trajectory of fame and celebrity has almost naturalized it to the extent that serial killers can be consumed in exactly the same way as pop, rock, or film stars in terms of merchandise and cultural products. However, a further dimension to this analysis of extreme fame is the reflective awareness of some serial killers of the ways in which their crimes can lift them out of anonymity and enable them to achieve fame through murder.

CONTACTING THE MEDIA: DAVID 'SON OF SAM' BERKOWITZ AND DENNIS RADER

Currently serving six life sentences for the murder of six people and the wounding of seven others, using a .44 calibre pistol, from 1976 to 1977 in New York City, David Berkowitz is especially significant because of the close linkages between his murders, the media coverage of them, and Berkowitz's reaction to his 'fame' and public interest in his actions. After his arrest, Berkowitz commented that:

> I finally had convinced myself that it was good to do it, necessary to do it, and that the public wanted me to do it. The latter part I believe until this day. I believe that many were rooting for me. This was the point at which the papers began to pick up vibes and information that something big was happening out in the streets. Real big! (Schmid, 2005: 307)

As Schmid continues, on one level it would be simple to reject the killer's explanation as merely the result of insanity. Indeed, Berkowitz's self-imposed nickname, 'Son of Sam', was derived from the name of his neighbour, Sam Carr. On his arrest, Berkowitz explained to the arresting police officers his belief that Sam Carr was a 'high demon' who could transmit his diabolical powers to Berkowitz through Carr's dog, a black Labrador (although he later recanted on this story, claiming that he simply wished to punish his neighbour for the noise that his dog made). Thus, Berkowitz stands as one of the key 'celebrity killers' due to the extent that he was reflectively aware of his 'fame', and he was intimately embroiled with the media coverage of his crimes to the extent that he was convinced that the public supported his murders because 'the media chronicled his every deed in a state of mounting excitement' (2005: 307). In particular, Berkowitz posted a series of letters to the *New York Post* columnist, Jimmy Breslin, which even included clues and support for the police actively hunting him – 'P.S, Please inform all the detectives working on the case that I wish them luck. Keep them digging, drive on. Think positive' (Fox and Levin, 2012: 9) – and on his capture he cried out to the arresting officers 'You finally got me!' (Hickey, 2013: 351). As Robert Ressler (who conducted interviews with the incarcerated killer) states, Berkowitz's relationship with the media instilled within him a palpable desire to achieve notoriety and even went as far as him designing a 'Son of Sam' logo to accompany his letters.

In Ressler's view, Berkowitz reacted to his publicity, and thus it 'was clear to everyone . . . that Berkowitz wished to be famous (or infamous) and was murdering in order to impress and shock society and thereby gain attention and identity' (Ressler and Shachtman, 1992: 84). Nevertheless, Ressler identifies, and criticizes, the uneasy relationship that developed between Berkowtiz's avowed desire for renown and the media coverage of his crimes, to the extent that the FBI detective ruefully concluded: 'it has always been clear to me that Berkowitz kept on killing so he would continue to be the focus of columnists such as Jimmy Breslin' (1992: 84).

David Berkowitz is not the only serial killer to be conscious of both media coverage and the way in which murder can lead to a form of celebrity status. For instance, Dennis Rader, aka the 'BTK' killer (BTK stood for bind, torture, kill), murdered ten people between 1974 and 1991. With regard to fame-seeking, in 1978, Rader sent a letter to a Wichita television station to bemoan the lack of media coverage that his acts of murder had garnered, writing: 'How many do I have to kill . . . before I get my name in the paper or some national attention?' (Fox and Levin, 2012: 9). Rader stopped killing and effectively disappeared for over a decade following his last murder, reappearing in 2004 to continue his demand for media attention, an action that actually led to his capture. In 2004, Rader began to send puzzles to the police and media that purported to reveal his identity if solved (a practice similar to the 1970s Zodiac Killer, who was never captured and whose identity remains unknown). Rader's game-playing provided the authorities with a vital link to him as police were able to trace the Internet Protocol (IP) address of the computer used to create the puzzles and they arrested Rader in 2005. Yet, as Hickey notes, this outcome might have been the desired conclusion as it 'was as if he wanted to be caught just so he could take public acknowledgement for his murders' (2013: 254). Directly citing the case of Rader, Leo Braudy places the attention-seeking behaviour of serial killers in the context of the human drive to be unique that has intensified since World War II through mass-media technologies that greatly expanded the ways in which individuals can seek and acquire fame, but as far as criminal routes to renown, and especially the acts of serial killers in this regard are concerned, 'the concept of fame has been grotesquely distended, and the line between public achievement and private pathology grown dimmer as the claims grow more bizarre' (1986: 3).

SERIAL KILLING AND THE PURSUIT OF FAME

To demonstrate just how explicit this pursuit of fame through murder has become, Rojek (2001) cites the example of David Copeland, who, in June 2000 in London, was given six life sentences for committing a series of bombings that ultimately killed three people and injured 139. Named 'the Soho Nail Bomber' by the media, the dominant theme of Copeland's arrest and his subsequent trial was that he was pleased to have been arrested because of the public attention that he would receive through the media coverage of his trial. As he stated of his capture: 'I've been dreaming about this for ages. Doing what I did, getting caught, going to court – it's my destiny. If no one remembers who you were, you never existed' (2001: 143). The significance of Copeland's actions is that they served as an example of an individual subverting the conventional nature of acquiring the status of achieved celebrity, with its resultant public acclamation. In this regard, the act of serial murder was a compensation for the lack of a talent that might result in the procurement of fame, and, consequently, if the drive for fame cannot be met through conventional routes, then 'some individuals will have a compelling propensity to use violence as a means of acquiring fame through notoriety' (2001: 146). The impetus for such behaviour is that many social actors experience what Rojek calls 'achievement famine'. This is a specific psychological state that springs from an acute sense of frustration at being seemingly barred from the rewards of fame and celebrity, from enhanced wealth status to the degree to which celebrities can form romantic/sexual relationships with other, invariably physically attractive, celebrity figures.

While the rhetoric of the development of fame through various communication mediums and technologies has pointed towards a democratization of fame, a perception exacerbated by the rise of Reality TV and forums such as YouTube by which talent is *not* necessary to gain public interest and adulation, the reality for most is that the 'democratic ideal of being recognized as extraordinary, special or unique collides with the bureaucratic tendency of modern societies to standardize and routinize existence' (2001: 149). In this perspective, criminal activity arguably provides a means for an individual to stand out from the general population. Consequently, many who commit criminal acts are not merely opportunistic, but are driven by a desire to confront conventional morality and stand against the forces of law and order, deriving a palpable sense of superiority and engaging in a deliberate process of 'one-upmanship' against conventional society, a quality that is linked to some serial killers and their desire for fame.

To illustrate this, a prime example is that of Ted Bundy, whose handsome and seemingly 'well-educated' qualities (at one stage he studied law in Salt Lake City) frequently deflected attention away from his crimes, the murder of up to 40 young women committed from the 1960s to the late 1970s. Having engaged in murder for over a decade, Bundy was arrested and found guilty of aggravated kidnapping in 1976 and sentenced to prison. However, he escaped, twice, from custody to assault and murder again before being arrested by police – quite accidentally, as they had simply been 'puzzled by his erratic driving' (Wilson and Seaman, 2007: 265). With regard to fame, Rojek argues that psychiatric investigations carried out on Bundy when in custody reported that part of his motive to murder was a desire to be arrested so that he could set himself up against authority at his trial. Indeed, his desire to take centre stage was such that he conducted his own defence and was 'reported to have behaved with a careless, nonchalant charm' (2001: 153), although he was found guilty, sentenced to death, and executed on 24 January, 1989. Reports suggest that during his trial, Bundy was a charismatic and narcissistic figure, whose 'charms' were effective. In addition to attracting a number of Ted 'groupies', women declaring sexual attraction and devotion to serial killers, Bundy's appeal even extended to his judge, Edward Cowart, who, upon sentencing him to death, stated:

> You're a bright young man. You'd have made a good lawyer, and I'd have loved to have you practice in front of me – but you went another way, partner. Take care of yourself. I don't have any animosity to you, I want you to know that. (Schmid, 2005: 216)

However, as Ressler (who interviewed the killer) notes, attitudes such as that of Judge Cowart together with newspaper coverage established a 'romanticized' image of Bundy that effectively and successfully obscured the true nature of his crimes, which were horrific and which involved strangulation, sexual assault, bodily dismemberment, and necrophilia (and one of his last victims was a 12-year-old girl). Yet Bundy is not alone in explicitly linking murderous activity to a desire to achieve celebrity status. For example, Charles Starkweather, who killed 11 people between 1957 and 1958, resisted the chance to mitigate his case with a plea of insanity at his trial because he felt that he would rapidly be forgotten by the public if he was judged to be insane. Rather, Starkweather emphasized his association with the 'rebel without a cause' film star James Dean, and justified his murderous actions as a deliberate act of 'revenge' on the American social system that limited his life chances and blocked any authentic paths to celebrity status. But perhaps the most stark motivation to acquire fame through an act of murder was reflectively stated by Mark David Chapman, the man who shot and killed John Lennon in 1981, and who later justified his action to the American US TV interviewer Barbara Walters stating that: 'I thought by killing him I would acquire his fame . . . I was Mr Nobody until I killed the biggest somebody on earth' (Rojek, 2001: 154). It is interesting to note, bearing in mind the degree to which media discourses 'created' serial killers, that the Russian serial killer Andrei Chikatilo's crimes were unknown to the public due to the political suppression of news coverage. Dubbed the 'Rostov Butcher', Chikatilo murdered 52 women and children between 1978 and 1990, but his crimes were hidden from public knowledge as Soviet authorities did not publicize the murders (and consequently potential victims were unaware of the presence of a killer within their community) in order to 'convince the world that compared to the 'decadent West', Russia was virtually free of crime' (Wilson and Seaman, 2007: 311).

FICTIONAL SERIAL KILLER 'STARS'

The corollary, argues Schmid, to real-life killers gaining media attention and celebrity status is a pop cultural fascination with serial killers that covers fiction, music, cinema, and television. While the serial killer biopic *Monster* (2003) secured Charlize Theron a Best Actress Oscar for her portrayal of Aileen Wuornos (and there have been biopics of Charles Manson, Ed Gein, John Wayne Gacy, Ted Bundy, Jeffrey Dahmer, and Richard Ramirez), fictional serial killers have also gained Academy Awards. The most notable example is *The Silence of the Lambs* (1990), based upon Thomas Harris' novel, which won multiple Oscars, including best actor for Anthony Hopkins' portrayal of the urbane serial killer, Hannibal 'the Cannibal' Lecter. While the Lecter character would feature in further films such *Hannibal* (2001), *Red Dragon* (2002), *Hannibal Rising* (2007), and the television series, *Hannibal* (2013–), and represents a purely fictitious figure, the issue is that the prominence and enthusiastic fandom of Lecter 'reconfirmed the continuing status of the serial killer as a form of "superstar" and demonstrates the widespread and persistent fascination that exists with serial killers' (2005: 114). Moreover, this fascination has extended beyond Lecter with further cult characters such as Bret Easton Ellis' Patrick Bateman, the body image-and-status-obsessed Wall Street trader whose savage acts of murder and mutilation serve equally as an exploration of Bundy-esque charisma and a presentation of the serial killer as a metaphor for 1980s neoliberal rapacious and hyper-consumerist capitalism (Jarvis, 2007). Within contemporary television the figure of the serial killer has found frequent expression in crime shows such as *C.S.I.*, *Criminal Minds*, and *The Mentalist*, and programmes which explicitly deal with the cult-like attraction of serial murderers, such as *The Following*. Furthermore, characters such as Dexter Morgan, the eponymous 'hero' of *Dexter*, with his 'code' that diverts him from murder of the general public to target instead fellow serial killers that, argues Schmid, made the character 'a sympathetic, even identificatory, figure to the audience' (2010: 133).

So, although Hannibal Lecter and Dexter are fictional characters, they contribute to the pervasive cultural presence and accessibility of the serial killer and are part of a fandom spectrum that, for some, includes their real-life counterparts who have transcended notoriety to be little, if any, different from many other celebrity figures. Indeed, at one macabre level, they are individuals who would not be in possession of fame without their pathological acts of murder – their own alternative form of achievement.

CONCLUDING POINTS

As communication media developed, from the printing press, portraiture, mass-circulation newspapers, and the chief audio-visual technologies of the Graphic Revolution, what stands as being worthy of fame and who constitute the famous have widened. Furthermore, the apparent dissolution of the conventional divide between infamy and fame, conjoined with the primacy of public visibility, has resulted in a celebrity culture whereby criminality is as likely a qualification to fame as acting, musical talents, or achievements of merit. But, of course, Braudy's conception of the urge to be unique predates the mechanical reproduction of print and images and, when we return to the themes raised in Chapter 1, crime, brutality, and violence, from Herostratus' fame-guaranteeing act of arson, through to the military campaigns and conquests of Alexander the Great and Julius Caesar, the line between achievement, merit, heroism, and brutality is rooted within the history of fame and casts the serial killer's presence within the pantheon of fame as not quite as unprecedented as it might first seem, a conclusion Schmid proffers in his observation that 'we might best interpret celebrity serial killers as continuous, rather than discontinuous, with the history of fame' (2005: 10). Although, it is important to acknowledge that not all serial killers do achieve high levels of celebrity, especially non-American perpetrators.

For instance, British murderers such as Peter Sutcliffe (the 'Yorkshire Ripper'), Dennis Nielsen (whose crimes bore some similarities to those of Jeffrey Dahmer), Fred and Rose West, and Harold Shipman (who, with a body count of at least 250 victims, killed more people than any previous serial killer) remain firmly within the notorious category of fame, while Myra Hindley and Ian Brady, both known as the 'Moors Murderers' for their murders of five young people committed between 1963 and 1965, are vehemently beyond 'celebrification', with popular cultural and artistic projects featuring references to them and their imagery eliciting critique, condemnation, and even sometimes displays of public violence (the vandalism of artworks bearing Hindley's face, for example).

Nevertheless, the figure of the serial killer continues to have considerable cultural appeal and fascination, and especially those associated with the 'Golden Age' of serial murder have been, and continue to be, regarded not as notorious, but as 'stars'. In this regard, Fox and Levin have no doubts concerning the ease with which serial killers have assumed a position within celebrity status, and the implications this admission has:

> By granting celebrity status to villains . . . we may be inadvertently providing young people with a dangerous model for gaining national prominence. We may also be giving to the worst among us exactly what they hope to achieve – celebrity status. (2012: 16)

FURTHER READING

The chapter has examined serial killers largely in relation to media and celebrity culture and has due to necessity omitted much that explores the crime of serial killing from criminological, sociological, and psychological perspectives. To gain a wider perspective and understanding of the complex psychological and sociocultural issues, theories, and debates that surround the crime of serial killing and the differing patterns that such crimes take, readers should consult:

- Hickey, E.W. (2013) *Serial Murderers and Their Victims*. Andover: Cengage Learning.

- Miller, L. (2014a) 'Serial killers: I. Subtypes, patterns, and motives', *Aggression and Violent Behaviour*, 19(1); 1–11.

- Miller, L. (2014b) 'Serial killers: II. Development, dynamics, and forensics', *Aggression and Violent Behaviour*, 19(1): 12–22.

CELEBRITY CULTURE: CONCLUSIONS

Evaluating the status of fame in the mid-1990s, the science fiction author, J.G. Ballard, author of books such as *Crash* and *The Atrocity Exhibition* (both of which are concerned with icons of fame), observed that although celebrity was a crucial factor within the media landscape, to the extent that it constituted the 'fuel' that pushed the media machine forward, nevertheless it was beginning to falter. This was the result of the steady decline in the lack of admiration for individuals truly worthy of public praise. Thus, where once approbation was directed towards world leaders of the stature of JFK, in the 1990s it had alternatively drifted towards celebrities of the stature of television personalities, individuals whose fame was not built upon any firm foundation of substantial achievement. Consequently, the cache of fame had diminished to such an extent that Ballard stated that the celebrity 'system is entropic, energy is running down. It may be that we're nearing the end of celebrity' (quoted in Vale and Ryan, 2004: 80).

Suffice to say, Ballard's predication was highly inaccurate, indeed, far from ending in this period, celebrity culture was gathering pace and intensifying as a cultural force, aided not only by the development of new media communication technologies and platforms, but also by the rise of entirely new genres that radically changed perceptions of who could be a celebrity, namely Reality TV. Indeed, the genre of Reality TV has, in little over a decade, graduated from formats such as once-a-year media spectacles like *Big Brother*, to dominating entire television channels, most notably TLC (The Learning Channel). As such, the twenty-first century has seen celebrity develop and proliferate to the extent that it is transmitted by and embedded into media to an unprecedented degree, and on a global scale. To reinforce the centrality of this culture (and to dispel the persistent cultural reactions to both celerity and its study on the grounds that it is a trivial subject that lacks seriousness and weight), Graeme Turner stresses its economic significance in relation to its centrality within the entertainment industries. This is because

> Celebrity has become a central structural component of the contemporary political economy of the media; take away celebrity and the industries which feed it, and some of the basic support systems for contemporary commercial media production go with them. (2014: 145)

Celebrity matters, then, and its economic force is not, as Chapter 7 argued, a W
phenomenon. Celebrity culture is very much a global culture and there are
industries and cultural forms (such as Bollywood or K-pop) that have little or no need
for Western consumers, but possess indigenous celebrity cultures with extensive and
devoted fanbases, both nationally and abroad in the form of receptive diasporic communities. However, the economic nature of celebrity is not limited to enterprises that
are directly involved with it (the film, television, music, advertising, or modelling
industries, for example), but as Chapter 3 explored, celebrities are intimately linked
with the capitalistic system in more complex ways.

For example, while leading brand manufacturers employ celebrities to endorse
their products and lend their glamour and appeal to advertising campaigns, many
such figures juxtapose their lucrative endorsement deals with the business of establishing themselves as brands and producing products for public consumption in their
own name. Consequently, the fashion and fragrance industries have seen a marked
increase in celebrity brands, predicated on the pressure that the toughest challenge
that a new brand faces in the marketplace, namely getting its branded identity
noticed among its numerous competitors, is overcome due to the instant recognizabil-
ity of the celebrity on whom the brand is based. As such, the contemporary economic
landscape is now populated by a growing number of individual celebrity business
empires, from Beyoncé and Jay-Z, to Justin Timberlake and the Kardashians. And
while there are critical perspectives that can be taken towards this development,
that it arguably validates Adorno's view of the machinations of an insidious culture
industry, or indeed a potent form of Marxist 'commodity fetishism' that seduces consumers with celebrity glamour and fidelity while maximizing profits, the centrality of celebrity culture within the economic system is undeniable and potent. For
instance, a middle way between endorsement and brand ownership is the degree to
which celebrities take roles as Creative Directors within the brands they advertise.
However, few such endorsements yield success (for example, Pharrell Williams' work
with the MTV alternative music channel, Karmaloop TV, or Lady Gaga's creative
relationship with Polaroid). Thus, celebrity endorsement is not all-powerful and consumers are discerning.

To emphasize the social centrality of celebrity culture, this book has explored it
through reference to major facets of the contemporary world, such as economics, but
also through the ways in which the political system is, on the one hand, adopting the
visual performative and image-dominated motifs of the celebrity world, while on the
other, it is serving as a space in which celebrities are increasingly involving themselves.
Accordingly, while celebrity advocacy of political causes is laudable with regard to
raising awareness of issues, fund-raising, and engaging social actors with the political process (P. Diddy's 'Vote of Die' initiative, for example), Cooper Lawrence's concept of the 'Celebritocracy' is, nevertheless, a pertinent means by which to evaluate
the centrality of such political involvement, and to be cautious in light of the weight
that celebrity citizens' voices have in relation to the general citizenry. Of course, the
cynical view of Ilan Kapoor (that involvement in political causes is frequently related

to celebrity brand enhancement rather than pure philanthropy) cannot be overlooked regarding the potentially deleterious effect of celebrity political activity (risking rendering politics as a further branch of the entertainment industry), and the degree to which Alberoni's assertion that the influence of the famous would never extend into institutional power is now far less clear-cut than it was when he formulated it.

The major theme that runs throughout *Celebrity Cultures: An Introduction* is the way in which celebrity resonates with key aspects of modern culture and communicative practices, and how it is at the heart of vicissitudes within the communication industries. For example, as Chapter 6 examined, its historical symbiosis with professional journalism shows continuities (the edgy relationship between publicity-seeking and privacy protection through recourse to the law) and distinctive transformations (celebrity content increasingly displacing hard news and social media sites, and Internet-based insiders (such as Perez Hilton) rendering newspaper gossip columnists increasingly redundant).

Therefore, given the economic and political presence and multidimensional nature of celebrity, it is no surprise that the monolithic critical view, that celebrity is imposed upon a passive population simply for profit creation, is limited as individuals use celebrity in myriad ways. For instance, the modes by which fan behaviour towards celebrities has been transformed in relation to social media reflects the centrality of such technologies and the ways in which communicative practices have distinctly altered throughout the twenty-first century.

So, while Henry Jenkins' conception of the fan as a 'textual poacher' retains its significance, the evolution of this status into that of the 'collaborator' (as explored in Chapter 5) expresses the degree to which the effort of labour expended in being an active fan in an 'analogue' culture has been profoundly modified in the digital world. Via social media networks the classic para-social relation distance has diminished due to the immediacy of messages from celebrities and the regular posting of information and images, some of a candid and personal nature seldom seen in pre-digital media cultures or contemporary mainstream journalism (Rihanna, Kim Kardashian, Nicki Minaj, or Miley Cyrus' 'Selfies' on Instagram or Vin Diesel's bedroom karaoke), or to witnessing celebrities engaging in public feuds in real time. And while the chance of a personal message from a major celebrity is unlikely (One Direction, Katy Perry, and Lady Gaga's Facebook and Twitter accounts have tens of millions of followers), the networks are spaces in which fans can gather, express, and share their fandom directly with each other.

Although that a minority of fans seeking to transcend the para-social relation and sometimes engaging in celebrity stalking behaviour represent an element of extreme fandom, the idea that celebrity culture acts as a form of social currency (as Carol Brooks suggests) is a further indicator of the ways in which social actors use celebrity in a variety of ways. Hence, far from being uniformly in thrall to celebrity culture, individuals utilize, criticize, reject, and evaluate it. Therefore, as unlikely as it may appear, the function of social solidarity, as expressed over 100 years ago by the French sociologist Émile Durkheim, can be discerned in how we relate to celebrity, and how, within complex and fast-paced societies, talking about celebrities and their antics arguably constitutes a potent form of 'social glue'. This is especially significant the 'liquid' quality of many cultures and, even here, the pace of social transformation and innovation is reflected within accelerating media systems and the velocity in which celebrities break into the public eye. For example, although both prime examples of Chris Rojek's 'achieved' category, the young pop/hip-hop stars Lorde and Iggy Azalea have emerged as significant and globally famous figures purely on the basis of their musical debuts.

This is not to suggest that the critical evaluations of celebrity culture are without validity. The issue of celebrity influence raises perennial cultural fears concerning the effects that this culture can have on wider populations; although, as Chapter 9 stresses, the reasons why individuals develop eating disorders are complicated, within these debates the role of celebrities perceived to have 'perfect' bodies is a potent one, and this becomes even more complicated when the validity of many celebrity-based fashion and advertising images are questioned with regard to the extent to which they have been digitally altered to present illusions of perfection.

Furthermore, while serial killers are a comparatively rare criminal phenomenon, the degree to which some killers achieve a mode of celebrity status does raise issues regarding the nature of celebrity. As argued in Chapter 10, the once clear boundary between good and bad forms of fame has become progressively blurred. This process has led to concerns regarding fame in the contemporary world whereby media discourses are unconcerned with the issue of merit, and celebrity status can result from anti-social or scandalous behaviour. For instance, Lindsay Lohan's personal problems and driving under the influence convictions and Justin Bieber's various criminal charges have not resulted in either individual disappearing from the public eye, but they find themselves at the heart of more intensive media attention and coverage. Indeed, anti-social behaviour can act as a potent means to raise a public profile, as illustrated by Solange Knowles' (the considerably less famous sister of Beyoncé) physical attack on Jay-Z in May 2014, an act that dramatically raised her profile due to extensive media coverage and public media-based debate surrounding the motivations of her behaviour.

Ultimately, although it has its roots in the ancient world as evidenced by the deliberate and ingenious fame-seeking strategies of military leaders such as Alexander the Great and Julius Caesar, celebrity is a cultural force that developed as a specific cultural force apace throughout the twentieth century and is now a multi-faceted global cultural phenomenon, and whether the object of devotion, scorn, or bewilderment, it intersects with the dominant social and cultural institutions and values of the modern world. As such, it is difficult to imagine any contemporary commentator confidently predicting the end of celebrity culture in the near future.

BIBLIOGRAPHY

Aaker, D.A. (2010) *Building Strong Brands*. London: Pocket Books.

Adorno, T.W. (1954) 'How to look at television', *The Quarterly of Film and Television*, 8(3): 213–35.

Adorno, T.W. (2006) *The Culture Industry*. London and New York: Routledge.

Adorno, T.W. and Horkheimer, M. (1997) *Dialectic of Enlightenment*. London: Verso Books.

Alberoni, F. (1972) 'The powerless "elite": theory and sociological research on the phenomenon of the stars', in D. McQuail (ed.), *Sociology of Mass Communications*. Harmondsworth: Penguin, pp. 75–99.

Allan, S. (2006) 'Citizen journalists on the scene: the London bombings and Hurricane Katrina', *Online News*. London: Open University Press, pp. 143–69.

Allen, S. (2013) *Citizen Witnessing: Revisioning Journalism in Times of Crisis*. Cambridge: Polity.

Amper, S. (2010) 'The serial killer as superhero', in S. Waller (ed.), *Serial Killers – Philosophy for Everyone: Being and Killing*. Oxford: Wiley-Blackwell.

Anden, K. (2013) *Amateur Images and Global News*. London: Intellect.

Andrejevic, M. (2002) 'The kinder, gentler gaze of Big Brother: Reality TV in the era of digital capitalism, *New Media and Society*, 4(2): 251–70.

Ang, I. (1996) *Living Room Wars: Rethinking Media Audiences for a Postmodern World*. London: Routledge.

Anonymous. (2013) 'U2 frontman chased down street by German anarchists shouting "Make Bono history"'. *Independent*, Tuesday 24 September.

Atkins, C. (2012) 'How to fool the tabloids over and over again', in R. Keeble and J. Mair (eds), *The Phone Hacking Scandal: Journalism on Trial*. Suffolk: Abramis, pp. 25–37.

Augustine, St. (1984) *City of God*. London: Penguin.

Baglow, J.S. (2007) 'The rights of the corpse'. *Mortality*, 12(3): 223–39.

Bailey, S. (2005) *Media Audiences and Identity: Self-Construction in the Fan Experience*. Basingstoke: Palgrave Macmillan.

Banks, D. and Hanna, M. (2009) *McNae's Essential Law for Journalists*. Oxford: Oxford University Press.

Barker, C. (1999) *Television, Globalization and Cultural Identities*. Buckingham: Open University Press.

Barnes, R.D. (2010) *Outrageous Invasions: Celebrities' Private Lives, Media, and the Law*. Oxford: Oxford University Press.

Barron, L. (2007) 'The habitus of Elizabeth Hurley: celebrity, fashion, and identity branding', *Fashion Theory*, 11(4): 443–61.

Baudrillard, J. (1990) *Fatal Strategies*. New York: Semiotext(e)/Pluto.

Baudrillard, J. (1994) *Simulacra and Simulation*. Ann Arbor, MI: The University of Michigan Press.

Baudrillard, J. (2005) *The System of Objects*. London and New York: Verso.

Bauman, Z. (2000) *Liquid Modernity*. Cambridge: Polity Press.

Bauman, Z. (2003) *Liquid Love*. Cambridge: Polity Press.

Bauman, Z. (2005) *Liquid Life*. Cambridge: Polity Press.

Bauman, Z. (2007) *Liquid Times: Living in an Age of Uncertainty*. Cambridge: Polity Press.

Baym, N.K. (2012) 'Fans or friends? Seeing social media audiences as musicians do', *Participations: Journal of Audience and Reception Studies*, 9(2): 286–316.

BBC, Asia Pacific. (2011) 'Indonesia sex tape star is jailed'. 31 January 2011, http://www.bbc.co.uk/news/world-asia-pacific-12321215 (accessed 16 January 2014).

Beck, U. (1992) *Risk Society: Towards a New Modernity*. London: SAGE.

Becker, H.S. (1982) *Art Worlds*. Berkeley, CA: University of California Press.

Bell, D. (1974) *The Coming of Post-Industrial Society*. London: Heinemann.

Bell, L. and Seale, C. (2011) 'The reporting of cervical cancer in the mass media: a study of UK newspapers', *European Journal of Cancer Care*, 20(3): 389–94.

Beltrán, M.C. (2007) 'The Hollywood Latina body as site of social struggle: media constructions of stardom and Jennifer Lopez', in S. Redmond and S. Holmes (eds), *Stardom and Celebrity: A Reader*. Los Angeles, CA and London: SAGE: 275–87.

Benjamin, W. (2008) 'The work of art in the age of its technological reproducibility', in M.W. Jennings, B. Doherty and T.Y. Levin (eds) *The Work of Art in the Age of its Technological Reproducibility and Other Writings on Media*. Cambridge and London: Belknap Press, pp. 19–56.

Bennett, L. (2013) 'Researching online fandom', *Cinema Journal*, 52(4): 129–34.

Best, S. and Kellner, D. (1991) *Postmodern Theory: Critical Interrogations*, London: Macmillan.

Bignell, J. (2005) *Big Brother: Reality TV in the Twenty-First Century*. Basingstoke: Palgrave Macmillan.

Biltereyst, D. (2004) 'Reality TV, troublesome pictures and panics: reappraising the public controversy around Reality TV in Europe', in S. Holmes and D. Jermyn (eds), *Understanding Reality Television*. London and New York: Routledge, pp. 91–111.

Biressi, A. and Nunn, H. (2005) *Reality TV: Realism and Revelation*. London: Wallflower.

Bishop, J. (2012) 'Scope and limitations in the Government of Wales Act 2006 for tackling Internet abuses in the form of "flame trolling"', *Statute Law Review*, 33(2): 207–16.

Bisley, N. (2007) *Rethinking Globalization*. Basingstoke: Palgrave Macmillan.

Blond, A. (2008) 'Impacts of exposure to images of ideal bodies on male body dissatisfaction: a review', *Body Image*, 5(3): 244–50.

Boorstin, D. (1992) *The Image: A Guide to Pseudo-Events in America*. London: Penguin.

Boorstin, D. (2006) 'From hero to celebrity: the human pseudo-event', in P.D. Marshall (ed.), *The Celebrity Culture Reader*. London and New York: Routledge, pp. 35–55.

Boorstin, J. (2005) The scent of celebrity. *Fortune*, Vol. 152, Issue 10: 67–70.

Bordo, S. (1993) *Unbearable Weight: Feminism, Western Culture and the Body*. Berkeley, CA: University of California Press.

Bourdieu, P. (1984) *Distinction: A Social Critique of the Judgement of Taste*. London: Routledge & Kegan Paul.

Boyle, L. (2013) '"It's a messed-up situation when Miley gets a laugh and Phil gets Suspended": Louisiana governor defends Duck star – as backlash grows over his sacking for homosexual rant'. *Mail Online*, 19 December, http://dailymail.co.uk/news/article-2526619/Duck-Dynasty-star-Phil Robertson (accessed 13 February 2014).

Boyle, R. and Kelly, L.W. (2010) 'The celebrity entrepreneur on television: profile, politics and power', *Celebrity Studies*, 1(3): 334–50.

Brand, R. (2014) *Revolution*. London: Century.

Braudy, L. (1986) *The Frenzy of Renown*. New York: Vintage Books.

Braudy, L. (2006) 'The longing of Alexander', in D.P. Marshall (ed.), *The Celebrity Culture Reader*. London and New York: Routledge, pp. 35–55.

Brock, G. (2012) 'The Leveson Inquiry: there's a bargain to be struck over media freedom and regulation', *Journalism*, 13(4): 519–28.

Brockes, E. (2012) 'Kim Kardashian: My life as a brand', *The Guardian*, Friday, 7 September.

Brockington, D. (2009) *Celebrity and the Environment: Fame, Wealth and Power in Conservation*. London and New York: Zed Books.

Brooker, W. (2002) *Using the Force: Creativity, Community and 'Star Wars' Fans*. London: Continuum.

Brooks, C. (2004) What celebrity worship says about us. USATODAY.com http://www.usatoday.com/news/opinion/editorials/2004–09–13-celebrity-edit_x.htm (accessed 19 June 2013).

Brown, C.G. (2009) *The Death of Christian Britain: Understanding Secularisation, 1800–2000*. London and New York: Routledge.

Brown, W.J., Michael, B.D., and Bocarnea, M.C. (2003) 'Social influence of an international celebrity: responses to the death of Princess Diana', *Journal of Communication*, 53(4): 587–605.

Burgess, J. and Green, J. (2009) *YouTube: Online Video and Participatory Culture*. Cambridge: Polity.

Burke, E. (2008) *A Philosophical Enquiry*. Oxford and New York: Oxford University Press.

Burke, P. (1992) *The Fabrication of Louis XIV*. New Haven and London: Yale University Press.

Burns, K.S. (2009) *Celeb 2.0*. California: Greenwood Publishing Group.

Burr, C. (2009) *The Perfect Scent: A Year Inside the Perfume Industry in Paris and New York*. New York: Picador.

Caesar, J. (1967) *The Civil War* (translated by J.F. Gardner). London: Penguin Books.

Caesar, J. (1982) *The Conquest of Gaul* (translated by S.A. Handford). London: Penguin.

Carey, P. and Verow, R. (1998) *Media and Entertainment: The Law and Business*. Bristol: Jordan Publishing.

Carroll, R. (2006) 'Rights row as Jolie and Pitt prepare Namibian nest', guardian.co.uk (*Guardian* online service), 1 May, http://www.guardian.co.uk/world/2006/may/01/film.filmnews (accessed 11 March 2012).

Cartledge, P. (2004) *Alexander the Great: The Hunt for a New Past*. London: Pan Books.

Cashmore, E. (2002) *Beckham*. Cambridge: Polity.

Cashmore, E. (2006) *Celebrity/Culture*. Abingdon: Routledge

Castells, M. (1996) *The Rise of the Network Society*. Oxford: Blackwell.

Cathcart, B. (2012) *Everybody's Hacked Off*. London: Penguin.

Chang, S. (2005) 'The prodigal "son" returns: an assessment of current "son of Sam" Laws and the reality of the online murderabilia marketplace', *Rutgers Computer & Technology Law Journal,* 31(2): 430–58.

Chattopadhyay, D. and Subramanian, A. (2010) 'SRK Inc.'. *Business Today*. 21 February, http://businesstoday.intoday.in/story/srk-inc./1/5200.html (accessed 13 January 2014).

Cheadle, D. and Prendergast, J. (2007) *Not On Our Watch: the Mission to End Genocide in Darfur and Beyond*. Dunshaughlin: Maverick House.

Chin, B. and Hills, M. (2011) 'Restricted confessions? Blogging, subcultural celebrity and the management of producer-fan proximity', in S. Redmond (ed.), *The Star and Celebrity Confessional*. London and New York: Routledge, pp. 142–62.

Chopra, A. (2007) *King of Bollywood: Shah Rukh Khan and the Seductive World of Indian Cinema*. New York, and Boston, MA: Warner Books.

Church Gibson, P. (2012) *Fashion and Celebrity Culture*. London and New York: Berg.

Cicero, M.T. (2009) *Political Speeches*. Oxford: Oxford University Press.

Clifford, J. (1994) Diasporas. *Cultural Anthropologist*, 9(3): 302–38.

Cohen, S. (1980) *Folk Devils and Moral Panics: The Creation of the Mods and Rockers* (2nd edn). Oxford: Martin Robertson.

Cohen, J. (2005) 'Global and local viewing experiences in the age of multichannel television: the Israeli experience', *Communication Theory*, 15(4): 437–55.

Cohen, S. (2007) *Decline, Renewal and the City in Popular Music: Beyond the Beatles*. Aldershot: Ashgate.

Conboy, M. (2010) *Journalism: A Critical History*. Los Angeles, CA and London: SAGE.

Conboy, M. (2011) *Journalism in Britain: A History Introduction*. Los Angeles, CA and London: SAGE.

Cos, G. and Norris Martin, K. (2013) 'The rhetoric of the hanging chair: presence, absence, and visual argument in the 2012 presidential campaign', *American Behavioral Scientist*, 57(12): 1688–1703.

Cosgrave, B. (2008) *Made For Each Other: Fashion and the Academy Awards*. London: Bloomsbury.

Couldry, N. (2000) *The Place of Media Power: Pilgrims and Witnesses of the Media Age*. London and New York: Routledge.

Couldry, N. (2003) *Media Rituals: A Critical Approach*. London: Routledge.

Cox, N.B. and Proffitt, J.M. (2012) 'The housewives' guide to better living: promoting consumption on Bravo's "The Real Housewives"', *Communication, Culture & Critique*, 5: 295–312.

Craik, J. (1994) *The Face of Fashion: Cultural Studies in Fashion*. London and New York: Routledge.

Cummings, D., Clark, B., Mapplebeck, V., Dunkley, C., and Barnfield, G. (2002) *Reality TV: How Real is Real?* London: Hodder & Stoughton.

Cunningham, H. (2002) 'Prodigal bodies: pop culture and post-pregnancy', *Michigan Quarterly Review*, 41(3): 428–54.

Cywinski, S. (2011) *Kate: Style Princess*. London: John Blake.

Davies, O. (2009) *The Haunted: A Social History of Ghosts*. Basingstoke: Palgrave Macmillan.

deCordova, R. (2001) *Picture Personalities: The Emergence of the Star System in America*. Urbana and Chicago, IL: University of Illinois Press.

DeMello, M. (2014) *Body Studies: An Introduction*. London and New York: Routledge.

Denison, R. (2010) 'Bollywood blends: genre and performance in Shah Rukh Khan's post-millennial films', in C. Cornea (ed.), *Genre and Performance: Film and Television*. Manchester: University of Manchester Press, pp. 184–204.

Dhaliwal, N. and Rowe, J. (2013) 'Shah Rukh Khan interview: "I had no method to become a star, I just did whatever made me happy"', theguardian.com, Thursday 8 August, http://www.theguardian.com/film/2013/aug/08/shah-rukh-khan-interview (accessed 13 January 2014).

Diaz, C. and Bark, S. (2014) *The Body Book*. London: HarperCollins.

Drake, P. and Higgins, M. (2006) '"I'm a celebrity, get me into politics": the political celebrity and the celebrity politician', in S. Holmes and S. Redmond (eds), *Framing Celebrity: New Directions in Celebrity Culture*. London and New York: Routledge, pp. 87–101.

Duchesne, S. (2010) 'Stardom/fandom: celebrity and fan tribute performance', *Canadian Theatre Review*, 141: 21–7.

Durkheim, É. (1897–2002) *Suicide*. London and New York: Routledge.

Durkheim, É. (1984) *The Division of Labour in Society*. Basingstoke: Macmillan.

Dutton, K. (2013) *The Wisdom of Psychopaths*. London: Arrow Books.

Dyer, R. (1982) *Stars*. London: British Film Institute.

Eells, J. (2013) 'Miley Cyrus on why she loves weed, went wild at the VMAs and much more', *Rolling Stone*, 27 September, http://www.rollingstone.com/music/news/miley-cyrus-on-why-she-loves-weed-went-wild-at-the-vmas-and-much-more-20130927#ixzz2jOIhobut (accessed 1 November 2013).

Evans, J. (2004) 'Celebrity, media and history', in J. Evans and D. Hesmondhalgh (eds), *Understanding Media: Inside Celebrity*. Maidenhead: Open University Press, pp. 11–57.

Faina, J. (2012) 'Twitter and the new publicity', *ETC: A Review of General Semantics*, 69(1): 55–71.

Farid, H. (2009) 'Seeing is not believing', *IEEE Spectrum*, August, pp. 44–51.

Feasey, R. (2006) 'Get a famous body: star styles and celebrity gossip in *Heat* magazine', in S. Holmes and S. Redmond (eds), *Framing Celebrity: New Directions in Celebrity Culture*. London and New York: Routledge, pp. 177–95.

Featherstone, M. (1995) *Undoing Culture: Globalization, Postmodernism and Identity*. London: SAGE.

Fenster, M. (2012) 'Disclosure's effects: WikiLeaks and transparency', *Iowa Law Review*, 97(3): 753–807.

Ferris, K.O. and Harris, S.R. (2011) *Stargazing: Celebrity, Fame and Social Interaction*. London and New York: Routledge.

Figueiredo, S.M. (2009) 'Branding catastrophe', *Places: Forum of Design for the Public Realm*, 21(1): 1–6.

Foreman, A. (1998) *Georgiana, Duchess of Devonshire*. London and New York: Harper Perennial.

Foucault, M. (1978) *The History of Sexuality*, Vol. 1. London: Allen Lane.

Fox, J.A. and Levin, J. (2005) *Extreme Killing: Understanding Serial and Mass Murder*. Thousand Oaks, CA: SAGE.

Fox, J.A. and Levin, J. (2012) *Extreme Killing: Understanding Serial and Mass Murder* (2nd edn). Thousand Oaks, CA: SAGE.

Franklin, B., Hogan, M., Langley, Q., and Mosdell, N. (2009) *Key Concepts in Public Relations*. London: SAGE.

Fries, L. (2005) Britney and Kevin: chaotic. Variety.com, Wednesday 18 May.

Frisby, D. (1985) *Fragments of Modernity*. Cambridge: Polity.

Fung, A. (2008) 'Western style, Chinese pop: Jay Chou's rap and hip-hop in China', *Asian Music*, 39(1): 69–80.

Furedi, F. (2013) *Moral Crusades in an Age of Mistrust: The Jimmy Savile Scandal*. Basingstoke: Palgrave Macmillan.

Fuqua, J.V. (2011) 'Brand Pitt: celebrity activism and the Make It Right Foundation in post-Katrina New Orleans', *Celebrity Studies*, 2(2): 192–208.

Gabler, N. (1995) *Walter Winchell: Gossip, Power and the Culture of Celebrity*. London: Alfred A. Knopf.

Gabler, N. (2001) *Toward a New Definition of Celebrity*. Los Angeles, CA: The Norman Lear Center.

Galbraith, P.W. and Karlin, J.G. (2012) *Idols and Celebrity in Japanese Media Culture*. Basingstoke: Palgrave Macmillan.

Gamson, J. (1994) *Claims to Fame: Celebrity in Contemporary America*. Berkeley, CA: University of California Press.

Gamson, J. (2007) 'The assembly line of greatness: celebrity in twentieth-century America', in S. Redmond and S. Holmes (eds), *Stardom and Celebrity: A Reader*. Los Angeles, CA and London: SAGE, pp. 141–56.

Gardner, E. (2013). 'Lady Gaga concert promoters sue "despicable", insurer over terrorism-related cancellation', *The Hollywood Reporter*, 6 March, http://www.billboard.com/biz/articles/news/legal-and-management/1550715/lady-gaga-concert-promoters-sue-despicable-insurer (accessed 14 January 2014).

Garland, R. (2010) 'Celebrity ancient and modern', *Society*, 47(6): 484–8.

Gauntlett, D. (2004) 'Madonna's daughters: girl power and the empowered girl-pop breakthrough', in S. Fouz-Hernandez and F. Jarman-Ivens (eds), *Madonna's Drowned*

World: New Approaches to her Cultural Transformations, 1983–2003. Aldershot: Ashgate, pp. 161–76.

Gauntlett, D. (2008) *Media, Gender and Identity: An Introduction.* London and New York: Routledge.

Geldof, B. (2006) *Geldof in Africa.* London: Arrow Books.

Gerth, H.H. and Wright Mills, C. (1961) *From Max Weber: Essays in Sociology.* London: Routledge & Kegan Paul.

Giddens, A. (1998) *The Third Way.* Cambridge: Polity.

Giddens, A. (1999) *Runaway World: How Globalisation is Reshaping Our Lives.* London: Profile Books.

Giles, D. (2000) *Illusions of Immortality: A Psychology of Fame and Celebrity.* London: Macmillan.

Gitlin, T. (2003) *The Whole World is Watching: Mass Media in the Making and Unmaking of the New Left.* Berkeley, CA, Los Angeles, CA and London: University of California Press.

Gledhill, C. (1991) *Stardom: Industry of Desire.* London: Routledge.

Goffman, E. (1959) *The Presentation of Self in Everyday Life.* London: Penguin Books.

Goldman, R. and Papson, S. (1998) *Nike Culture: The Sign of the Swoosh.* London: SAGE.

Gonzalez, E. (2005) 'Britney and Kevin: chaotic'. *Slant Magazine.com*, 18 May.

Goody, J. (2006) *Jade: My Autobiography.* London: HarperCollins.

Gray, J. (2004) *Heresies: Against Progress and Other Illusions.* London: Granta Books.

Greenslade, R. (2013) 'Angelina Jolie illustrates the virtues of celebrity power', Guardian. co.uk (accessed 17 May 2013).

Griffen-Foley, B. (2004) From *Tit-Bits* to *Big Brother*: a century of audience participation in the media. *Media, Culture & Society*, 26(4): 533–48.

Grossberg, L. (1992) 'Is there a fan in the house? The affective sensibility of fandom', in L.A. Lewis (ed.), *The Adoring Audience: Fan Culture and Popular Media.* London and New York: Routledge, pp. 50–69.

Gruger, W. (2012). 'PSY's "gangnam style" hits 1 billion views on YouTube, *Billboard*, 21 December, http://www.billboard.com/articles/columns/k-town/1481275/psys-gangnam-style-hits-1-billion-views-on-youtube (accessed 17 January 2014).

Guinn, J. (2009) *Go Down Together: The True Untold Story of Bonnie and Clyde.* London: Pocket Books.

Hafez, K. (2007) *The Myth of Media Globalization* (translated by Alex Skinner). Cambridge: Polity.

Haggerty, K.D. (2009) 'Modern serial killers', *Crime, Media, Culture*, 5(2): 168–87.

Hague, S., Street, J., and Savigny, H. (2008) 'The voice of the people? Musicians as political actors', *Cultural Politics*, 4(1): 5–24.

Haig, M. (2011) *Brand Success.* London: Kogan Page.

Hall, S. (1980) Encoding/decoding. In S. Hall, D. Hobson, A. Loew and P. Willis, (eds) *Culture, Media, Language.* London: Hutchinson, pp. 117–28.

Hampton, M. (2012) 'The fourth estate ideal in journalism history', in S. Allan (ed.), *The Routledge Companion to News and Journalism.* London and New York: Routledge, pp. 3–13.

Harris, D. (2010) 'Celebrity sex scandals', *Salmagundi* 166/167: 146–56.

Harris, N.-E. (2013) 'The Angelina Jolie effect: surge in women patients requesting double mastectomies, even when they don't carry BRCA1 gene', *Medical Daily*, 3 October, http://www.medicaldaily.com/angelina-jolie-effect-surge-women-patients-requesting-double-mastectomies-even-when-they-dont-carry (accessed 13 May 2014).

Harvey, D. (1989) *The Condition of Postmodernity.* Oxford: Blackwell.

Harvey, D. (2007) *A Brief History of Neoliberalism*. Oxford: Oxford University Press.

Healey, M. (2008) *What Is Branding?* Hove: Rotovision.

Heelas, P. (1996) *The New Age Movement*. Oxford: Blackwell.

Hermida, A. (2010) 'Twittering the news', *Journalism Practice*, 4(3): 297–308.

Hewer, P. and Hamilton, K. (2012) 'Exhibitions and the role of fashion in the sustenance of the Kylie Brand mythology: unpacking the spatial logic of celebrity culture', *Marketing Theory*,12: 411–25.

Hickey, E.W. (2013) *Serial Murderers and Their Victims*. Andover: Cengage Learning.

Hill, A. (2005) *Reality TV: Audiences and Popular Factual Television*. London and New York: Routledge.

Hills, M. (2002) *Fan Cultures*. London and New York: Routledge.

Hills, M. (2006) 'Not just another powerless elite? When media fans become subcultural celebrities', in S. Holmes and S. Redmond (eds), *Framing Celebrity: New Directions in Celebrity Culture*. London and New York: Routledge, pp. 101–19.

Hills, M. (2010) *Triumph of a Time Lord: Regenerating Doctor Who in the Twenty-First Century*. London: I.B. Taurus.

Hills, M. (2012) '"Twilight" fans represented in commercial paratexts and inter-fandoms: resisting and repurposing negative fan stereotypes', in A. Morey (ed.), *Genre, Reception, and Adaptation in the 'Twilight' Series*. Aldershot: Ashgate, pp. 113–31.

Hillyer, M. (2010) Underexposed Overexposure: *One Night in Paris*. Velvet Light Trap, 65: 20–21.

Hoare, P. (1999) *Icons of Pop*. London: Booth-Clibborn Editions.

Hoe-Lian Goh, D. and Sian Lee, C. (2011) An analysis of tweets in response to the death of Michael Jackson. *Aslib Proceedings: New Information Perspectives*, 63(5): 432–44.

Hoffman, J. and Sheridan, L. (2008) 'Celebrities as victims of stalking', in J. Meloy, S. Reid, L. Sheridan, and J. Hoffman (eds), *Stalking, Threatening and Attacking Public Figures: A Psychological and Behavioural Analysis*. Oxford: Oxford University Press, pp. 195–213.

Hollander, P. (2010a) 'Michael Jackson, the celebrity cult, and popular culture', *Culture and Society*, 47: 147–52.

Hollander, P. (2010b) 'Slavoj Žižek and the rise of the celebrity intellectual', Springer. com, http://link.springer.com/article/10.1007/s12115–010–9329-z/fulltext.html (accessed 1 May 2013).

Holmes, R.M. and Holmes, S.T. (1998) *Serial Murder*. London: SAGE.

Holmes, S. (2004) 'All you've got to worry about is the task, having a cup of tea, and doing a bit of sunbathing': approaching celebrity in "Big Brother"', in S. Holmes and D. Jermyn, (eds), *Understanding Reality Television*. London and New York: Routledge, pp. 111–36.

Holmes, S. (2006) 'It's a jungle out there! Playing the game of fame in celebrity Reality TV', in S. Holmes and S. Redmond (eds), *Framing Celebrity: New Directions in Celebrity Culture*. London and New York: Routledge, pp. 45–65.

Holmes, S. (2009) '"Jade's back, and this time she's famous": narratives of celebrity in the Celebrity Big Brother "race" row. *Entertainment and Sports Law*, 7(1): http://www2.warwick.ac.uk/fac/soc/law/elj/eslj/issues/volume7/number1/holmes (accessed 5 January 2014).

Holmes, S. and Jermyn, J. (2204) *Understanding Reality Television*. London and New York: Routledge.

Holmlund, C. (2010) Celebrity, ageing and Jackie Chan: middle-aged Asian in transnational action. *Celebrity Studies*, 1(1): 96–112.

Horkheimer, M. and Adorno, T.W. (1973) *The Dialectic of Enlightenment* (translated by John Cumming). London: Allen Lane.

Horton, D. and Wohl, R.R. (1956) 'Mass communication and para-social interaction', *Psychiatry*, 19: 215–29.

Houran, J., Navik, S., and Zerrusen, K. (2005) 'Boundary functioning in celebrity worshippers', *Personality and Individual Differences*, 38: 237–48.

How, A. (2003) *Critical Theory*. Basingstoke: Palgrave Macmillan.

Howard, A. (2010) 'A timeline of serial killers', in S. Waller (ed.), *Serial Killers – Philosophy for Everyone: Being and Killing*. Oxford: Wiley-Blackwell.

Hyde, M. 'Apocalypse Brangelina', 22 April 2006, http://www.guardian.co.uk/commentisfree/2006/apr/22/comment.mainsection1 (accessed 11 March 2012).

Hyde, M. (2009) *Celebrity: How Entertainers Took Over the World and Why We Need an Exit Strategy*. London: Harvill Secker.

Hylland Eriksen, T. (2007) *Globalization*. Oxford and New York: Routledge.

Iezzi, T. (2010) *The Idea Writers: Copywriting in a New Media and Marketing Era*. Basingstoke: Palgrave Macmillan.

Inglis, F. (2010) *A Short History of Celebrity*. Princeton, NJ: Princeton University Press.

Jackson, T. and Shaw, D. (2009) *Mastering Fashion Marketing*. Basingstoke: Palgrave Macmillan.

Jarvis, B. (2007) 'Monsters Inc.: serial killers and consumer culture', *Crime, Media, Culture*, 3(3): 326–44.

Jenkins, H. (1992) *Textual Poachers: Television Fans and Participatory Culture*. New York: Routledge.

Jenkins, H. (2008) *Convergence Culture: Where Old and New Media Collide*. New York: New York University Press.

Jenner, K. (2011) *Kris Jenner . . . and All Things Kardashian*. London and New York: Simon and Shuster.

Jermyn, D. (2012) '"Get a life, ladies. Your old one is not coming back": Ageing, ageism and the lifespan of female celebrity' (Editor's Introduction to special edition) *Celebrity Studies*, 3(1): 1–12.

Johnson, R. (2006) 'Exemplary differences: mourning (and not mourning) a princess', in D.P. Marshall (ed.), *The Celebrity Culture Reader*. London and New York: Routledge.

Jolie, A. (2003) *Notes From My Travels: Visits with Refugees in Africa, Cambodia, Pakistan, and Ecuador*. New York and London: Pocket Books.

Jolie, A. (2013) 'My medical choice', *The New York Times*, 14 May, http://www.nytimes.com/2013/05/14/opinion/my-medical-choice.html?_r=0 (accessed 13 May 2014).

Jones, R.B., Soler-Lopez, M., Zahra, D., Shankleman, J., and Trenchard-Mabere, E. (2013) 'Using online adverts to increase the uptake of cervical screening amongst "real Eastenders": an opportunistic controlled trial', *BMC Research Notes*, 6(117): 1–8.

Jung, S. (2011) 'K-pop, Indonesian fandom, and social media', *Transformative Works and Cultures*, 8, http://journal.transformativeworks.org/index.php/twc/article/view/289/219 http://journal.transformativeworks.org/index.php/twc/article/view/289/219 (accessed 31 October 2013).

Kapoor, I. (2013) *Celebrity Humanitarianism: The Ideology of Global Charity*. London and New York: Routledge.

Karmini, N. (2010) 'Ariel, Luna Maya sex tape: Indonesia's first celebrity sex tape scandal', *HuffPost World*, 6 June, http://www.huffingtonpost.com/2010/06/13/ariel-luna-maya-sex-tape-indonesia_n_610446.html (accessed 16 January 2014).

Katz, J., Rice, E., and Ronald, E. (2002) *Social Consequences of Internet Use*. Cambridge, MA: MIT Press.

Kellner, D. (2003) *Media Spectacle*. London and New York: Routledge.

Kellner, D. (2012) 'The Murdoch media empire and the spectacle of scandal', *International Journal of Communication*, (6): 1169–200.

Kershaw, I. (1998) *Hitler. 1889–1936 – Hubris*. London: Allen Lane.

King, B. (2010) 'Stardom, celebrity, and the money form', *The Velvet Light Trap*, 65: 7–19.

King, B. (2011) 'Stardom, celebrity, and the para-confession', in S. Redmond (ed.), *The Star and Celebrity Confessional*. London and New York: Routledge, pp. 7–25.

King, N., Touyz, S., and Charles, M. (2000) 'The effect of body dissatisfaction on women's perceptions of female celebrities', *The International Journal of Eating Disorders*, 27(3): 341–7.

Kissling, E.A. (2006) 'I don't have a great body, but I play one on TV: the celebrity guide to fitness and weight loss in the United States', in P.D. Marshall (ed.), *The Celebrity Culture Reader*. London and New York: Routledge, pp. 551–7.

Kristof, N.D. (2007) Wretched of the Earth. *The New York Review of Books*, 54(9), May, 1.

Kumar Dudrah, R. (2002) 'Vilayati Bollywood: popular Hindi cinema-going and diasporic South Asian identity in Birmingham', *Javnost*, 9(1): 19–36.

Kurzman, C., Anderson, C., Key, C., Lee, Y.O., Moloney, M., Silver, A., and Van Ryn, M.W. (2007) 'Celebrity status', *Sociological Theory*, 25(4): 347–67.

Lai, A. (2006) 'Glitter and grain: aura and authenticity in the celebrity photographs of Jürgen Teller', in S. Holmes and S. Redmond (eds), *Framing Celebrity: New Directions in Celebrity Culture*. London and New York: Routledge: 215–31.

Lam, A. (2013) '"Gangnam style": crossing over in the new world', *World Literature Today*, 87(2): 4.

Lane Fox, R. (1997) *Alexander the Great*. London: The Folio Society.

Lawrence, C. (2009) *The Cult of Celebrity*. Guilford, CT: skirt!

Lechner, F.J. (2009) *Globalization: The Making of World Society*. Oxford: Wiley-Blackwell.

Leveson, Lord Justice. (2012) *An Inquiry Into the Culture, Practices and Ethics of the Press*, Vol. I. London: The Stationery Office.

Levitt, L. (2010) Death on display: reifying stardom through Hollywood's dark tourism. *The Velvet Light Trap*, 65: 62–70.

Lewis, L.A. (ed.) (1992) *The Adoring Audience: Fan Culture and Popular Media*. London and New York: Routledge.

Lie, J. (2012) 'What is the K in K-pop? South Korean popular music, the culture industry, and national identity', *Korea Observer*, 43(3): 339–63.

Lim, G. (2005) *Idol to Icon: The Creation of Celebrity Brands*. Singapore: Cyan.

Littler, J. (2011a) 'Celebrity and the transnational', *Celebrity Studies*, 2(1): 1–5.

Littler, J. (2011b) '"I feel your pain": cosmopolitan charity and the public fashioning of the celebrity soul', in S. Redmond (ed.), *The Star and Celebrity Confessional*. London and New York: Routledge, pp. 127–41.

Luckett, M. (2010) 'Toxic: the implosion of Britney Spear's star image', *The Velvet Light Trap*, 65: 39–41.

Lukes, S. (1973) *Emile Durkheim: His Life and Work*. London: Allen Lane and the Penguin Press.

Lupton, D. (2013) *Fat*. London and New York: Routledge.

Lyotard, J.-F. (1984) *The Postmodern Condition: A Report On Knowledge*. Manchester: Manchester University Press.

McCarthy, E. (2012) 'Tokyo is trending: the rise of J-pop'. *London Evening Standard*, 23 January, http://www.standard.co.uk/lifestyle/london-life/tokyo-is-trending-the-rise-of-jpop-7310536.html (accessed 17 January 2014).

McChesney, R.W. (2004) *The Problem of the Media: U.S. Communication Politics in the 21st Century*. New York: Monthly Review Press.

McDonald, P. (2000) *The Star System: Hollywood's Production of Popular Identities*. London: Wallflower .

McDonald, P. (2013) *Hollywood Stardom*. Oxford: Wiley-Blackwell.

MacGillivray, A. (2006) *Globalization*. London: Robinson.

McLuhan, M. (1994) *Understanding Media: The Extensions of Man*. Cambridge, MA: MIT Press.

McNair, B. (2009) *News and Journalism in the UK*. London and New York: Routledge.

McNair, B. (2012) 'WikiLeaks, journalism and the consequences of chaos', *Media International Australia*, 144: 77–86.

McQuail, D. (1994) *Mass Communication Theory*. London: SAGE.

Maltby, J. and Giles, D. (2008) 'Toward the measurement and profiling of celebrity worship', in J.R. Meloy, L. Sheridan, and J. Hoffman (eds), *Stalking, Threatening and Attacking Public Figures: A Psychological and Behavioural Analysis*. Oxford: Oxford University Press, pp. 271–85.

Maltby, J., Giles, D.C., Barber, L., and McCutcheon, L.E. (2005) 'Intense-personal celebrity worship and body image: Evidence of a link among female adolescents', *British Journal of Health Psychology*, 10(1): 17–32.

Maltby, J., Houran, J., and Lange, R. (2002) 'Thou shalt worship no other gods – unless they are celebrities: the relationship between celebrity worship and religious orientation', *Personality and Individual Differences*, 13(6): 1157–72.

Marche, S. (2010) 'The glittering skull: celebrity culture as world religion', *Queen's Quarterly*, 117(1): 9–21.

Maréchal, A.J. (2012) 'Rubes ramp ratings', *Daily Variety*, Thursday, 27 September: 1 and 25.

Marr, A. (2004) *My Trade: A Short History of British Journalism*. London: Pan Books.

Marshall, P.D. (1997) *Celebrity and Power: Fame in Contemporary Culture*. Minneapolis, MN and London: University of Minneapolis Press.

Marshall, P.D. (2005) 'Intimately intertwined in the most public way: celebrity and journalism', in S. Allan (ed.), *Journalism: Critical Issues*. Berkshire: Open University Press, pp. 19–30.

Marshall, P.D. (ed.) (2006) *The Celebrity Culture Reader*. London and New York: Routledge.

Marshall, P.D. (2010) 'The promotion and presentation of the self: celebrity as marker of presentational media', *Celebrity Studies*, 1(1): 35–48.

Marwick, A. and boyd, D. (2011) 'To see and be seen: celebrity practice on Twitter', *Convergence*, 17(2): 139–58.

Marx, K. and Engels, F. (1985) *The Communist Manifesto*. London: Penguin.

Mauss, M. (1972) *A General Theory of Magic*. London: Routledge & Kegan Paul.

Mayer, C. (2012) Time 100: Catherine, Duchess of Cambridge, and Pippa Middleton. *Time Magazine*, Wednesday, Apr. 18, http://content.time.com/time/specials/packages/article/0,28804,2111975_2111976_2111952,00.html (accessed 29/11/2013).

Mears, A. (2010) 'Size zero high-end ethnic: cultural production and the reproduction of culture in fashion modelling', *Poetics*, 38: 21–46.

Mehta, R.B. (2010) 'Bollywood, nation, globalization: an incomplete introduction', in R.B. Mehta and R.V. Pandharipande (eds), *Bollywood and Globalization: Indian Popular Cinema, Nation, and Diaspora*. London and New York: Anthem Press.

Meikle, G. and Young, S. (2012) *Media Convergence: Networked Digital Media in Everyday Life*. Basingstoke: Palgrave Macmillan.

Mercer, R. (2007) *Angelina Jolie: The Biography*. London: John Blake.

Merrin, W. (2005) *Baudrillard and the Media: A Critical Introduction*. Cambridge: Polity.

Metcalfe, D., Price, C., and Powell, J. (2011) 'Media coverage and public reaction to a celebrity cancer diagnosis', *Public Health & Epidemiology*, 33(1): 80–5.

Meyer, D.S. and Gamson, J. (1995) 'The challenge of cultural elites: celebrities and social movements', *Sociological Inquiry*, 65(2): 181–206.

Miller, D. and Dinan, W. (2008) *A Century of Spin*. London: Pluto Press.

Miller, L. (2014a) 'Serial killers: I. Subtypes, patterns, and motives', *Aggression and Violent Behaviour*, 19(1): 1–11.

Miller, L. (2014b) 'Serial killers: II. Development, dynamics, and forensics', *Aggression and Violent Behaviour*, 19(1): 12–22.

Mishra, V. (2002) *Bollywood Cinema: Temples of Desire*. London and New York: Routledge.

Mitford, N. (1966) *The Sun King*. London: Hamish Hamilton.

Moore, M. (2008) '"Guns 'n' roses", Chinese democracy banned in China', *The Telegraph*, 24 November, http://www.telegraph.co.uk/news/worldnews/asia/china/3511767/Guns-N-Roses-Chinese-Democracy-banned-in-China.html (accessed 16 January 2014).

Morris, S. (2013) 'Ian Watkins gets 35-year sentence for child sex crimes', theguardianbeta. http://www.theguardian.com/uk-news/2013/dec/18/ian-watkins-jailed-child-sex-crimes (accessed 1 March 2014).

Nederveen Pietrese, J. (2009) *Globalization and Culture*. New York and Toronto: Rowman & Littlefield Publishers, Inc.

Nelson, J. (2012) *Airbrushed Nation: The Lure and Loathing of Women's Magazines*. Berkeley, CA: Seal Press.

Nelson, M.R. and Devanathan, N. (2006) 'Brand placements Bollywood style', *Journal of Consumer Behaviour*, 5: 211–21.

Nicholl, K. (2011) *The Making of a Royal Romance*. London: Arrow Books.

Nicholl, K. (2013) *Kate: The Future Queen*. New York: Weinstein Books.

NME.com (2013) Lily Allen continues Twitter feud with Azealia Banks: 'Bet my album comes out first', http://www.nme.com/news/lily-allen/71426 (accessed 25 October 2013).

Nussbaum, E. (2005) 'My so-called blog', in D. Kline and D. Burstein (eds), *Blog!: How the Newest Media Revolution is Changing Politics, Business, and Culture*. New York: CDS Books: 349–62.

Okonkwo, U. (2007) *Luxury Fashion Branding: Trends, Tactics, Techniques*. Basingstoke: Palgrave Macmillan.

Olins, W. (2003) *Wally Olins on Brand*. London: Thames & Hudson.

Oppenheimer, J. (2006) *House of Hilton*. New York: Crown Publishers.

Orbach, S. (2010) *Bodies*. London: Profile.

Ouellette, L. and Hay, J. (2008) *Better Living Through Reality TV*. Oxford: Blackwell.

Paltrow, G. (2011) *Notes from my Kitchen Table*. London: Boxtree.

Parekh, B., Gurharpal, S., and Vertovee, S. (eds) (2003) *Culture and Economy in the Indian Diaspora*. London and New York: Routledge.

Parke, M. and Wilson, N. (eds) (2011) *Theorizing Twilight*. Jefferson: McFarlane & Company, Inc.

Peppiatt, R. (2012) 'The story factory: infotainment and the tabloid newsroom', in R. Keeble and J. Mair (eds), *The Phone Hacking Scandal: Journalism on Trial*. Suffolk: Abramis, pp. 16–25.

Petty, R.D. and D'Rozario, D. (2009) 'The use of dead celebrities in advertising and marketing', *Journal of Advertising*, 38(4): 37–49.

Pilger, J. (ed.) (2005) *Tell Me No Lies: Investigative Journalism and its Triumphs*. London: Vintage Books.

Plutarch. (1998) *Selected Lives*. Hertfordshire: Wordsworth Classics.

Podneiks, E. (2009) 'Celebrity bio blogs: hagiography, pathography, and Perez Hilton', *a/b: Auto/Biography Studies*, 24(1): 53–73.

Pringle, H. (2004) *Celebrity Sells*. Chichester: John Wiley & Sons Ltd.

Punathambekar, A. (2005) 'Bollywood in the Indian-American diaspora', *International Journal of Cultural Studies*, 8(2): 151–73.

Quinn, F. (2013) *Law For Journalists*. Harlow: Pearson.

Redmond, S. (2010) 'Avatar Obama in the age of liquid celebrity', *Celebrity Studies*, 1(1): 81–95.

Redmond, S. (2011) 'Pieces of me: celebrity confessional carnality', in S. Redmond, (ed.), *The Star and Celebrity Confessional*. London and New York: Routledge, pp. 41–53.

Redmond, S. (2014) *Celebrity and the Media*. Basingstoke: Palgrave Macmillan.

Rees, L. (2012) *The Dark Charisma of Adolf Hitler*. London: Ebury Press.

Reid Meloy, J. (1998) 'The psychology of stalking', in J. Reid Meloy (ed.), *The Psychology of Stalking: Clinical and Forensic Perspectives*. San Diego, CA and London: Academic Press, pp. 2–21.

Reid Meloy, J. (2002) 'Stalking and violence', in J. Boon and L. Sheridan (eds), *Stalking and Psychosexual Obsession: Psychological Perspectives for Prevention, Policing and Treatment*. Chichester: John Wiley and Sons, pp. 105–25.

Ressler, R.K. and Shachtman, T. (1992) *Whoever Fights Monsters*. London: Simon & Shuster.

Ritchie, J. (2000) *Big Brother: The Official Unseen Story*. London: Channel 4 Books.

Rivers, J. and Frankel, V. (2009) *Men Are Stupid . . . And They Like Big Boobs*. New York: Pocket Books.

Rogers, M.F. (1999) *Barbie Culture*. London: SAGE.

Rogers, R. and Chabrol, H. (2009) 'The impact of exposure to images of ideally thin models on body dissatisfaction in young French and Italian women', *Encephale*, 35(3): 262–8.

Rojek, C. (2001) *Celebrity*. London: Reaktion.

Rojek, C. (2012) *Fame Attack: The Inflation of Celebrity and its Consequences*. London: Bloomsbury Academic.

Rojek, C. (2013) *Event Power: How Global Events Manage and Manipulate*. Los Angeles and London: SAGE.

Rooney, J.A. (1995). 'Branding: a trend for today and tomorrow', *Journal of Product & Brand Management*, 4(4): 48–55.

Roscoe, J. (2001) 'Big Brother Australia: performing the "real" twenty-four-seven', *International Journal of Cultural Studies*, 4(4): 473–88.

Rowe, D. (2012) 'Tabloidization of news', in S. Allan (ed.), *The Routledge Companion to News and Journalism*. London and New York: Routledge, pp. 350–62.

Rozenberg, J. (2005) *Privacy and the Press*. Oxford: Oxford University Press.

Russell, V. (2007) 'Make me a celebrity: celebrity exercise videos and the origins of makeover television', in D. Heller (ed.), *Makeover Television: Realities Remodelled*, London and New York: I.B. Tauris, pp. 67–79.

Saliba, J.A. (1995) *Perspectives on New Religious Movements*. London: Geoffrey Chapman.

Salvato, N. (2009) 'Out of hand: YouTube amateurs and professionals', *TDR: The Drama Review*, 53(3): 67–83.

Sánchez Abril, P. (2011a) 'A simple, human measure of privacy': public disclosure of private facts in the world of Tiger Woods', *Connecticut Public Interest Law Journal*, 10(2): 385–98.

Sánchez Abril, P. (2011b) 'The evolution of business celebrity in American Law and Society', *American Business Law Journal*, 48(2): 177–225.

Sansom, I. (2010) 'Family: great dynasties of the world: no. 17, Bollywood. Ian Sansom on the founding families behind Indian cinema', *The Guardian*, 10 July: 7.

Sayre, R.F. (1977) The proper study-autobiographies in American Studies. *American Quarterly*, 29(3): 241–62.

Scannell, P. (2002) '"Big Brother" as a television event', *Television & New Media*, 3(3): 271–82.

Schiller, H. (1969) *Mass Communication and the American Empire*. New York: Augustus M. Kelly.

Schmid, D. (2005) *Natural Born Celebrities: Serial Killers in American Culture*. Chicago, IL: University of Chicago Press.

Schmid, D. (2010) 'The devil you know: Dexter and the "goodness" of American serial killing', in D.L. Howard (ed.), *Dexter: Investigating Cutting Edge Television*. London: I.B. Taurus, pp. 132–42.

Seale, C. (1998) *Constructing Death: The Sociology of Dying and Bereavement*. Cambridge: Cambridge University Press.

Shingler, M. (2012) *Star Studies: A Critical Guide*. London: British Film Institute.

Simmel, G. (1971) *On Individuality and Social Forms*. Chicago, IL and London: The University of Chicago Press.

Smart, B. (2005) *The Sport Star: Modern Sport and the Cultural Economy of Sporting Celebrity*. London: SAGE.

Smartt, U. (2006) *Media Law for Journalists*. London: SAGE.

Smartt, U. (2011) *Media and Entertainment Law*. London and New York: Routledge.

Smit, C. (2013) *The Exile of Britney Spears: A Tale of 21st Century Consumption*. London: Intellect.

Spitzberg, B.H. and Cupach, W.R. (2008) 'Fanning the flames of fandom: celebrity worship, parasocial interaction, and stalking', in J.R. Meloy, L. Sheridan, and J. Hoffman (eds), *Stalking, Threatening and Attacking Public Figures: A Psychological and Behavioural Analysis*. Oxford: Oxford University Press, pp. 287–321.

Springer, K. (2012) 'Indonesian police may cancel "Satanic" Lady Gaga concert', *Time*, 15 May, http://newsfeed.time.com/2012/05/15/indonesian-police-may-cancel-satanic-lady-gaga-concert/ (accessed 14 January 2014).

Stacey, J. (1994) *Star Gazing: Hollywood Cinema and Female Spectatorship*. London and New York: Routledge.

Stephens, M. (2007) *A History of News* (3rd edn). Oxford and New York: Oxford University Press.

Stever, G.S. and Lawson, K. (2013) 'Twitter as a way for celebrities to communicate with fans: implications for the study of parasocial interaction', *North American Journal of Psychology*, 15(2): 339–54.

Stiglitz, J. (2013) *Globalization and Its Discontents*. London: Penguin.

Stratton, J. (1996) 'Serial killing and the transformation of the social', *Theory, Culture & Society*, 13(1): 77–98.

Street, J. (1997) *Politics and Popular Culture*. Cambridge: Polity.

Street, J. (2001) *Mass Media, Politics, and Democracy*. Basingstoke: Palgrave Macmillan.

Street, J. (2004) Celebrity politicians: popular culture and political representation. *British Journal of Politics and International Relations*, 6(4): 435–52.

Street, J. (2006) 'The celebrity politician: political style and popular culture', in P.D. Marshall (ed.), *The Celebrity Culture Reader*. London and New York: Routledge, pp. 359–71.

Sweney, M. (2011) 'L'Oréal's Julia Roberts and Christy Turlington ad campaigns banned', TheGuardianBeta, Wednesday 27 July, http://www.theguardian.com/media/2011/jul/27/loreal-julia-roberts-ad-banned (accessed 1 May 2014).

Taddeo, J.A. and Dvorak, K. (2010) *The Tube Has Spoken: Reality TV and History*. Lexington, KY: The University Press of Kentucky.

Taib, S. (2009) 'Top 10 influential celebrities in Malaysia: stars with the X-factor sizzle', *The New Straits Times*, 7 September, http://news.asiaone.com/News/Latest+News/Showbiz/Story/A1Story20090907–166131.html (accessed 14 January 2014).

Taylor, M.E. (2012) *Charisma: Why Obama Will Beat Romney*. Grand Rapids, MI: Edenridge Press.

Thimsen, A.F. (2010) 'Populist celebrity in the election campaigns of Jesse Ventura and Arnold Schwarzenegger', *The Velvet Light Trap*, 65: 44–57.

Thomas, D. (2008) *Deluxe: How Luxury Lost its Lustre*. London: Penguin.

Thompson, P. (2012) '"Somebody could kill me": Kristen Stewart fears fame may lead to her death', MailOnline, 14 October, http://www.dailymail.co.uk/tvshowbiz/article-2217640/Kristen-Stewart-fears-fame-lead-death.html#ixzz2lOWgKvil (accessed 22 November 2013).

Thornborrow, J. and Morris, D. (2004) 'Gossip as strategy: the management of talk about others on reality TV show "Big Brother"', *Journal of Sociolinguistics*, 8(2): 246–71.

Thorpe, V. (2011) 'Meet Chris Crocker: Britney's champion and YouTube sensation', *The Observer*, 21 August, http://www.theguardian.com/media/2011/aug/21/chris-crocker-britney-spears-youtube-blog (accessed 1 November 2013).

Thurman, N. and Walters, A. (2013) 'Live blogging – digital journalism's pivotal platform? A case study of the production, consumption, and form of live blogs at Guardian.co.uk', *Digital Journalism*, 1(1): 82–101.

Tierney, T. (2013) *The Public Space of Social Media: Connected Cultures of the Network Society*. London and New York: Routledge.

Till, B.D. and Heckler, D. (2008) *The Truth About Brands*. Harlow: Pearson Education Limited.

Tincknell, E. and Raghuram, P. (2002) 'Big Brother: reconfiguring the "active" audience of cultural studies?', *European Journal of Cultural Studies*, 5(2): 199–216.

Tincknell, E. and Raghuram, P. (2004) '*Big Brother*: reconfiguring the "active" audience of cultural studies?', in S. Holmes and D. Jermyn (eds), *Understanding Reality Television*. London and New York: Routledge, pp. 252–69.

Toffoletti, K. (2014) 'Baudrillard, postfeminism, and the image makeover', *Cultural Politics*, 10(1): 105–19.

Tomlinson, J. (1991) *Cultural Imperialism*. London: Pinter Publications.

Toth, C. (2008) 'J-pop and performances of young female identity: music, gender and urban space in Tokyo', *Young*, 16(2): 111–29.

Tremayne, M. (2006) *Blogging, Citizenship, and the Future of Media*. London and New York: Routledge.

Tungate, M. (2008) *Fashion Brands: Branding Style from Armani to Zara*. London: Kogan Page.

Tunstall, J. (1977) *The Media are American: Anglo-American Media in the World*. London: Constable.

Turner, G. (2004) *Understanding Celebrity*. London: SAGE.

Turner, G. (2006) The mass production of celebrity: 'Celetoids', reality TV and the 'demotic turn'. *International Journal of Cultural Studies*, 9(2): 153–65.

Turner, G. (2014) *Understanding Celebrity* (2nd edn). London: SAGE.

Turnock, R. (2000) *Interpreting Diana: Television Audiences and the Death of a Princess*. London: British Film Institute.

Vale, V. and Ryan, M. (2004) *J.G. Ballard: Quotes*. San Francisco: RE/Search.

Van Krieken, R. (2012) *Celebrity Society*. London and New York: Routledge.

Vermorel, F. and Vermorel, J. (1985) *Starlust: The Secret Life of Fans*. London: Comet.

Vince, J. (2012) 'Kate Middleton's style by numbers: the "duchess effect"', *Grazia Fashion*, http://www.graziadaily.co.uk/fashion/archive/2012/05/16/kate-middletons-style-by-numbers (accessed 20 November 2013).

Vincent, J., Hill, J.S., and Lee, J.W. (2009) 'The multiple brand personalities of David Beckham: a case study of the Beckham brand', *Sport Marketing Quarterly*, 18: 173–80.

Virilio, P. (2005) *The Information Bomb*. London and New York: Verso.

Walter, T. (2010) 'Jade and the journalists: media coverage of a young British celebrity dying of cancer', *Social Science and Media*, 71(5): 853–60.

Waters, M. (1995) *Globalization*. London and New York: Routledge.

Watson, C.W. (1997) '"Born a lady, became a princess, died a saint": the reaction to the death of Diana, Princess of Wales', *Anthropology Today*, 13(6): 3–7.

Weber, B.R. and Spigel, L. (2009) *Makeover TV: Selfhood, Citizenship, and Celebrity*. Durham, NC: Duke University Press.

Weber, M. (1978) *Economy and Society: An Outline of Interpretive Sociology*, Vol. 1. Berkeley, CA and London: University of California Press.

Weber, M. (2006) 'The sociology of charismatic authority and the nature of charismatic authority and its routinization', in P.D. Marshall (ed.), *The Celebrity Culture Reader*. London and New York: Routledge, pp. 55–71.

Whannel, G. (2002) 'David Beckham, identity and masculinity', *Sociology Review*, 11: 2–4.

Whannel, G. (2010) 'News, celebrity, and vortextuality: a study of the media coverage of the Michael Jackson verdict', *Cultural Politics*, 6(1): 65–84.

Wheeler, M. (2010) 'Celebrity diplomacy: United Nations goodwill ambassadors and messengers of peace', *Celebrity Studies,* 2(1): 6–8.

Willinge, A., Touyze, S., and Charles, M. (2006) 'How do body-dissatisfied and body-satisfied males and females judge the size of thin female celebrities?', *International Journal of Eating Disorders*, 39(7): 576–82.

Wilson, C. and Seaman, D. (2007) *The Serial Killers: A Study in the Psychology of Violence*. London: Virgin.

Wolf, N. (1990) *The Beauty Myth*. London: Vintage.

Woods, V. (2008) 'From boy band to megabrand', *Vogue*, 98(9): 746–8.

Wright Mills, C. (1959) *The Power Elite*. London, Oxford and New York: Oxford University Press.

Wring, D. (2012) '"It's just business": the political economy of the hacking scandal', *Media, Culture & Society*, 34(5): 631–6.

Wykes, M. and Gunter, B. (2005) *The Media and Body Image: If Looks Could Kill*. London and California: SAGE.

Young, J. (2007) *The Vertigo of Late Modernity*. Los Angeles, CA and London: SAGE.

INDEX

Gordian knot 15–16
gossip
    and business leaders 62
    in journalism 98–9, 100, 106, 114, 125, 165,
        182
    as 'social bridge' 44–5, 46
    social media 38, 112, 113, 114
GQ magazine 159
Graf, Steffi 92
Graphic Revolution 16, 24, 26, 33
Gray, John 66–7, 134
Grazia 100, 104, 105
Green Hornet, The 124
Greenslade, Roy 77
Greig, Geordie 104
Griffith, D.W.
    The Birth of a Nation 25
Groban, Josh 90
Grossberg, Lawrence 84
Guardian, The 102, 107
Guinn, Jeff 168
Guns 'N' Roses 124, 173

H&M 56
habitus 149, 183
Hafez, Kai 118–19
Haggerty, K.D. 172–3
Hague, William 77
Haig, Matt 54
Hall, Jenny 150
Hannibal 177
Hannibal (military leader) 19
Hannibal Rising 177
Harding, Sarah 106
Harris, Anthony 177
Harris, Daniel 125, 126, 165
Hathaway, Anne 35
health and fitness 151, 152–3
Hearst, William Randolph 98, 99
Heat 100
Hello! 99, 100, 104, 105, 110
Henry VIII 70
Hepburn, Audrey 56, 75
Here Comes Honey Boo Boo 143
heroism 14–15, 24, 33
Herostratus 12
Hickey, E.W. 175
Hilfiger, Andy 59
Hills, Matt 84, 88, 91
Hilton, Paris 52–3, 126, 137
    Confessions of an Heiress 52
    One Night in Paris 52, 126, 166
Hilton, Perez 114
Hinckley, John 93
Hindi films 121
Hindley, Myra 178–9
Hitler, Adolf 30

Hollander, P. 43–4, 47
Hollywood
    marketing 119
    power of 117, 119, 120
    star system 2, 26, 32, 50–1, 53, 117
    see also Bollywood; cinema; film stars
Hollywood Fan Magazine 99
Holmes, H.H. 170
Holmes, Katie 59
Holmes, Su 133, 134
Homer: *Iliad* 14, 17
Horkheimer, Max and Adorno, Theodor 34
Horton, Donald and Wohl, R. Richard 37, 87
Hottie and the Nottie, The 52
House of Wax 52
Houston, Whitney 43
How, Alan 35
Howard, Amanda 169, 170
Hurley, Elizabeth 58–9, 151
Hurricane Katrina 77
Hyde, Marina 79

'Identity Brands' 57
Identity Thief 160
I'm a Celebrity, Get Me Out of Here 136–7
image 18, 23, 70
    and achievement 33
    body image 150, 151, 154, 156–7, 159
    demystification 139, 140
    manipulation 26–7, 158–60
    and Reality TV 137–9
Independent 102
India 119–20, 121, 122–3
    economic power 120
individualism 3, 99–100
    and body enhancement 154–5
    growth of 14, 38
    suppression of 22
Indonesia 125, 126, 127–8
Inglis, Fred 5, 22–3, 29, 98
inscriptions 24
Instagram 113
Internet *see* blogging; social media
Internet celebrity 86–7
Irham, Nazril 8, 9, 126
Islamic culture 124–5
Israel 79

J-pop 128–9
Jack the Ripper 169–70
Jackson, Michael 43, 105, 155, 167
James, E.L.: *Fifty Shades of Grey* 36
Japan 127, 128–9
    J-pop 128
    national idols 128–9
Jenkins, Henry 7, 84, 91
Jenner, Bruce 61